Education for Sustainable Development

Education for Sustainable Development

Challenges, Strategies, and Practices in a Globalizing World

Edited by

Anastasia Nikolopoulou
Taisha Abraham • Farid Mirbagheri

Copyright © Anastasia Nikolopoulou, Taisha Abraham and Farid Mirbagheri, 2010

All rights reserved. No part of this book may be reproduced or utilized in any form or by any means, electronic or mechanical, including photocopying, recording or by any information storage or retrieval system, without permission in writing from the publisher.

First published in 2010 by

SAGE Publications India Pvt Ltd
B 1/I-1 Mohan Cooperative Industrial Area
Mathura Road, New Delhi 110044, India
www.sagepub.in

SAGE Publications Inc
2455 Teller Road
Thousand Oaks, California 91320, USA

SAGE Publications Ltd
1 Oliver's Yard, 55 City Road
London EC1Y 1SP, United Kingdom

SAGE Publications Asia-Pacific Pte Ltd
33 Pekin Street
#02-01 Far East Square
Singapore 048763

Published by Vivek Mehra for SAGE Publications India Pvt Ltd, typeset in 10/12.5 pt Minion by Star Compugraphics Private Limited, Delhi and printed at Chaman Enterprises, New Delhi.

Library of Congress Cataloging-in-Publication Data

Education for sustainable development: challenges, strategies, and practices in a globalizing world/edited by Anastasia Nikolopoulou, Taisha Abraham, and Farid Mirbagheri.
    p. cm
  Includes bibliographical references and index.
  1. Environmental education. 2. Sustainable development. 3. World citizenship. 4. Education–Social aspects. I. Nikolopoulou, Anastasia. II. Abraham, Taisha. III. Mirbagheri, Farid.

GE70.E398   338.9'27071—dc22   2010   2009044223

ISBN: 978-81-321-0293-9 (HB)

The SAGE Team: Rekha Natarajan, Manali Das, Mathew P.J. and Trinankur Banerjee

Contents

List of Tables   vii
List of Figures   ix
Acknowledgements   x

Introduction   xi
    Anastasia Nikolopoulou, Farid Mirbagheri, and *Taisha Abraham*

Part I   Globalization and the Politics of Exclusion

1. Caste, Exclusion, and Marginalized Groups in India: Dalit Deprivation in India   3
   Sukhadeo Thorat

2. Education in a Globalizing Era: Implications for Disabled Girls   28
   Anita Ghai

Part II   From Rio to Indigenous Cultural Resources: Education for Sustainable Development

3. Education for Sustainable Development: The Concept and Its Connection to Tolerance and Democracy   47
   Michael J. Scoullos

4. Education for Sustainable Tribal Development   64
   Archana Prasad

5. Premodern Indigenous Practitioners' Dilemmas in a Postmodern Globalized World   81
   Janet Chawla

Part III Empowering the Human Capital: Challenges and Strategies in India

6 Market, Deprivation, and Education in the Age of Globalization   95
   Ravi Kumar

7 Literacy Instruction in Indian Schools   117
   Shobha Sinha

8 Empowering Pedagogy: Potentials and Limitations   129
   Sadhna Saxena

9 Squaring National Pride with Tolerance: A Lesson for School Textbooks   152
   Narayani Gupta

10 Indian School Textbooks   161
   Teesta Setalvad

Part IV Ethical Paths to Global Citizenship

11 Global Ethical Options in the Framework of Development: Gandhian Perspectives   175
   Neelakanta Radhakrishnan

12 Reconciling Identity and Citizenship: A Case for Moral Cosmopolitanism in a Divided World   188
   M. Satish Kumar

13 Islam and Liberal Peace   204
   Farid Mirbagheri

About the Editors and Contributors   221
Index   228

List of Tables

A1.1	Occupational Pattern: Scheduled Caste and Others	16
A1.2	Percentage of Landless and Near Landless Households among Scheduled Castes	16
A1.3	Land Ownership Background of Rural Labour Households	17
A1.4	Employment Rate 1999–2000—All India	17
A1.5	Unemployment Rate (Age 5 years and above) in Rural Areas	18
A1.6	Unemployment Rate (Age 5 years and above) in Urban Areas	19
A1.7	Poverty Social Groups in Rural Area 1993–1994 and 1999–2000	20
A1.8	Percentage of Persons Below-Poverty-Line by Household Type for Each Social Group	20
A1.9	Average MPCE of Rural Households Classified by Household Type, Social Group (in rupees) 1999–2000	21
A1.10	Literacy Rate of Scheduled Caste and Others	21
A1.11	Infant Mortality—1998–99	21
A1.12	Morbidity—1998–99	22
A1.13	Women's Health—1998–99	22
A1.14	Crimes and Atrocities against Scheduled Castes, 1981–2000	23
A1.15	Practice of Untouchability—Andhra Pradesh	23
A1.16	Social Discrimination: Orissa	24
A1.17	Economic Discrimination: Orissa	25
A1.18	Orissa, 1987–88	25

4.1	Drop-out Rates of Tribal Students	72
4.2	Enrolment Rates of Scheduled Tribes at Different Levels	72
4.3	Pattern of Expenditure on Education Schemes	73
4.4	Number of Beneficiaries for Different Schemes	74
4.5	Pattern of Enrolment of Scheduled Tribes in Undergraduate and Postgraduate Courses	75
4.6	Percentage of Scheduled Tribe Students Enrolled at Various Stages	76
4.7	Impact of Reservations on Scheduled Tribes (STs)	76
4.8	Work Participation of Scheduled Tribes, 1991–2001	77
4.9	Performance of Schemes for Self Employment: Coverage of Scheduled Tribe Youth	78

List of Figures

3.1 The 'Classical' Representation of Sustainable Development with Its Three Pillars — 51
3.2 The International Conference of Thessaloniki (1947) Suggested the Position of Education as Basis of the Three Pillars — 51
3.3 The Tetrahedron of Sustainable Development as Evolution of Figure 3.2 — 52
3.4 The Tetrahedron of Sustainable Development Where Governance is the Basis — 52
3.5 The Analysis of Governance and the Direct Connection between Democracy and Tolerance to Some of Its Components — 53
3.6 Components of Sustainable Development and the Means to Approach it (combination of Figure 3.4 and Figure 3.5) — 54
3.7 Implementing ESD through Relevant Perspectives — 54

Acknowledgements

We would like to thank *Social Change* for the permission to reprint Dr Anita Ghai's essay (Vol. 36, Number 3, September 2006). An earlier version of Dr Ravi Kumar's essay appeared in *Social Change* (Vol. 36, Number 3, September 2006). We would also thank *The Bulletin of Oriental Philosophy*, Japan, for the permission to reprint Dr M. Satish Kumar's essay 'Reconciling Identity and Citizenship: A Case for Moral Cosmopolitanism in a Divided World' (Vol. 22, 2006). We are grateful to Dr N. Balakrishnan, the deputy director of Nehru Memorial Museum and Library, New Delhi, India, for his encouragement and support for the conference 'The Challenge to Globalization: Education for Tolerance, Democracy and Sustainable Development,' which took place at the Nehru Memorial Museum and Library, 20–22 January 2005, and resulted in the present volume of essays. Finally, we want to thank Professor Michael Hays for his insightful suggestions on this volume.

Introduction

Anastasia Nikolopoulou, Farid Mirbagheri, and Taisha Abraham

THE LANGUAGE OF UNIVERSALISM

Two of the events that marked 1997 as an important year for education were the independent Earth Charter Commission and the Thessaloniki Declaration. After the 1992 Rio Summit failed to reach an agreement on how governments should protect the earth, the Commission undertook the task of drafting the Earth Charter, calling governments to commit themselves to the welfare of future generations: 'Humanity is part of a vast evolving universe. Earth, our home, is alive with a unique community of life....It is imperative that we, the people of Earth, declare our responsibility to one another, to the greater community of life, and to future generations'[1]. The significance of the Earth Charter rests on its bold use of a universal language that claims to embrace all, especially the marginalized and the poor. As Amartya Sen notes, the utopian connotations of this universal language can be traced 200 years back to its historical counterpart, the universal radicalism of the 1790s, when Mary Wollstonecraft's and Thomas Paine's writings, among others, triggered an unprecedented outpouring of populist fervour for emancipation of the oppressed—women, slaves, and workers: 'It is justice, not charity, that is wanting in the world' (Mary Wollstonecraft, 1996 quoted in Sen and Anand 1994). Even though this utopian universal language was soon superseded by nationalism, imperialism, and working class (male) emancipation rhetoric, it is doubtful that it ever disappeared. As Sen reminds us, the language of Wollstonecraft and Paine is actually a call for 'human development' (Sen and Anand 1994). Remarkably, this language returns now at the height of worldwide environmental and security crises to claim a universal emancipation as though it could, through its utopian trajectory, convince governments that only a moment separates the 1790s from the early 21st century and that we could turn the clock of modernity backwards and start anew a society whose priority is the happiness of all.

The Thessaloniki Declaration, couched in a language similar to the Earth Charter's universalist rhetoric and drafted the same year the Earth Charter was created, was presented at the 'International Conference on Environment and Society: Education and Public Awareness for Sustainability', organized by United Nations Educational, Scientific and Cultural Organization (UNESCO) and the Government of Greece (December 1997).[2] The Declaration places universalist language into the service of an educational imperative with demanding ethical aims. It is not governments, non-governmental organizations (NGOs), or civil society that will be at the forefront of an alternative conceptualization of our relationship to modernity and the environment; only through 'collective learning process[es]' and 'equal participation' can we expect to instil among learners '[a] change in behaviours and lifestyles'. Education is an indispensable means to give to all women and men in the world the capacity to own their own lives, to exercise personal choice and responsibility, to learn throughout life without frontiers, be they geographical, political, cultural, religious, linguistic, or gender.

The Declaration summons all educational forces, formal and non-formal, to put a stop to humanitarian crises:

> The reorientation of education as a whole towards sustainability involves all levels of formal, non-formal, and informal education in all countries. The concept of sustainability encompasses not only environment but also poverty, health, food security, democracy, human rights, and peace. Sustainability is, in the final analysis, a moral and ethical imperative in which cultural diversity and traditional knowledge need to be respected.[3]

The Thessaloniki Declaration tried to unite two contesting discourses: the discourse of environmental education, especially as this had been defined in Tbilisi, in 1977, and the discourse of sustainable development, as was defined 10 years later in the Brundtland Report, *Our Common Future* (The World Commission on Environment and Development 1987).

Taking the notion of environmental education out of its 'outdoors' and 'nature' context and uniting it with the notion of sustainable development was not an easy task. Since World War II, 'sustainable development' has been identified with economic progress. By placing the notion of sustainable development in the context of environmental education and a broader universalist discourse, the Thessaloniki Declaration succeeded, without detaching the definition from its previous economic connotation, in expanding sustainability's universalist, historical, and ethical dimensions. The Declaration proposed, in a sense, a new definition for sustainable development by linking it directly with education. Education for Sustainable Development (ESD) could be addressed through economics, politics, and culture, despite epistemological and ideological differences.

As a response to documents such as the Thessaloniki Declaration and the Earth Charter, we decided to plan a conference 'The Challenge to Globalization: Education for Tolerance, Democracy and Sustainable Development'. We found these documents to be challenging, yet remote from the current realities of tertiary education, with its insular view of research and growing emphasis on corporate-oriented technology. After a series of meetings in Cyprus in 2003 and 2004, facilitated by Taisha's appointment as a visiting professor at the University of Cyprus, in Nicosia, we three agreed to organize a conference on education and sustainable development in Delhi.

In January 2005, 'The Challenge to Globalization: Education for Tolerance, Democracy and Sustainable Development' was held at the Nehru Memorial Museum and Library, in New Delhi, India, under the encouragement of its Deputy Director, Dr Balakrishnan, who hosted the conference. Through Taisha's resourceful energy we were able to attract scholars and activists from diverse disciplines, in the hope of generating a discourse to tackle the problem of education and sustainable development from multiple disciplinary perspectives. This conference resulted in the present volume of revised essays as well as a growing awareness of the necessity to continue similar initiatives in Delhi and in other areas in the world[4] and to give educators and activists opportunities to address sustainable development from multiple disciplinary and institutional perspectives.

In the same year, the United Nations declared the beginning of the Decade of Education for Sustainable Development (DESD 2005–14). The website of UNESCO emphasizes the integrative character of DESD:

> The overall goal of the DESD is to integrate the principles, values, and practices of sustainable development into all aspects of education and learning. This educational effort will encourage changes in behaviour that will create a more sustainable future in terms of environmental integrity, economic viability, and a just society for present and future generations.[5]

The DESD announcement seemed to signal that. At last, the moment had arrived for an international organization such as UNESCO to put the utopian universalism and holistic philosophy of the Thessaloniki Declaration and the Earth Charter into practice or at least to call on governments to make this reality palpable by placing educational reform at the forefront of their agendas.

The DESD also promises that a new beginning may yet be possible, despite the criticism that UNESCO-sponsored conferences fail to deliver. The World Conference on Education for All in Jomtien (1990), for example, has been criticized for leading the Indian government to further lower the status of the teacher, marginalizing the role of women's education and offering no substantial opportunities for educating poor children. Jomtien and the Dakar Framework (2000), argues Anil Sadgopal, offer evidence of how market forces, while claiming to promote literacy skills, in effect reserve 'critical thinking, creativity, scientific temper, analytical abilities, sense of history or philosophy, aesthetic appreciation and other such educational attributes...for the privileged few' (Sadgopal 2003: 6). The implications for education for sustainable development necessitate a careful reconsideration of how globalization and the commodification of education put pressure on international conferences and hinder them from fulfilling their promises. As Krishna Kumar states, globalization has brought previous theories of education under enormous stress, rendering questions of equality, 'dignity of individuals, and room for social justice exceedingly difficult to handle' since for many, education in a globalized society signifies a desperate means to find a job in a competitive market' (Kumar 2005: 7).

Konai Thaman, UNESCO Chair in Teacher Education and Culture at the University of the South Pacific, Suva, Fiji Islands, singles out three areas in which UNESCO and other organizations need to work hard if they want to salvage trust and faith in educational initiatives, especially in regions where empowering educational practices are most urgently needed. International initiatives, Thaman argues, will fail if *(a)* they don't operate in the language of the culture they address, *(b)* they don't disassociate themselves from the cultures and languages of colonial and imperialist traditions, and *(c)* they downplay regional and local memories and traditions (Thaman 2002: 236).

Culture, language, memory—these three threads hold the key, argues Thaman, in bridging the internationalist discourse of sustainable development with cultural difference, preserving the latter's distinct identity.

Introduction

Neither the reduction of poverty nor human rights can be achieved when one turns his or her back on the cultural, linguistic, and historical specificities that comprise the memory and daily experiences of people in the world. To ignore the cultural and historical specificities of a region, village, or ethnic community would mean that education for sustainable development is just a pretext to further marginalize and disempower the poor by robbing them first of their identity and then of their resources.

Sen suggests that although the 'demand for sustainability' is, in fact, 'a particular reflection of universality of claims—applied to the future generations vis-à-vis us', it is important that 'in trying to prevent deprivation in the future we must not ignore the deprived people of today'(Sen and Anand 1994).

THE ECONOMICS OF NATURE

Kevin Watkins and Riccardo Petrella point out the dismal prospects of international conferences and their inflated (in their view) promises to radically reduce illiteracy and poverty in the world. Since the 1970s, it has become apparent that the goals of international conferences such as Dakar (2000), Jomtien (1990), Rio (1992) and Tbilisi (1977) are unreachable. Watkins notes that there is little evidence that by 2015 governments will achieve the goal they set at the World Education Forum (2000: 2) in Dakar, Senegal, to reduce the number of illiterate people in the world (Watkins 2000: 2). Petrella further argues that the treaty signed by governments in the Johannesburg summit in 2002 to halve the number of extremely poor people by the year 2015 (the 1.3 billion living on less than US$ 1 per day) is simplistic and couched in deceptive calculations (Petrella 2003: 133).

What are the obstacles to achieving these goals? Is it, as Joseph Stiglitz suggests, a question of changing the mind-set of finance ministers and central bank governors, in whose hands many decisions of these international conferences arrive in the hopes of funding and further implementation. (Stiglitz 2002: 225)? Initiatives such as Education for All (Jomtien 1990) must also include the re-education of the holders of power, finance ministers, and governors towards developing a holistic vision. Such initiatives can further counter the desensitization process whereby the learner gets used to looking at poverty through abstract data and statistics without a sense of ethical obligation. Isn't our current global financial system proof of how past educational traditions placed profit above value creation?

The educational system of wealthy nations does not suffer only from leaving millions of children without basic education and literacy skills, thus condemning them to a life of poverty; this educational system is itself suffering from a poverty of thought.

The current education system, with its emphasis on scientific-technocratic advances in particular, is at the centre of our inability to grasp the whole. The technocratic mentality of the prevailing educational philosophy borrows from the need after World War II to promote economic achievements, something that led many to assume that by becoming experts in the narrow disciplines they serve, they would be able to grasp the whole. For the sake of scientific progress, tertiary education in particular became preoccupied with a disciplinary mentality leading to spatial claims and an explosion of specialization. This has given rise to 8,530 different disciplines, according to the UNESCO Symposium organized by the Division of Philosophy and Ethics in 1998, 'Transdisciplinarity: Stimulating Synergies, Integrating Knowledge' (UNESCO 1998). Daisaku Ikeda (2001) notes that while this emphasis on expertise has produced impressive results in the physical realm, it has also 'created a condition in which the cords that once connected individual to individual, to say nothing of individual and nature, have been severed. Individuals groan in the small, enclosed, and lonely space to which they have been driven' (Ikeda 2001: 127).

Surely not all scientific thinking has evolved along these lines; yet it seems that the quantification and codification of poverty and disease is representative of a mode of thinking that, as Spariosu argues, is hierarchical and reductionistic rather than interactive and reciprocal. The techno-scientific reduction of poverty to numbers and statistics, which prevails in tertiary, research-oriented institutions in particular, and emerges in international conferences, is an example. Numerical and statistical approaches to poverty, suggests Petrella (2003: 133), are not necessarily sending a clear message as to the need to re-examine our policies of sustainable development. For example, he points out that halving the 1.3 billion of extremely poor people 'means that it is acknowledged that there will still be 650 million extremely poor people in 2014 living on less than $1 per day'. He further concludes that by 2015, the estimate of those who live with less than US$ 2 or US$ 1 will reach a total of 3 billion and 50 million, respectively.

The extent of these staggering figures may be difficult to grasp because the poor seem to exist in a place remote from the daily experiences of wealthy nations. Surely, it is not the fault of the techno-scientific discourse

Introduction

bringing about a singular preoccupation with commercial and financial interests as opposed to caring about the environment and the poor. Yet the techno-scientific discourse, when cut off from the learner's sense of value and capacity for grasping the notion of sustainability holistically, is insufficient to conceptualize alternative communities of learning and living. Ikeda points out this problem through an example that might strike closer to home for those living in wealthy nations:

> The fact is that nearly 24,000 people die every day because of extreme poverty and the resulting lack of access to nutrition, clean drinking water, and basic medical care. The next hour will claim another 1,000 lives. To make a stark comparison, this toll is the equivalent of a passenger jet carrying 500 people crashing every 30 minutes. And in this case, three of four of the victim 'passengers' are children aged five or under. (Ikeda 2006)

What Ikeda suggests with the example of the passenger jet crashing every 30 minutes is not that indices and statistical tables hinder our capacity to grasp the problem of poverty in its entirety. He means that these indices are not sufficient if they do not incorporate the perspective of value creation, but are simply read as abstract data. What these numbers do not address is the human being's tendency to use nature as a means for personal profit rather than as a resource that we all share with future generations. Nor do they address the need to change our personal lifestyles, learning habits, and systems.

Since World War II, the idea of development has become equated with the idea of economic advancement, not equal distribution of economic resources. The notions of wealth and nature have, however, a much older relationship. Since the late 17th century, the idea of 'wealth' has implied economic as well as personal improvement. At the same time, the idea of 'nature' as 'natural history' provided a historical and ideological ground on which the middle class claimed its prerogative to assume a leading socio-political role, disregarding earlier beliefs in the divine right of kings. For the nascent bourgeoisie, moral and individual improvement went along with economic improvement, strengthening the belief that capitalism would activate the benign proclivities of individuals while suppressing their malignant ones. Such were the views of the cultural defenders of early capitalism such as Montesquieu and James Steurt, as Sen (2001) points out.

The historicity of sustainable development needs to be understood further within the context of the articulation of value in the discourses of wealth and nature in the 17th century. Both of these discourses assumed their authority not by translating value for humanity's benefit but by translating (and transforming) nature into wealth (for example, metal to merchandise), servicing, in turn, theoretical and political aims. Michel Foucault (1970: 206, 255), who analyzes the linguistic emergence of these discourses in *The Order of Things*, focuses on the preoccupation of economists and natural historians with establishing the authority and mastery of their objects of inquiry by breaking down their components into their minutest detail: from 'genera, families, sub-kingdoms' to flow of money, rising and falling prices, growing or diminishing production. The linguistic codification and structuring of natural history and the discourse of wealth—through highly rigid, stratified, and taxonomic ways of analysis—reduced them into principles and facts, leaving out questions that 'spontaneous' ('everyday' language) might include, such as issues pertaining to social justice or ethics. As natural history and wealth depended upon ideas coded in a well tabulated space, their use for the service of humanity was taken for granted: 'Natural history, since it must of necessity be a science, and the circulation of wealth, since it is an institution created by men and also controlled by them, are bound to escape the perils inherent in spontaneous language' (Foucault 1970: 204). Any other language, notes Foucault, would render both of these discourses vulnerable to the 'perils' of a language open to diverse social, ethical, and political questions. To safeguard its authority, the language of wealth and nature had to be 'exact and definite' through 'structure and character, value, and money': 'Where the disordered order of language implies the continuous relation to an art and its endless tasks, the orders of nature and wealth are expressed in the mere existence of structure and character, value, and money' (ibid.: 204–05).

What is of interest in this historical convergence between the two discourses of 'natural history' and 'wealth' is that they both emerged as scientific discourses. One could not speak about them ambiguously, spontaneously, or from personal experience. Their validity was exemplified in the linguistic codification and structuring of their objects of inquiry. Both developed highly rigid, stratified, and taxonomic ways of analysis, reducing their findings into principles and facts. By drawing on Foucault, we offer a glance at the epistemological, historical, and ideological complexities of the notions of economics and nature, notions that became central in the formation of modern Western subjectivities. The 18th century approaches to wealth and nature aspired towards the emergence of the beneficent and

Introduction

moral person of fortune who shares the greater part of his revenue with others. Yet, as Adam Smith was prone to diagnose, the case was often that the person would spend 'the whole upon his own person' and give nothing to the other (Smith 1993: 212). The celebration of industrialization and technology as the ultimate revolution in learning and well-being solidified further modern desire and consumer-oriented subjectivities, while privileging even further the domain of science research in education.

However, the discourse of the economics of nature is not impenetrable and invincible. Since its emergence in the 17th and 18th centuries, it has been threatened from several fronts. The first time was during the late part of the 18th century when experience, personal narrative, and a utopian universalism dominated the radical public sphere for almost 40 years (1790–1830). Anticipated by the universalist language of Wollstonecraft, Godwin, Paine, and others, the late 18th century public sphere, as Sen notes, was open to all, 'irrespective of class, gender, race, community, or generation'. Like ours, the world of the 1790s was characterized by 'enormous inequities of contemporary living conditions and real threats to the prospects of human life in the future' (Sen and Anand 1994).

Since the late 18th century, the scientific-industrial establishment has been challenged on several occasions, not the least being from within its own ranks (Spariosu 2005: 103). Has the time come to place science at the forefront of humanitarian concerns? Scientists must ask themselves what connection their learning has with the challenges that threaten humankind, argues Daisaku Ikeda (2001: 129). Certainly, many academicians resist being influenced by other-than-scientific imperatives, particularly those related to military and economic power. But while some academicians warn of the effects of chemical industry on human health or oppose a value-free education, there are still many academicians and institutions linked to potentially biased affiliations with large private pharmaceutical, chemical, and agri-food companies (Petrella 2003: 127–30). Market-driven scientific knowledge, claims Anil Sadgopal, lacks a 'critical and holistic epistemological relationship with social reality' while its tendency to control nature and maximize profits rather than to 'co-exist with nature' renders it a threat to human welfare (Sadgopal 2004: 8).

Education for sustainable development necessitates an ethical struggle to transform knowledge into what Ikeda calls a 'propelling force for an eternally unfolding humanitarian quest' (Ikeda 2001: 99). 'This ethical struggle' has now taken on an ever greater urgency, notes Petrella. 'Academics must therefore exercise their responsibility in a forceful, clear, and uncompromising manner' in the areas of war and injustice (Petrella 2003: 132). To disconnect its interests from private enterprise, financial capital, and world markets, higher education must reformulate a discourse that goes against a 'denuded, aseptic' philosophy and instead links knowledge to the fate of humankind. The calls of the Earth Charter and the Thessaloniki Conference for an ethical imperative that implies respect 'for cultural diversity and traditional knowledge' mark a breakthrough in the economistic discursive tradition of nature and wealth (The Thessaloniki Declaration 2002). Surely they are not the only discourses that attempt to de-regulate the historically reductionist discourse of the economics of nature. They are important because they have been sanctioned by international governments and NGOs, thus signaling that Western traditions of the economics of nature might be ready for a change.

If maintained, this change in looking at economics, nature, and profit from a broader ethical framework could provide an unparalleled and historic opportunity for empowering people to take concrete action and resolve the issues they face (Ikeda 2001: 127). According to Masao Miyoshi (2001: 295), this is the first time in human history where 'one single common ality involves all those living on the planet: environmental deterioration as a result of the human consumption of natural resources'. Education has now a common goal: 'to nurture our common bonds to the planet' (ibid: 295).

THE POLITICS OF SUSTAINABLE DEVELOPMENT

Sustainable development is no longer only an attractive project to the developing world. It is now a necessity for the whole of humanity, including the advanced societies of the West. The holistic and inclusive nature of sustainable development encompasses a wide range of issues as interconnected parts of a whole and addresses the entire population of the globe rather than the conventional differentiating state-centric model. The pressing question of the environment, for example, and the serious challenges it poses require a cosmopolitan outlook and international solutions beyond the requirements of the current statist model.

The conception and the establishment of the state over three and a half centuries ago in a continent ravaged by religious wars was an answer to a specific set of problems peculiar to that time and geography. It is hardly reasonable to assume that it can provide solutions to the question of governance everywhere, all of the time. Today, the most challenging threat to world peace, religious fundamentalist terrorism, can no longer be met by the state. Civilizational worldviews and not national outlooks, though over-simplifying in some respects, are increasingly more able to explain mindless violence committed by non-state actors internationally.

State policies are axiomatically and philosophically shaped by concern for national interests where pedantic rationality forms the core criterion of policy making. In an era, however, when the interests of all communities are evidently interconnected, humanity as a whole and its constituent parts can only benefit from a holistic outlook pursuing international interests. The questions of environment, terrorism, drugs, migration, and so on can no longer be viewed as national or even regional concerns alone. They are international problems requiring international solutions, a task for which the state is ill-equipped. Its particularistic and pedantic trait, fundamental to its very existence, prohibits or at least limits states' capacity to engage in all-inclusive, non-discriminatory approaches to international life. Sustainable development is no exception. As an issue that requires a cosmopolitan approach and international cooperation, it needs dialogic communities committed to a global outlook and not infused with indifference or even hostility towards one another brought about by statehood.

However, we may be a long way from a stateless world, where an alternative and more inclusive system of governance would replace sovereign statehood. Such a fundamental shift in political life and radical change in the status quo, would, in all probability, not arrive anytime soon or easily. In the meantime, sustainable development cannot be put on hold. We have to strive for the best we can achieve in the present conditions and under the rule of the sovereign state. Greater efforts would therefore have to be made to converge the local and the global; that would mean what is deemed to be in the national interest of the state should also be assessed in terms of international interests of humanity as a whole. In that endeavour we can be aided by some aspects of globalization, where the sharp edges of statehood are gradually eroded and a better harmony between the micro and the macro is brought about. However, the harmonization of the local and the global through globalization should not be achieved at the expense of the local. Diversity should not be sacrificed but preserved and in fact celebrated. Minimizing cultural differences in the world in order to boost financial benefits, that is, increase the relative gap between the rich and the poor, would not only not assist sustainable development but is in fact harmful to the cause. Thus, more investment in the developing world, greater transparency in financial transactions, more egalitarian approach to human communities, applying free market rules to agriculture, narrowing the gap between realist foreign and liberal domestic approaches, and promoting tolerance can be emphasized whilst the marginalization of the majority of humanity, based solely on insufficient purchasing power, should be avoided. The poor of the 21st century know what they are missing and are aware how some of those riches were compiled. They are cognizant of the exploitation that they and their land were subjected to for the prosperity that has now befallen a minority in the human community.

However, there is also a serious need to engage the younger generations, particularly in the Islamic communities, in a culture of tolerance. The nature and the scale of violence committed, or the threat of its use, against innocent civilians are symptomatic of indoctrination by intolerant ideologies based on a fundamentalist interpretation of the faith. Although socio-political factors cannot be discarded altogether, the greater part of the cause must lie in the exposure of young fertile minds to terrorist propaganda. In that sense alone sustainable development faces a formidable challenge. Development cannot be based upon monopoly of understanding as is practiced by fundamentalist groups. Combating this ideology is not a military operation but rather a cultural affair. International cultural institutions such as UNESCO should take it upon themselves to promote policies that encourage tolerance of difference. As a suggestion perhaps some passages of the Universal Declaration of Human Rights relating to basic freedoms can be posted on the first page of every school textbook throughout the world. That could be a simple but effective way of exposing young minds, throughout their primary and secondary education, to the importance of respecting the other(s).

The world cannot continue along the path it is currently treading. Environmental pressures aside, the threat of terrorism, cultural intolerance, and the increasing frustration of the poor will lead to serious disruptions of global arrangements. There is a pressing need to engage the less well-off and the impoverished in world affairs, which would require in part some redistribution of the planet's resources and more equitable ways of addressing global issues. Those are the bedrock of sustainable development. In parallel, the younger members of the human race should be educated to respect one another. That respect can provide the basis for learning from and understanding one another and the world we live in. Failure can mean not just the continuation of the unjust status-quo but perhaps the decline and the possible demise of humanity altogether. Sustainable development therefore must be given every chance to succeed.

Introduction

GLOBALIZATION AND SUSTAINABLE DEVELOPMENT

The title of our volume, *Education for Sustainable Development: Challenges, Strategies, and Practices in a Globalizing World* merits some elaboration. It asks the reader to take the everyday issue of globalization and link it to the seemingly disparate issues of education for sustainable development. In what way do the challenges, strategies, and practices of the latter arise within and even depend on the ongoing phenomenon of globalization?

Since the largely economic discourse of globalization has been foregrounded over its other variables, it is best to address this aspect of globalization first before linking it to the field of education. Globalization is seen as an epoch-defining phenomenon both in its descriptive and in its prescriptive aspects. In its descriptive aspect it is seen as the international flow of capital, investments, and technological developments. The Transnational Corporations (TNCs) along with the World Bank, the International Monetary Fund (IMF), and the World Economic Forum are the main organizational conduits of policing this new economic order in the interest of the Western powers. Through the Structural Adjustment Programme (SAP) these organs streamline world economies to align them to the changing needs of the new economic order. In its prescriptive aspect the so-called 'developmental' paradigm of globalization (and this despite the fact that large constituencies of people have been marginalized by the new economic world order) is seen as inevitable rather than as contingent upon capitalism. What has to be noted is that ultimately financial pressures determine both the descriptive and prescriptive aspects of globalization.[6]

Global capitalism under the guise of distribution (in which mass consumerism is encouraged) creates an ostensibly democratic space that diffuses any resistance to it. Since the neo-liberal politics of globalization has identified the field of education as an important site for its contestation, it has commodified education by offering commercial benefits and employment opportunities and luring the state into its economic vortex.

Ravi Kumar in his essay, 'Market, Deprivation, and Education in the Age of Globalization' states that this has resulted in the shift from welfare to market models in education by the state in India. What is disturbing about this shift, as Kumar delineates, is that 'when the purchasing capacity of the majority remains low, it becomes difficult to buy education and therefore the majority of Indians—poor, dalits and the girl child—are getting alienated from education' (Kumar 2005: 106). He is critical of Amartya Sen's position on globalization where Sen states that one cannot 'reverse the economic predicament of the poor across the world by withholding from them the great advantages of contemporary technology, the well established efficiency of international trade and exchange, and the social as well as economic merits of living in an open society' (Sen 2002). Sen insists upon a balance between the market and the state in the form of multiple institutions in society that should reflect it. Kumar asks what if the state itself has succumbed to neo-liberal market politics of globalization. He points out that the very rule of capital, which is always exploiting surplus does not allow for a human face to globalization as Sen seems to indicate.

One of the crucial points to note about globalization and its system of interdependencies (in which the West is always privileged) is that it creates responsive models of development in the developing nations. These responsive models basically adjust to the demands placed upon them by the West for which they get short-term spin-offs with its allied ripple effects in limited spheres, which becomes self-perpetuating. Given this fact, what may be useful is to make interventions through a renewed and stronger state into this responsive model of development. The idea is to maintain a high growth rate but with distributive justice and without surrendering democracy. This will open up an alternative system that will be socially inclusive of all.

Interestingly, since the 1990s, education has been made into an international issue. (In 1990 the first Global Conference on Basic Education in Jomtien, Thailand, which universalized basic education, followed the first Child Rights Convention (1989).) However, the evaluation made by the Education For All (EFA) showed that although progress was made in the field of education, the marginalized were still left out. The Dakar 2000 framework of action focused on this disadvantaged group and the United Nations in its Millennium Development Goals interlinked basic education and poverty reduction (Govinda 2003).

Sen's book, *Development as Freedom*, is in many ways an elaboration on this idea. In his book he argues that sustainable development should not see poverty in an economic context alone but also as 'capability deprivation'. He states that in a country like India for an individual to exercise freedom to develop his/her capabilities, there are other constraining social factors such as illiteracy, caste, and physical disability—to name three among others—that affect the conversion rate of money. That is, even if individuals from disadvantaged backgrounds get a high income, social

Introduction

factors such as caste prevent them from gaining the benefits that others from non-disadvantaged groups get. Sen insists that although poverty as income and poverty as 'capability deprivation' are interrelated, it is important to distinguish between them. What the 'capability' perspective does, according to Sen is that it shifts from (economic) means to ends 'that people have reason to pursue, and correspondingly, to the freedoms to be able to satisfy these ends' (Sen 1999: 90). Sen liberates development from 'pure' economics to 'impure' social factors, which forces 'ethical considerations'.

Education and sustainable development are not merely concepts but are intervening tools as well. Sen shows the role of education in alleviating poverty and in sustaining development by foregrounding caste, class, region, gender, and other markers that act as 'glass ceiling' in the development of the marginalized.

Interestingly, Sukhadeo Thorat in his chapter, 'Caste Exclusion, and Marginalized Groups in India: Dalit Deprivation in India' underscores the point made by Sen on poverty and development. He states that social discrimination of the lower castes and the untouchables deprives these communities of educational and employment opportunities resulting in 'high levels of economic deprivation and poverty'. He insists that for education to be sustainable it has to be seen in conjunction with other developmental sectors such as health, sanitation, and so on. For him the discriminatory caste politics also influence 'private economic market' that is very competitive and searches for highly educated and skilled workers. This further perpetuates the cycle of poverty.

For Thorat, reducing 'economic discrimination' can be a good starting point for uplifting the community. 'Re-adjustment' of employment avenues for the untouchables, who have been traditionally associated with 'socially degrading' jobs, can provide 'optimal labour' for market efficiency. He says that the failure of the market to accommodate the lower castes—even when they have been qualified—should be countered by interventions made by the state through affirmative action programmes, particularly in the field of education since the literacy rates are the lowest among the Dalits. Apart from better productive possibilities this will also eventually break the cycle of social injustices against the untouchables, and more importantly, 'minimize the potential for conflict' between the 'haves' and the 'have-nots' that is rapidly widening within globalization.

Anita Ghai extends the argument of social and economic ostracization to the issue of disablity in her chapter, 'Education in a Globalizing Era:

Implications for Disabled Girls'. In the face of the fiercely competitive market of global capitalism, where market models are privileged over welfare models run by the state, Ghai argues that there is a shift in power from the public domain of politics associated with the state to the private realm of economics. Since in market models only the most skilled and qualified get selected for educational benefits and employment opportunities, the disabled remain unskilled and unemployed. Arguing that disability cannot be seen as singular but as plural since it interfaces with caste, class, religion, and gender, Ghai advocates an inclusive system of education that does not marginalize differences.

Shobha Sinha's chapter on 'Literacy Instruction in Indian Schools' hones in on cultural and social specificities in educational projects. She states that a distinction has to be made between literacy as a technical skill and literacy as something that is 'embedded in a system of social functions and cultural processes'. She points out that although there is an increase in the rate of literates in the country (18.33 per cent to 64.8 per cent from 1951 to 2001 Census), in terms of absolute numbers keeping the increase in population in mind, there is no increase. This is further compounded by factors such as gender, caste, region, and disparity between urban-rural populations. Tracing the history of literacy teaching in India, Sinha argues that 'poor pedagogy' is largely responsible for a system that teaches 'not to seek meaning while reading'. Quoting Paulo Freire, who saw education as a liberating tool rather than as a mechanical skill, Sinha says, one has to teach students to read the world and not just to read the word. It is being increasingly understood now that literacy has to be related to social learning. That is, 'there is a need to recognize that there is not one literacy but many literacies' (Diwan 2003: 304).

Sadhna Saxena's essay, Empowering Pedagogy: Potentials and Limitations engages this issue. Her chapter discusses the experience of running a small pilot literacy programme Jan Shikshan Abhiyan in the late 1980s in 25 villages of Bankhedi block of Hoshangabad district in Madhya Pradesh. This area had hardly any schools and even where there were schools, they were dysfunctional. Reading without comprehension was the most basic problem that the group encountered while conducting literacy classes in the region. This was mainly due to the fact that the sanskritized version of Hindi was privileged over the local language. This alienated the learner from his/her own local language and culture, which was seen as backward. Saxena argues that it is not linguistic ability that has created failure in the literacy programmes since most children by the age of five have 'full

Introduction

command of the grammatical systems of their own language'. Rather it is the undervaluing of contextualized cultural readings that has done so. As Saxena states, ultimately it is the social context that moulds the content and pedagogical approaches have to take this factor into account.

But these contextualized cultural readings should extend to other spheres of learning as well such as the portrayal of religious groups in history textbooks where an inclusive approach would reach out to the marginalized and the disadvantaged groups. Narayani Gupta's chapter, 'Squaring National Pride with Tolerance: A lesson for School Textbooks' talks about the kinds of challenges faced by the historian in writing history books in the context of South Asia. Given the various stages of the partition of the sub-continent, new problems of language, ethnicity, and religion were thrown up and history was re-written from biased perspectives by India, Pakistan, and Bangladesh. Gupta states that histories of the partitioned nations should be inclusive of the larger history of the sub-continent. This would forge ties for unity among its people across religious and cultural differences, and across borders.

Teesta too argues that history as a subject has been used politically for sectarian ends in textbooks. In her chapter, 'Indian School Textbooks' she says most books on history reflect the ideological orientation of the ruling party. This includes the demonization of Muslims, the silence on India's partition, and a refusal to acknowledge the contribution of the Dalits, lower castes and tribes, and other minorities in official history. This is compounded by the hierarchical caste system in India. For Setalvad the equality project of democracy must include the rewriting of history of both pre- and post-independence India so that it is inclusive of India's different 'life-worlds'.

Underscoring the need for this holistic approach, Farid Mirbagheri in his chapter 'Islam and Liberal Peace' explains some key concepts of Islam against their media distortions. He distinguishes between two dominant schools of Islamic thinking: the Epistemic and the Jurisprudential in relation to the 'Shari'a' or the rules of Islam. If the first school is open to a pluralist and evolving human interpretation of the Quran within the changing historical and social contexts of human existence, the second sees God's words as perfect with the 'clerical-hierarchy' as the sole authority to hand down readings of the Quran; a reading immune to epistemology of knowledge. It is within these debates that Mirbagheri examines the links between Islam and liberal peace. He gives the example of the interpretation of 'Jihad' as indicative of the debates. The term 'Jihad' Mirbagheri states means 'struggle' in Islam. Since the Jurisprudential School in Islam sees peace more as an external condition, which may require the use of violence, Jihad is linked by this school to armed conflict. This is the lesser struggle, explains Mirbagheri. The greater struggle in 'Jihad' refers to the struggle within each individual to obtain peace, which is what the Epistemic School upholds.

Contrasting Kantian and Hobbesian notions of peace as man-made and rational for security and development, with the Islamic notion of peace, as divine, Mirbagheri foregrounds the more inclusive approach in Islam towards peace. He explains that the word Islam means 'surrender', and the surrender is to God for peace. It is only when there is peace that human development can take place.

Michael J. Scoullos in his chapter, 'Education for Sustainable Development: The Concept and Its Connection to Tolerance and Democracy' argues that when we speak of education for sustainable development we have to take into account Environmental Education (EE) with all its cultural and regional challenges by negotiating between the local and the global. This is where the role of tolerance comes in. Tracing the history of the concept of environmental education from the 1960s, Scoullos points out the changing strategies adopted by the United Nations Economic Commission for Europe (UNECE) in order to make the concept a reality not only for the member states but also beyond them to other states as well. The thrust of the UNECE Scoullos states is for an inclusive framework. The prerequisite for any economic development is to create an awareness of preserving natural resources and environment protection.

Archana Prasad in her chapter 'Education for Sustainable Tribal Development' illustrates the need for such an approach. She traces historically the various educational and development projects started for the tribals in India. She states that educational projects in the tribal region have ignored the connection of the tribal people with their natural resources. This has resulted in uneven development. Although after India's independence the state played a crucial role in the development of the region, with privatization and the withdrawal of the state from agriculture and social welfare the impact on the community has been disastrous. Prasad states that globalization continues to do what colonialism had done earlier by divesting the tribal people from their 'rights to natural resources' and offering them an education that is not culturally or socially specific to their regional needs.

Janet Chawla's chapter, 'Premodern Indigenous Practitioners' Dilemmas in a Postmodern Globalized World' exemplifies the point by discussing the need to negotiate between indigenous knowledge forms and modern medicalization in the context of midwifery and childbirth in the Indian subcontinent. Basing her findings on the research of MATRIKA (an NGO that documents and interprets traditional midwifery), she argues that the assumption that western medicine with its scientific basis is better than 'indigenous, culturally appropriate, affordable and sustainable' ethno medicines leaves many poor people outside the ambit of any kind of medical assistance. Mediating between the ethno medical and the biomedical is important in preserving cultural resources for sustainable development.

The shift from learning as skill to learning as practice is the thrust of Neelakanta Radhakrishnan in his chapter, 'Global Ethical Options in the Framework of Development—Gandhian Perspectives'. In it he draws upon Gandhi's ideas on education for life knowledge. He argues how Gandhi's *Nai Talim* (New Education), which had the village children as its primary subjects, stressed on the holistic development of the body, mind, and soul. In this new educational endeavour, where manual and vocational training would be combined with knowledge of various subjects, both parents and teachers would have an important role to play. This would act as an effective antidote to the influence of the media where commercial values are propagated and it would also create an ethical framework within globalization to undermine its dehumanizing drives.

It is the need for a moral vision and an ethical dimension to education that M. Satish Kumar also focuses on in his essay, 'Reconciling Identity and Citizenship: A Case for Moral Cosmopolitanism in a Divided World'. He says in today's globalized world an overemphasis on science and technology as instruments that search for truth has de-humanized people. He underscores Daisaku Ikeda's ideas that good education leads to true humanity. Kumar locates his argument within the current debate on identity and citizenship that informs today's world. Globalization, he states, has fractured identities along the lines of race, gender, ethnicity, and other such markers. Negotiating between the positions taken by the communitarian and liberal thinkers in which the former talk of the individual in relation to the community, and the latter talk of the importance of the individual's sovereignty and freedom with the state as its arbiter, he offers the de-politicized notion of 'civic republicanism' in which the individual can retain his/her identity and yet connect with people across class, race, and religion towards a global citizenship and without the impeding presence of the state. The 'moral scope' of this form of citizenship is vast since it combines individual goals with the larger good of all humanity. When such a paradigm of value-based development and growth is transferred into the realm of education, Kumar states, the returns are invaluable.

NOTES

1. The Earth Charter was created during the late 1980s and its manifesto was completed in 2000 under the auspices of the United Nations. It has been endorsed by organizations representing millions of people. Its aims are to promote 'a just, sustainable and peaceful global society in the 21st century. It seeks to inspire in all people a new sense of global interdependence and shared responsibility for the well-being of the whole human family, the greater community of life, and future generations'. The final text was aproved by UNESCO in 2000. The text is available on the Earth Charter website in 77 languages. Available online at http://www.earthcharter.org/files/charter/charter.pdf.
2. For the Thessaloniki Conference see also the essay in this volume by Michael J. Scoullos, who was the principal coordinator of the Thessaloniki Conference.
3. The Thessaloniki Declaration was drafted in December 1997, during an international conference held in Thessaloniki, Greece, to celebrate the 20th anniversary of the Tbilisi Doctrine and to reorient education for sustainability in the 21st century. The conference was attended by participants from governmental, intergovernmental, non-governmental organizations (NGOs) and the civil society at large from 85 countries. The International Conference on Environment and Society: Education and Public Awareness for Sustainability was organized by UNESCO and the government of Greece, from 8 to 12 December 1997. The culmination of this event was the Thessaloniki Declaration—a charter for the future of education for sustainability (http://portal.unesco.org/.../ev.php-URL_ID=37610&URL_DO=DO_TOPIC&URL_SECTION=201.html).
4. The second conference on education and sustainable development took place at the university of Cyprus, 15–18 November 2007. The conference, sponsored by UNESCO and the University of Cyprus, focused on the Mediterranean. The Education for All movement was launched by UNESCO at the World Conference on Education for All in Jomtien in 1990. 155 countries and 150 organizations pledged to provide education for all by 2000 and signed the World Declaration on Education for All.
5. See UNESCO, Education for Sustainable development, United Nations Decade (2005–14), 'Objectives'. Available online at http://portal.unesco.org/education/en/ev.php-URL_ID+27234&URL_DO=DO_TOPIC&URL_SECTION=201.html
6. For an overview of the various aspects of globalization see Dower and Williams 2002 and Scholte 2000.

BIBLIOGRAPHY

Diwan, Rashmi. 2003. 'Learning for Sustainable Development: The Global Challenge and Opportunities for India', Compiled by Josephine Yazali. *Globalization and Challenges for Education: Focus on Equity and Equality NIEPA*. Delhi: Shipra.

Introduction

Dower, Nigel and John Williams (eds). 2002. *Global Citizenship: A Critical Reader*. Edinburgh: Edinburgh, UP.
Foucault, Michel. 1970. *The Order of Things*. New York: Vintage.
Govinda, R. 2003. 'Basic Education. Making it Work for the Poor. Experiences from the South', Compiled by Josephine Yazali. *Globalization and Challenges for Education: Focus on Equity and Equality NIEPA*. Delhi: Shipra.
Ikeda, Daisaku. 2001. *Soka Education*. Santa Monica: Middleway Press.
———. 2002. 'The Challenge of Global Empowerment: Education for a Sustainable Future'. Available online at http://www.sgi.org./ngo_sd-proposal.html.global.htm (accessed on 7 April 2003).
———.2004. 'Inner Transformation: Creating a Global GroundswellforPeace'. Available online at http://www. sgi-uk.org/index.php/sgi/Ikeda_Peace_Proposal (accessed on 5 September 2005).
———. 2006. 'Extreme Poverty: The Gravest Violation of Human Rights'. *The Japan Times*, 14 December. Available online at http://search.japantimes.co.jp/cgi-bin/eo20061214a1.html (accessed on 25 August 2009).
Kumar, Krishna. 2005. 'Quality of Education at the Beginning of the 21st Century—Lessons from India', *Indian Educational Review*, 41(1): 1–24. UNESCO doc. 2005/ED/EFA/MRT/PI/24. Available online at http://Portal.Unesco.org/Education/en (accessed on 18 May 2007).
Miyoshi Masao. 2001. 'Literature, Diversity, and Totality. Return to the Planet', *Comparative Literature*, 53, Autumn (4): 283–97.
Petrella, Riccardo. 2003. 'The Global Knowledge Wall', in Gilles Breton and Michael Lambert (eds), *In Universities and Globalization: Private Linkages, Public Trust*, pp. 127–35. Laval: Universite Laval/UNESCO.
Sadgopal, Anil. 2003. 'Education for Too Few', *Frontline*, 20(24). Available online at http://www. educationforallinindia.com/anilsadgopalnew.htm (accessed on 28 May 2007).
———.2004. 'Globalisation and Education. Resisting Appropriation and Distortion of Knowledge', *The People's Movement*, (May–June). Available online at http://www.doccentre.net/eldoc/n00_/01may04tpm4.html (accessed on 25 May 2007).
Scholte, Jan Aart. 2000. *Globalization: A Critical Introduction*. New York: St Martin's Press, 2000.
Scoullos, Michael. 2004. 'Evolution and Progress in Key Issues of Education for Sustainable Development (ESD)', *Soka Gakkai Quarterly*, No. 38, p. 11.
Sen, Amartya. 1999. *Development as Freedom*. Oxford: Oxford University Press.
———.2001. 'Culture and Development,' World Bank Tokyo Meeting, 13 December. Available online at www.info.worldbank.org/etods/docs/voddoes/354/688/sen_tokyo.pdf (accessed on 25 May 2007).
———. 2002. 'How to Judge Globalism', *The American Prospect*, 13(1) January 1–14. Available online at http://www.prospect.org/print/V13/1/sen-a.html (downloaded on 21 June 2006). Cited in Ravi Kumar.
Sen, Amartya and Sudair Anand. 1994. 'Sustainable Human Development: Concepts and Priorities', Occasional Paper no. 9, pp. 6–10, Human Development Report Office, UNDP, New york. Available online at http://www.undp.org/hdro/oc8a.htm (accessed on 21 May 2007).

Smith, Adam. 1993. *Wealth of Nations*. Book II, Chapter III, World Classics edition. Oxford: Oxford University Press.

Spariosu, Mihai. 2005. *Global Intelligence and Human Development. Towards an Ecology of Global Learning*. Cambridge: MIT Press.

Stiglitz, Joseph. 2002. *Globalization and Its Discontents*. New Delhi: Penguin.

Thaman Konai H. 2002. 'Shifting Sights. The Cultural Challenge of Sustainability, *International Journal of Sustainability in Higher Education*, 3(3): 233–42.

The Earth Charter, 'The Earth Charter Initiative'. Available online at http://www.earthcharter.org/files/charter/charter.pdf.

The Thessaloniki Declaration. 2002. Available online at www.mio-ecsde.org/old/Thess/declar_en.htm(accessed on 31 December 2002).

The World Commission on Environment and Development. 1987. *Our Common Future*. Oxford: Oxford University Press.

UNESCO. 'Education for Sustainable Development, United Nations Decade (2005–2014), "Objectives"'. Available online at http://portal.unesco.org/education/en/ev.php-URL_ID+27234&URL_DO=DO_TOPIC&URL_SECTION=201.html

UNESCO. 1998. 'Transdisciplinarity. Stimulating Synergies, Integrating Knowledge', Division of Philosophy and Ethics, UNESCO. Available online at http://unesdoc.unesco.org/images/0011/001146/114694eo.pdf (accessed on 3 January 2007).

Watkins, Kevin. 2000. *The Oxfam Report*. London: Oxfam.

Wollstonecraft, Mary. 1796. *A Vindication of the Rights of Women*. p. 156. London: J Johnson.

PART I
GLOBALIZATION AND THE POLITICS OF EXCLUSION

1
Caste, Exclusion, and Marginalized Groups in India: Dalit Deprivation in India

Sukhadeo Thorat

Historically, the caste system has formed the social and economic framework for the life of people in India. In its essential form, caste as a system of social and economic governance is based on certain principles and customary rules, which are distinct and unique. It involves division of people into social groups (or castes) in which the social and economic rights of each individual caste are predetermined by birth. The assignment (or division) of these rights among castes is unequal and hierarchical.

The unequal and hierarchical (graded) access to economic and social rights implies that every caste, except those at the top of the caste hierarchy, suffers from unequal division of rights. The untouchables or Scheduled Castes (SCs) or Dalits who are placed at the bottom of caste hierarchy suffered the most. They are excluded from access to property rights and social rights except for providing labour or service to the castes above them. The disadvantages of low-caste untouchables are so severe that they are physically and socially segregated from the rest of the Hindu society through the institution of untouchability. This adds an additional dimension to the physical, social, and economic exclusion of this social group. It is these comprehensive and multiple exclusions of the low-castes and untouchables, which have a severe consequence on their poverty and deprivation.

Much of the modern abhorrence of the caste system is due to the legitimate dislike of the social and economic inequality it perpetuates.

The idea of equality is completely alien to its basic governing principles and ethic. Indeed the government has recognized the inequalities, exclusion, and severe deprivation of the SCs, and many anti-discriminatory policies have been developed after the adoption of Constitution in 1950. Though these have brought about some positive changes in the economic and social condition of the SCs, they still continue to suffer from a high degree of economic deprivation resulting in disparities between them and the dominant high castes.

The main purpose of this chapter is to develop an understanding of caste-based exclusion/discrimination and its impact on lack of access to sources of income and poverty. To begin with, drawing from the theoretical interpretation, we will discuss the governing principles of the caste system that involve exclusion and discrimination; develop some insights on the concept of exclusion/discrimination—the way it has evolved in the modern economic literature; and the consequences of exclusion on poverty and economic growth. Then, we will discuss the impact of exclusion and discrimination on economic deprivation of the SCs by presenting an empirical account of their present economic and social conditions, including the evidence on continuing economic and social discrimination and exclusion.

INTERPRETING CASTE AND ITS CONSEQUENCES— INSIGHTS FROM THEORIES

In its essential form, caste as a system of production, organization, and distribution is governed by certain customary rules and norms, which are unique and distinct. In general, the caste-based economy is one in which occupations (or property rights) are hereditary, compulsory, and endogamous. The organizational scheme of the caste system is based on the division of people into social groups (or castes) in which the occupations and property rights of each individual caste are predetermined by birth and heredity. The assignment or division of occupations and property rights across castes is unequal and hierarchical. Some occupations are also considered socially inferior (or polluting), with low social status, for those engaged in them. And finally, the caste economy is maintained or enforced through the instruments of social ostracism (system of social and economic penalties) with justification and support from philosophical elements in Hindu religion (Akerlof 1976; Ambedkar 1987a; Lal 1984; Romer 1984; Scoville 1991).

In this systemic framework, the concept of 'human rights' assumes a specific meaning. Unlike many other human societies, the caste system does not recognize the individual and his/her distinctiveness as the centre of the social purpose. In fact, when it comes to rights and duties, the individual is not considered as a unit of the Hindu society. Even the family is not regarded as a unit of society except for the purposes of marriages and inheritance. The primary unit is caste and hence the rights and privileges (or lack of rights) of the individual are on account of him/her being a member of a particular caste.

The caste system is based on a graded hierarchy. Various castes are artfully interlined with each other (in their rights and duties) in such a manner that the rights and privileges of higher castes become the disadvantages of the lower castes, particularly the untouchables. In this sense, a caste cannot exist in isolation but only in tandem with other castes. Castes exist as a system of interlinked endogenous groups with inequitable rights in all walks of life. Castes at the top of the order enjoy more rights at the expense of those located at the bottom; untouchables at the bottom of caste hierarchy have much less economic and social rights. This is also due to a particular concept (or perspective) of 'human hood' involved in the caste system, under which the untouchables are considered as 'inferior human beings' and therefore are not entitled to any individual social, religious, political, and economic rights, while the high-caste Brahmins are considered as 'superior human beings' and are entitled to more rights and privileges (Ambedkar 1987a).

CONCEPT OF CASTE-BASED EXCLUSION AND DISCRIMINATION

Since the occupation and property rights of each caste are fixed and enforced, it necessarily involves forced exclusion of one caste from the occupations of other castes. Determination of occupation by birth obviously restricts the freedom of occupation, but does not necessarily lead to deprivation and poverty, provided there are reasonable sources of livelihood for each caste. However, in the case of untouchables, exclusion leads to deprivations in so far they are excluded from access to all sources of livelihood, except for the manual labour and services to the castes above them. Their exclusion is multiple, comprehensive, and complete.

The concept of 'exclusion and economic discrimination' in modern economic literature has been developed with respect to race, ethnicity, and gender. At a general level, social exclusion is considered to be a process through which individuals are wholly or partially excluded from full par-ticipation in the society in which they live. As de Haan (1997) points out, social exclusion is opposite to social integration. Sen (2000) also draws a distinction between the situation where some people are being kept out (at least left out) and where some people are being included—may even be forced to be included—in deeply unfavourable terms and described these two situations as unfavourable exclusion and unfavourable inclusion. The 'unfavourable inclusion' particularly that with unequal treatment or unacceptable arrangement may carry the same adverse effects as that of the unfavourable exclusion. This concept is quite close to the concept of 'economic discrimination' developed separately in recent economic literature related to race and gender, which recognized participation or access but with unequal treatment in labour and other markets.

Discrimination in labour markets, for instance refers to a situation of unequal treatment of the workers possessing same productivity in hiring or in wage payment due to non-economic group characteristics, such as race, colour, gender, or caste. Thus, the real relevance of an exclusionary perspective is conditional on the nature of the process of deprivation.

Banerjee and Knight (1985), among others, have applied the concept of labour market and occupational discrimination to caste. While applying the concept developed in context of race and gender to the caste, it is necessary to recognize the uniqueness of caste discrimination. The normative framework of the caste system involves exclusion and discrimination in multiple market and non-market transactions and social relations. Untouchables also suffer from social exclusion due to the practice of untouchability, which brings in an additional dimension to their discrimination and exclusion. Thus, exclusion and discrimination may involve:

1. Some groups being denied job opportunities, sale and purchase of factors of production (like agriculture land, non-land capital assets, and various factor inputs), consumer goods, social service (like education, housing, and health, including common property resources such as water bodies and land), and so on.
2. Differences between price charged or received and the market prices. This can include price of factor inputs and consumer goods, price of factors of production such as wages for labour, price of land or rent on land, interest on capital, rent on residential houses, charges or fees on services such as water and electricity.

3. The untouchables from participating in certain categories of jobs (like the sweeper being excluded from specific household jobs, such as cooking) and sale of certain consumer goods (such as vegetables/milk and similar items) because their occupation and physical touch is considered to be polluting.
4. The untouchables may also face discrimination and exclusion in the use of public services like road, temples, and water bodies.
5. Because of the physical (or residential) segregation and social exclusion due to the notion of untouchability (or touch-me-not-ism), they suffer from a general exclusion in what Sen (2000) would describe as 'constitutive relevance' of exclusion, in which the exclusion or deprivation has an intrinsic importance of its own—for instance, not being able to relate to others and take part in the life of the community can directly impoverish a person's life, in addition to the further deprivation that it may generate.

CONSEQUENCES OF DISCRIMINATION AND EXCLUSION

Economists maintain that efficient functioning of markets is of central importance in the developmental process, and can have a profound impact on economic growth and the distribution of income. Since private economy markets are the places where people get access to factors of production, employment, consumer goods and services, the exclusion and discrimination of some groups in the market transactions on the basis of their caste is a serious case of market failure. Market discrimination adversely affects both economic efficiency and income distribution. Thus, discrimination is an issue not only of equity but also of economic growth (Birdsall and Sabot 1991).

The consequences of caste system, however, are pronounced in income distribution and poverty of the excluded groups. Since the property rights are assigned unequally across the castes, the income distribution is generally skewed on caste line. The impact on the SCs is far more serious as they are excluded from the access to property rights, including education. Restriction on mobility of labour also leads to unemployment among the SCs. By not permitting readjustment of employment, caste becomes a direct cause of much of involuntary unemployment among the low castes (Akerlof 1980; Ambedkar 1987a).

Labour market discrimination slows down economic growth due to sub-optimal allocation of labour among firms and economy, by reducing job commitment and efforts of workers who perceive themselves to be the victims of discrimination and, by reducing the magnitude of investment in human capital by discriminated groups and return on this investment (Birdsall and Sabot 1991).

Further, the occupations of some castes are considered polluting and socially degrading. Forced into these occupations on account of their caste origin, people do not derive job satisfaction. In fact, such occupations constantly provoke them to aversion, ill will, and desire to evade, which also affect their efficiency. Finally, exacerbating current inequality between groups and by contributing to its perpetuation across generations, discrimination and exclusion may foster conflict. Caste-based discrimination in the access to sources of income, human development as well as discrimination of subordinate groups in civil and political arena thus has the potential for conflict.

REMEDIES AGAINST DISCRIMINATION AND EXCLUSION

Reducing economic discrimination is thus a worthwhile strategy as it is likely to increase economic growth, reduce inequality and poverty among groups, and also minimize the potential for conflict. One strand in economic theory argues that in highly competitive markets, discrimination will prove to be a transitory phenomenon as there are costs associated with discrimination to the firm/employer, which results in lowering the profits. However, others observe that market discrimination might persist over long periods for several reasons because not all markets are highly competitive and monopoly power is quite a significant feature in both developed and developing economies. Even in competitive markets, discrimination may persist if all firms practice discrimination. Therefore, correcting discrimination requires both improvements in market competitiveness and direct measures to overcome market failure. It calls for the state's interventions in various markets and non-market transactions, to provide protection against exclusion and discrimination. It also demands strategies to improve the ownership of fixed capital assets, including human capital which is remarkably deficient due to exclusion and discrimination in the past. Therefore, various measures, including compensation for exclusion in the past, figured prominently in the discussions on remedies.

ECONOMIC SITUATION OF SCHEDULED CASTES

Thus, the caste economy involves exclusion of low-caste untouchables (or Scheduled Castes) in multiple spheres, and high levels of economic deprivation and poverty. Based on the official data, we present a brief sketch of the socio-economic condition of the SCs—with respect to occupation, ownership of agricultural land and access to the non-land capital assets, education and health, employment and poverty.

The Scheduled Castes constitute about 17 per cent (equivalent to 138.2 million) of India's population in 1991. The 2001 estimate puts this figures at 18 per cent and 81 per cent of them live in rural areas spread all over the country.

OCCUPATION PATTERN

Data on occupation patterns capture the access of SC households to sources of income. The National Sample Survey Organisation (NSSO) provides data on economic activities or occupations in terms of proportion of self-employed and wage labour households. While the former is a measure of access to capital assets like agricultural land and non-land capital assets (from which SCs have been debarred historically), the latter indicate continuing dependence on the traditional occupation of wage labour (Table A1.1).

In 2000, of the total SC households in rural area, about 16.4 per cent pursued cultivation as an independent (self-employed) occupation. About 12 per cent were employed in some kind of non-farm, self-employment activities (or business). Thus, in rural areas, about 28.4 per cent of SC households had acquired some access to fixed capital assets (agricultural land and non-land asset). This was still a very low proportion compared with 55.9 per cent for other households (non-SC/ST households). In urban areas also, the access to capital assets to SC was low (27.3 per cent) as compared to other households (35.5 per cent) (Table A1.1).

Inadequate access to fixed capital assets, led to exceptionally high dependence of the SC households on manual wage labour. In 2000, the wage labour households accounted for 61.40 per cent of all SC households in rural area and 26.5 per cent in urban areas, compared to 25.3 per cent and 7.4 per cent for other households. In urban areas, 37.6 per cent of SC households also depend on regular wage and salaried jobs (see Table A1.1). Thus about 61.4 per cent of the SC households in the rural and 37.6 per cent in the urban areas continue to depend on wage employment and only about 27.3 per cent had acquired some access to fixed capital assets. As we shall see later, although close to one-third have acquired access to fixed capital assets, most of them are small and marginal farmers and petty business holders.

Information on the ownership of agricultural land by the SCs in rural area provides some insights on the low proportion of self-employed cultivators among the SC households in rural area. In 1992, about 13 per cent of SC households were landless and 87 per cent owned some land. Among the latter (that is, land-owning households), about 56 per cent owned less than one acre (of which 47.5 per cent owned less than half acre). Thus, the landless and near landless (that is, those owning less than one acre) accounted for nearly 70 per cent of the total SC households in 1991. Evidence for more recent year, 1999–2000, from an alternative source namely NSS Employment survey put the figures of landless and near landlessness among the SC in vicinity of 75 per cent (Table A1.2).

EMPLOYMENT/UNEMPLOYMENT

Since more than 60 per cent of the SC workers in rural and urban areas depend on wage employment, their earnings are determined by the level of employment and the type of wage earnings (that is, daily or regular). The SC workers seem to suffer from possible discrimination both in employment and wage earning in the labour market. The NSS data on employment for 1999–2000 indicate that the SC workers suffered from low employment. The differences in the employment rate based on usual principal status (which captures open employment/unemployment) between the SCs and others are not large. However, differences emerge clearly for employment rate based on current daily status (CDS) which capture the underemployment of the employed workers. In 2000, the CDS employment rate in the rural area was 46.2 per cent for SC male workers when compared with 47.6 per cent for other male worker. Similarly the CDS employment rate for SC workers in urban area was 45.8 per cent, compared to 49.9 per cent for other households (see Table A1.4). Disparities between the SCs and others are reflected in the unemployment rate. Unemployment rate based on CDS for SCs was about 5 per cent as compared to about 3.5 per cent for other workers in rural and urban area (Table A1.5 and Table A1.6).

The NSS data on the wage earning revealed the disparities between SC wage labour and other labour. For instance, in 1999–2000 the average weekly wage earning of an SC worker (at 1993–94 prices) was Rs 174.50 when compared to Rs 197.05 for other workers (Dubey 2003).

POVERTY

With high incidence of wage labour associated with high rate of underemployment and low wage earning, the SCs household suffer from low income and high incidences of poverty. This is reflected in the proportion of persons falling below a critical minimum level of consumption expenditure called the poverty line. In 1999–2000 about 35.43 per cent of SCs were below the poverty line in rural areas as compared to 21.14 per cent among others; in urban areas the gap was slightly larger; 39 per cent of SC and only 15 per cent among others (Table A1.7).

The variation in poverty ratio across household types or occupational groups is striking. In 1993–94 the incidence of poverty was about 60 per cent among agricultural labour followed by 41.44 per cent among non-agricultural labour. The level was relatively low for persons engaged in self-employed activities in agriculture (37.70 per cent) and in the non-agricultural sector (38.19 per cent). Poor SC households were overrepresented in these groups. In urban area, the incidence was astonishingly high among the casual labour (69.48 per cent). The poverty was also high among the self-employed households (54.60 per cent). High incidence of poverty among those SC households engaged in self-employment in agriculture and in non-agriculture indicates that they are normally concentrated in small farm and low-income petty businesses (Table A1.8). The recent data on monthly per capita expenditure (MPCE) for more recent year, 1999–2000 also bring out disparities between the two groups; practically for all household types the MPCE for the SC was lower than the other households (Table A1.9).

ACCESS TO EDUCATION AND HEALTH

In addition to property rights, SCs have been denied the right to education. There are large gaps in literacy rate and level of education between them and others. High drop-outs in school, poor quality of education, and discrimination in education, are some of the educational problems faced by the SCs. In 1991 (latest census year for which data are available), literacy rate among SCs was 37 per cent compared to 58 per cent among the non SC/ST. The literacy rate was particularly low among the females

(23 per cent), two times less when compared with other women. School attendance is about 10 per cent less among SC boys than other boys, while the difference is about 5 per cent among the girls. According to Nambissan and Sedwal (2002), discrimination in schools exists in various forms (Table A1.10).

Evidence based on National Family Health Survey data for 1998–99 revealed wide gaps between SCs and others in health status and access to health services (Tables A1.11, A1.12, and A1.13). Early marriage and high fertility characterized the SC population. The difference in the total fertility rate between them and others is more than a year. The percentage of SC women using any method of contraception and their exposure to family planning messages or media is comparatively low. Infant (83 per cent) and child mortality (39.5 per cent) among the SCs is higher than others, that is 61.8 per cent and 22.2 per cent respectively. In 1998–99, at least 56 per cent of SC women suffered from anaemia. More than 70 per cent deliveries took place at home. Only one-fourth of the deliveries took place in institution; of which more than 40 per cent were delivered by TBA (village *dais*). The incidence of morbidity among the children is high, that is more than three-fourth of the SC children are anaemic, 29.4 per cent suffered from fever, and another 19.6 per cent by ARI and diarrhoea. The extent of malnutrition and under nutrition among the SC children is high, as more than half of them suffered from this problem. High morbidity and child mortality among SCs is closely linked with poverty and low educational status, and also with discrimination in the access to health services. High incidence of illiteracy, poverty, and discrimination reduce the capacity of SC to demand and utilize the public health services.

UNTOUCHABILITY AND ATROCITIES

We now highlight SC's social disadvantages with particular reference to the practice of untouchability, and discrimination in public spheres and atrocities covered under the protection of Civil Right Act of 1955 and Prevention of Atrocities Act of 1989. Violation of civil rights include prohibition of SC to use public water bodies such as well, water tape, temple, tea stall, restaurant, community bath, road, and other social services (Table A1.14). Practice of untouchability and social discrimination continue to be of high magnitude. During the 16 year period between 1981 and 2000, a total of 3,43,461 cases of crime and atrocities were committed against the SC. Thus, annually an average of about 22,371 cases of general crimes and atrocities were committed on the SC during 1981–2000. The break-up of the atrocities and violence for the year 2000 include 486 cases of murder, 3,298 grievous hurt, 260 of arson and 1,034 cases of rape, and 13,586 cases of other offences.

EVIDENCE ON ECONOMIC DISCRIMINATION AND EXCLUSION

Preceding sections show the disparities in ownership of capital assets, employment, education, and access to health services between the SC and other households. Although there has been some improvement in the ownership of capital assets, a large proportion of SC households continue to depend on the traditional occupation of wage labour. To what extent are the disparities and segregation into traditional occupations with the legacy of the past exclusion and to what extent is it conditioned by continuing discrimination and exclusion in the market and non-market transactions or both is an important question? The issue of economic discrimination, particularly the market exclusion and discrimination has been almost neglected in the Indian social science research.

Very few studies have empirically examined the nature and magnitude of economic discrimination. Limited evidence points towards the presence of discrimination against the SC in labour and other factor markets. Studies observed that high landlessness could be due to weak resource position but also due to the discriminatory working of the land market which reduce the access of SC to purchase and leasing of agricultural land. Studies also provide evidence that discriminatory working of the labour market may explain low employment rate and wage earning of the SC workers. Banerjee and Knight (1985) observed that there is discrimination by caste, particularly on job discrimination. For example, Untouchables are disproportionately represented in poorly-paid and dead-end jobs. Even if the discrimination is no longer practised, the effects of past discrimination could be carried on to the present. This may help to explain why discrimination is the greatest in operative jobs, in which contacts are more important for recruitment, and not in white-collar jobs in which recruitment involves formal methods. The economic function which the system performs for favoured castes suggests that discrimination is based on economic interest, thereby making prejudice more difficult to eradicate.

Besides land and labour markets, some studies also found discrimination in occupation, credit, and other market transactions. A study on the practice of untouchability in Andhra Pradesh observed social ostracism being used against SCs in the change of occupation. In rural Karnataka, nearly 85 per cent of the respondents continued with their traditional occupation and only 15 per cent could make a switch over. In the urban areas, however, 56 per cent had experienced a shift from their traditional occupation (Khan 1983). A study on social/economic discrimination in Orissa by Tripathy (1985) observed discrimination in the land lease, credit, and labour markets in rural areas. Nearly 96 per cent of untouchable respondents in one village and all untouchable respondents in another village were discriminated in the wage payment; 28 per cent in one village and 20 per cent in the other faced discrimination in the share of rent. Discrimination in the interest rate charged by moneylenders was found in both the villages. A Coimbatore study by Harriss, Kannan, and Rodgers (1990) observed that caste contact played a major role in sources of information and means of access to the first jobs (also Tables A1.15, A1.16, A1.17, and A1.18).

PERSISTENCE DISCRIMINATION AND DEPRIVATION

How dynamic is the caste system? And what determines the continuity and change in caste economy? Theoretical literature by the economists underlined three elements involved in the dynamics of caste system. The changes in caste system will be influenced by the magnitude of social costs (in terms of social isolation/standing), economic cost (in terms of transaction and enforcement costs of enforcing the system), and economic gains (in term of profit and surplus appropriation to enforcer of the system). It also depends on what extent the modern ideas about human rights and equality support or contradict the one involved in the caste system. If changes in the caste system involve low social and economic costs and high economic gains, and also if a recognition and pursuit of modern concept of human rights based on equality and justice is predominant, then impulses and conditions for change would be much stronger. Conversely, traditional rules would persist or change partially if the alternative rules involve high social and economic cost and yield less economic gains to the higher caste, and that recognition and pursuit of modern ideas about human rights based on justice and equality are weak.

The caste economy has undergone changes but at the same time there is continuity in some of its traditional aspects. Empirical evidence revealed that about one-third of SC households in rural and urban areas have now acquired access to land and non-land capital assets, from which they were prohibited. In urban areas, about 38 per cent were also employed in regular/salaried jobs. The literacy rate has improved three-fold, from 10 per cent in 1961 to 37 per cent in 1991. This improvement needs to be seen in the background of traditional restrictions for SCs in the ownership of capital assets and education. The cumulative impact of this and other improvements is reflected in decline in poverty, from 59 per cent in 1983–84 to 35 per cent in 1999–2000 in rural areas.

Notwithstanding these gains, the disparities between them and other sections of Indian society still continue as they lag behind with respect to the number of development indicators. The access of SC to fixed capital assets is still very low and as a result, for employment a large majority of them depend on their traditional occupation, namely the wage labour. However, the employment rate and the wage earnings are low compared with other sections, as they face discrimination in the labour market. Disparities of a similar magnitude are observed in the case of education and access to health services. The cumulative impact of these deprivations was such that although the level of poverty among them had declined, the gap between them and the other sections (that is non-SC/ST) still continues. In order to reduce the disparities in poverty between SC and others, the poverty among the SC should necessarily decline at a faster rate than other. During 1983–2000, poverty among the SC had declined at lower per annum rate (–2.50 per cent) as compared to the others (–3.02 per cent) (preliminary observation by Dubey and de Hann, DFID [2003]).

APPENDIX

Table A1.1 Occupational Pattern: Scheduled Caste and Others (in Percentage)

Occupational category	1987–88 SC	1987–88 Other	1993–94 SC	1993–94 Other	1999–00 SC	1999–00 Other
Rural						
Self-employed in Agriculture	18.90	43.3	19.12	42.42	16.4	41.1
Self-employed in Non-agriculture	11.0	13.8	10.32	13.89	12.0	14.8
Self-employed (Total)	29.90	57.1	29.44	56.31	28.4	55.9
Agricultural Wage Labour	51.7	23.2	50.6	22.37	51.4	19.0
Non-agricultural Wage Labour	11.4	09.7	10.22	6.67	10.0	6.3
Wage Labour (Total)	63.1	32.9	60.82	29.04	61.4	25.3
Others	06.9	11.5	9.67	14.62	10.2	18.7
Urban						
Self-employed	28.0	35.2	24.08	35.05	27.3	35.5
Regular Wage/Salaries	39.4	45.0	39.27	43.11	37.6	46.5
Casual Labour	26.0	10.3	26.96	10.57	26.5	7.4
Others Wage	08.5	09.2	9.67	11.25	8.5	10.5

Source: NSS Employment/Unemployment Survey, 1987–88, and 1993–94 CSO, Delhi.
Note: SC = SCHEDULED CASTE; OTHERS = NON SC/ST (excluding Scheduled Caste and Scheduled Tribe).

Table A1.2 Percentage of Landless and Near Landless Households among Scheduled Castes (% to total rural households in India)

1982					1992					1999–2000				
Land Less	Less than Half Acre	Between Half and One Acre	Up to One Acre	Landless and up to One Acre	Land Less	Less than Half Acre	Between Half and One Acre	Upto One Acre	Land Less and upto One Acre	Land Less	Less than Half Acre	Between Half and One Acre	Upto One Acre	Land Less and upto One Acre
12.62	47.97	9.53	57.50	70.12	13.34	47.50	8.89	56.39	69.73	10.0	65.0	14.7	6.50	2.80

Source: Figures for 1982 and 1992 are based on NSS landholding survey, and the figures for 1999–2000 is based on NSS Employment/Unemployment Survey.

Table A1.3 Land Ownership Background of Rural Labour Households (in percentage)

	Other (Non-SC/ST)		SC	
	1974–75	1993	1974–75	1993
Without Land	55.97	81.19	44.38	35.05
With Land	44.02	18.81	55.65	64.95
Total	100.00	100.00	100.00	100.00
With Land by Size (in hectares)	1993–94			
	All Households	SC Households		
<0.4	59.60	68.00		
0.4–1	27.10	21.90		
>1	13.30	10.10		

Source: Labour Bureau, 1974–75, 1983–84, 1987–88, 1993–94.

Table A1.4 Employment Rate 1999–2000—All India

	Scheduled caste		Other	
	Male	Female	Male	Female
Rural				
Usual Principal Status	52.4	25.5	50.9	15.5
Usual Principal and Subsidiary	53.1	32.5	52.0	22.3
Current Weekly	50.5	27.0	50.1	19.1
Current Daily	46.2	21.2	47.6	149.0
Urban				
Usual Principal Status	49.8	15.2	51.4	9.0
Usual Principal and Subsidiary	50.3	18.5	51.8	10.8
Current Weekly	48.6	16.7	51.3	10.0
Current Daily	45.8	14.0	49.9	8.9

Source: Employment/Unemployment Survey, 1999–2000.

Table A1.5 Unemployment Rate (Age 5 years and above) in Rural Areas

Category/year	Male				Female			
	Usual principal status	Principal and subsidiary	Current weekly status	Current daily status	Usual principal status	Principal and subsidiary	Current weekly status	Current daily status
Scheduled Caste								
1999–2000	1.20	1.00	2.50	5.00	0.30	0.20	1.00	2.10
1993–94	0.90	0.60	1.90	4.30	0.30	–	1.10	2.00
1987–88	1.30	0.90	–	–	1.40	1.10	–	–
1983	1.10	0.76	3.22	7.16	0.40	0.23	2.16	2.23
1977–78	1.10	0.00	2.93	6.73	2.20	0.00	1.90	4.00
Others								
1999–2000	1.60	1.20	2.50	3.50	0.50	0.50	1.20	1.40
1993–94	1.20	0.90	1.60	2.70	0.44	–	0.80	1.11
1987–88	1.70	1.10	–	–	0.48	0.70	–	–
1983	1.30	1.90	2.15	4.03	0.43	0.29	0.91	1.72
1977–78	1.57	0.00	2.15	3.90	1.53	0.00	0.97	0.97

Source: NSS Employment/Unemployment Survey of Various Round, NSSO, Delhi.

Table A1.6 Unemployment Rate (Age 5 years and above) in Urban Areas

Category/year	Male				Female			
	Usual principal status	Principal and subsidiary	Current weekly status	Current daily status	Usual principal status	Principal and subsidiary	Current weekly status	Current daily status
Scheduled Caste								
1999–2000	2.80	2.70	3.70	5.20	0.60	0.60	0.70	1.20
1993–94	–	2.60	3.30	4.90	–	0.00	0.00	1.70
1987–88	–	3.50	–	–	–	1.10	–	–
1983	–	3.20	4.40	7.20	–	0.80	1.20	1.70
1977–78	–	3.40	4.50	7.37	–	3.40	1.10	4.20
Others								
1999–2000	2.70	2.50	3.00	3.50	1.00	0.90	1.10	1.10
1993–94	–	2.40	2.70	5.28	–	1.10	1.30	1.40
1987–88	–	3.20	–	–	–	1.20	–	–
1983	–	3.10	4.00	5.35	–	0.90	1.00	1.42
1977–78	–	3.33	4.24	5.35	–	2.60	0.00	0.00

Source: NSS Employment/Unemployment Reports 32nd, 38th, 43rd, and 50th Round.
Note: SC = Scheduled Caste; OT = non-SC/ST.

Table A1.7 Poverty Social Groups in Rural Area 1993–1994 and 1999–2000

States	1993–1994				1999–2000				Change 1993/1999			
	ST	SC	Others	All	ST	SC	Others	All	ST	SC	Others	All
Andhra Pradesh	26.94	26.01	11.79	15.95	23.07	16.47	7.39	10.54	-2.39	-6.11	-6.22	-5.65
Madhya Pradesh	59.59	47.92	27.46	39.28	57.19	39.22	22.22	33.74	-0.67	-3.03	-3.18	-2.35
Orissa	71.31	49.84	40.16	49.79	73.10	52.30	33.29	48.05	0.42	0.82	-2.85	-0.58
West Bengal	62.09	46.03	35.53	41.17	50.05	34.91	28.42	31.65	-3.23	-4.10	-3.34	-3.85
Total (all India)	47.05	48.31	31.19	37.28	44.33	35.43	21.14	26.50	-0.96	-4.44	-5.37	-4.82

Source: Dubey 2003.

Table A1.8 Percentage of Persons Below-Poverty-Line by Household Type for Each Social Group

Category	Self-employed in agriculture		Self-employment in non-agriculture		Agriculture labour		Non-agriculture		Others labour		All	
	87–88	93–94	87–88	93–94	87–88	93–94	87–88	93–94	87–88	93–94	87–88	93–94
Rural												
Scheduled Caste	41.21	37.70	41.60	38.19	59.77	60.00	46.49	41.44	29.98	29.00	50.07	48.14
Others	25.57	25.57	31.42	29.49	53.30	52.34	34.45	35.59	19.26	20.19	34.37	31.29

Category	Self-employed		Regular Service/wage earner		Casual labour		Others		All	
	87–88	93–94	87–88	93–94	87–88	93–94	87–88	93–94	87–88	93–94
Urban										
Scheduled Caste	61.48	54.60	43.69	35.28	73.45	69.48	56.84	45.00	56.84	49.90
Others	33.60	33.64	25.26	19.04	70.10	60.60	32.21	26.06	37.21	29.66

Source: Based on NSSO, 1987–88 and 1993–94, *Consumption Expenditure*, CSO, New Delhi.

Caste, Exclusion, and Marginalized Groups

Table A1.9 Average MPCE of Rural Households Classified by Household Type, Social Group (in rupees) 1999–2000

Average MPCE of rural households classified by household type and social groups (in Rupees)

Household type	Average MPCE (Rs) of households of social groups			
	SC	OBC	others	all
Rural				
Self-employed in Agriculture	435.46	495.09	557.19	502.28
Agricultural Labour	378.31	397.08	419.35	385.98
Other Labour	438.09	496.18	554.31	482.74
Self-employed in agriculture	442.22	488.02	602.81	519.53
Other Households	581.87	591.23	733.68	652.05
All households	418.51	473.65	577.22	485.88
Urban				
Self-employed	542.68	674.97	953.00	812.96
Regular Wage/salaried	754.69	859.34	1101.05	981.49
Casual Labour	463.58	608.23	548.65	540.66
Other Households	649.49	860.69	1207.74	1030.82
All Households	608.79	734.82	1004.75	854.70

Source: NSS, Consumption Expenditure Survey 55th Round—1999–2000.

Table A1.10 Literacy Rate of Scheduled Caste and Others

	1961	1971	1981	1991	2001
General (including SC & ST)	24.00	29.45	36.23	52.21	65.38
Non-SC/ST population	27.91	33.80	41.30	57.69	
SCs	10.27	14.67	21.38	37.41	
Gap between literacy rates among the SCs and non-SC/ST communities	17.64	19.13	19.92	20.28	

Source: Census of India, 1991.

Table A1.11 Infant Mortality—1998–99 (in percentage)

Indicators	Scheduled caste 1998–99	Other backward caste 1998–99	Others 1998–99
1. Infant Mortality	83.00	76.00	61.8
	(88)	(82)	(69)
2. Child Mortality	39.5	29.00	22.2
3. Under five Mortality	119	103	82

Source: International Institute of Population Studies, National Family Health Survey—1998–99, Mumbai.
Note: Figure in the bracket indicate the infant mortality in rural area.

Table A1.12 Morbidity—1998-99 (in percentage)

Indicators	Scheduled caste 1998-99	Other backward caste 1998-99	Others 1998-99
1. Prevalence of			
(i) ARI	19.6	19.1	18.7
(ii) Fever	29.4	28.1	30.4
(iii) Diarrhoea	19.8	18.3	19.1
2. Percentage of Children with Anemia	78.3	72.0	72.7
3. Percentage of children vaccinated			
4. Percentage of Public Medical Services as sources of childhood vaccination	87.2	83.0	77.3
5. Treatment of Diarrhoea from Public Health Facilities	64.6	63.8	66.1
6. Weight for age			
(i) % below 3SD	21.2	18.3	13.8
(ii) % below 2SD	53.5	47.3	41.1

Source: NFHS—1998-1999.

Table A1.13 Women's Health—1998-99 (in percentage)

Indicators	Scheduled caste 1998-99	Other backward caste 1998-99	Others 1998-99
1. Percentage of women with Anemia	56.0	50.7	47.6
2. Percentage of women with Antenatal check-up	61.8	65.2	72.1
3. Percentage of those received tetanus vaccination	74.2	76.8	80.0
4. Place of delivery (at Home)	72.1	62.0	59.0
5. Assistance during delivery			
(a) From TAB (Dia)	37.7	34.9	31.4
(b) From public health service	36.0	44.9	48.9
6. Postpartum check-up (within two month)	17.0	15.6	18.3

Source: National Family Health Survey—1998-99.

Caste, Exclusion, and Marginalized Groups

Table A1.14 Crimes and Atrocities against Scheduled Castes, 1981-2000

Year	Murder	Grievous hurt	Rape	Arson	Others	Crime under POA	Total
1981	493	1,492	604	1,295	10,434	14,318	28,636
1982	514	1,429	635	1,035	11,441	15,054	30,108
1983	525	1,351	640	993	11,440	14,949	29,898
1984	541	1,454	692	973	12,327	15,987	31,974
1985	502	1,367	700	980	11,824	15,373	30,746
1986	564	1,408	727	1,002	11,715	15,416	30,832
1989	556	1,630	830	51	12,080	–	–
1990	584	1,691	885	599	13,908	–	–
1991	610	1,706	784	602	13,944	–	–
1992	616	–	849	406	19,592	–	–
1995	571	4,544	837	500	11,056	13,925	31,433
1996	543	4,585	949	464	13,862	9,620	30,023
1997	504	3,462	1,002	384	12,149	7,831	25,338
1998	–	–	–	–	–	–	25,638
1999	506	3,241	1,000	337	14,925	5,084	25,093
2000	486	3,298	1,034	260	13,586	5,078	23,742

Source: Annual Reports of Commission for the Scheduled Caste and Tribe, Delhi.
Note: POA stands for Prevention of Atrocities Act.

**Table A1.15 Practice of Untouchability—Andhra Pradesh
(% to total respondents)**

Sl. No	Item	Very frequently	Frequently	Less frequently	Rarely	Did not do	Total
1.	Bar on temple entry	30.30	25.76	10.10	20.20	13.64	100.0
2.	Objection to sitting among upper caste Hindus in a public place	22.22	28.79	25.76	04.55	18.69	100.0
3.	Objections to entering upper caste Hindu houses	23.23	30.30	25.25	06.06	15.15	100.0
4.	Objection to taking a marriage procession in a upper caste Hindu locality	23.23	29.80	22.22	04.84	20.71	100.0
5.	Objection to a fetch water from a public well or tap	19.19	18.18	22.73	07.58	32.32	100.0
6.	Beating by upper caste Hindus	12.12	25.76	29.80	04.04	28.28	100.0
7.	Raiding	14.14	23.74	26.77	12.12	23.23	100.0

(Table A1.15 Continued)

(Table A1.15 Continued)

Sl. No	Item	Very frequently	Frequently	Less frequently	Rarely	Did not do	Total
8.	Looting	13.64	26.26	25.25	11.62	23.23	100.0
9.	Kidnapping	05.05	09.09	26.77	10.61	48.48	100.0
10.	Insults to Harijan Women	27.27	31.31	16.16	14.14	11.11	100.0
11.	Torture	11.11	17.17	35.35	20.20	16.16	100.0
12.	Attempt to Murder	05.56	14.14	18.18	11.11	51.01	100.0
13.	Refusal of a demand for higher wages	24.75	20.71	10.61	15.66	28.28	100.0
14.	Protest against occupational change	16.67	27.78	15.66	19.70	20.20	100.0
15.	Attempts to occupy lands	28.28	22.73	23.23	10.10	15.66	100.0
16.	Prevention from exercising franchise	25.25	18.18	21.72	11.62	23.23	100.0
17.	Prevention from participation in political activity	23.74	16.67	15.66	14.65	29.29	100.0
18.	Threats against not voting for their candidates	29.29	35.35	09.60	06.57	19.19	100.0
19.	Threats against contesting in an election	12.63	28.79	25.25	15.66	17.68	100.0
20.	Forced rendering of services in respect of a birth	15.15	21.78	31.82	07.58	23.74	100.0
21.	Forced rendering services in respect of a marriage	15.15	20.20	29.29	17.17	18.18	100.0
22.	Forced rendering of services in respect of death	16.16	19.19	35.35	14.14	15.15	100.0

Source: Venkateswarlu 1990.

Table A1.16 Social Discrimination: Orissa

	Kesharpur village		Jari village	
	No	Yes	No	Yes
(A) Are you prohibited water from any public well and public tube-well in village?	12	15	35	50
(B) Do you enjoy equal status?	Yes	No	Yes	No
(a) Village community feasts	–	15	–	50
(b) Marriages with non-harijans	–	15	–	50
(c) Village meetings and its decision-making process	–	15	17	50
(d) Taking drinks and snacks from the tea shops	3	15	10	50

(Table A1.16 Continued)

Caste, Exclusion, and Marginalized Groups

(Table A1.16 Continued)

	Kesharpur village		Jari village	
	Yes	No	Yes	No
(e) Getting groceries from grocery shops	3	15	15	50
(f) Worship in village temples	–	15	–	50
(g) Barber service	–	15	–	50
(h) Washer man service	–	15	–	50
(i) Cowherds man service	3	15	–	50
(j) Priest service (in marriage/death/ Festive occasions)	–	15	–	50
(C) Are you discriminated in? (Multiple response permissible)	Yes	No	Yes	No
(a) Schools	–	15	–	50
(b) Hospitals	–	15	–	50
(c) Transport services	3	15	23	50
(d) Village dramas	12	15	50	50
(e) Village festivals	12	15	37	50

Source: Tripathy 1990.

Table A1.17 Economic Discrimination: Orissa

No.	Are you discriminated against in case of the following? (Multiple response permissible)	Kesharpur village		Jari village	
		No	Yes	Yes	No
(a)	Wage rate	15	15	48	50
(b)	Share in rent renting	3	15	14	50
(c)	Interest rate in case of paddy loan	–	15	–	50
(d)	Interest rate from money lender	12	15	15	50

Source: Tripathy 1990.

Table A1.18 Orissa, 1987–88

	Yes	No
(a) Stop employing as labourers	50	50
(b) Prevent buying food and groceries from the shops	21	50
(c) Withdrawal of borrowing facilities	16	50
(d) Prevent the use of public well/tube wells	18	50
(e) Commit Atrocities (Arson/Rape/Murder/Violence)	50	50

Source: Tripathy 1990.
Note: If you protest against high caste discrimination, the above-mentoned steps might be taken against you by the high caste? (multiple response permissible)

BIBLIOGRAPHY

Akerlof, George. 1976. 'The Economic of Caste and of Rat Race and Other Woeful Tales', *Quarterly Journal of Economics*, XC (November): 599–617.

———. 1980. 'The Theory of Social Customs, of Which Unemployment May Be One Consequence', *Quarterly Journal of Economics*, XCIV (June): 749–75.

Ambedkar B. R. 1987a. 'Philosophy of Hinduism', in Vasant Moon (ed.), *Dr. Babasaheb Ambedkar Writings and Speeches*, pp 1–115. Bombay: Department of Education, Government of Maharashtra.

———. 1987b. 'The Hindu Social Order—Its Essential Features', in Vasant Moon (ed.), *Dr. Babasaheb Ambedkar Writing and Speeches*, pp. 95–115. Bombay: Department of Education, Government of Maharashtra.

Banerjee, Biswjit and J. B. Knight. 1985. 'Caste Discrimination in Indian Urban Labour Market', *Journal of Developing Economics*, 88(2): 292–300.

Birdsall, Nancy and Richard Sabot. 1991. 'Unfair Advantage—Labour Market Discrimination in Developing Countries', *World Bank Studies*.

Census of India. 1991. Final Population Total, Registrar General, New Delhi.

Darity, William and Steven Shulman. 1989. *Question of Discrimination—Racial Inequality in the U.S. Labour Market*. Middletown, Connecticut: Wesleyan University Press.

Deshi, A.K. and H. Singh. 1995. 'Education, Labour Market Distortions and Relative Earning of Different Religious—Caste Categories in India', *Canadian Journal of Development of Studies* (special issue).

DFID (Department for International Development). 2003. *Caste in South Asia and Economic Exclusion—Briefing for Secretary of State*. Delhi: DFID.

de Haan, Arjan. 1997. 'Poverty and Social Exclusion: A Comparison of Debates on Deprivation', Working Paper no. 2. Poverty Research Unit, University of Sussex, Sussex, Brighton.

———. 2003. 'Extreme Deprivation in Remote Areas in India: Social Exclusion as Explanatory Concept', Manchester Conference on Chronic Poverty. Session 'Social Exclusion, Rights and Chronic Poverty', Manchester, July.

Dubey, Ameresh. 2003. Note and Statistical Tables on Social Groups. Delhi: DFID Department for International Development.

Harriss, J., K. P. Kannan, and G. Rodgers. 1990. *Urban Labour Market Structure and Job Access in India: A Study of Coimbatore*. Geneva: International Institute of Labour Studies.

Khan, Mumtaz Ali. 1983. *Status of Rural Women in India: A Study of Karnataka*. Delhi: South Asia Books.

Lal, Deepak. 1984. *'Hindu Equalibrium', Cultural Stability and Economic Stagnation*. Carendor: Oxford.

Labour Bureau. 1974–75, 1983–84, 1987–88, 1993–94. *Rural Labour Enquiry, Report of General Characteristics of Rural Labour Households*. Shimla: Ministry of Labour.

Nambissan, G.B. and M. Sedwal. 2002. *Education for All: The Situation of Dalit Children in India*. Oxford: Oxford UP.

Randive, B.T. 1997. 'Caste, Class, and Property Relations', *Economic and Political Weekly*, Annual no. X (February): 20–30.

Romer, David. 1984. 'The Theory of Social Custom: A Modification and some Extension', *Quarterly Journal of Economics*, 8(5): 45–56.

Scoville, James G. L. 1991. 'Towards a Model of Caste Economy', in James G. Scoville (ed.), *Status Influences in Third World Labour Markets, Caste, Gender and Custom*, pp. 70–89. New York: Prentice.

———. 1996. 'Labour Market under Pinnings of a Caste Economy—Failing the Caste Theorem', *The American Journal of Economics and Sociology*, 55(4): 385–94.

Sen, Amartya. 2000. 'Social Exclusion: Concept, Application, and Scrutiny', Social Development Papers, presented at the Office of Environment and Social Development, Asian Development Bank, Manila.

Shah, Amita and D.C. Sah. 2004. 'Poverty among Tribals in South West Madhya Pradesh: Has Anything Changed over Time?' *Journal of Human Development*, 5(2): 249–263.

Thorat, S.K. 1996. 'Ambedkar on Economics of Hindu Social Order: Understanding its Orthodoxy and Legacy', in Walter Fernandes (ed.), *The Emerging Dalit Identity*, pp. 15–29. Delhi: Indian Social Institute.

———. 1996–1997. *Report of the Working Groups on Development and Welfare of Scheduled Castes during Eighth Five-year plan, 1990–95*. Government of India Ministry of Welfare, New Delhi.

———. 1998–1999. *Annual Report, 1997–98*. Government of India, Ministry of Social Justice and Empowerment, New Delhi.

———. 1999a. 'Caste and Labour Market Discrimination', *Indian Journal of Labour Economics*, Conference Issue (with R.S. Deshpande), pp. 7–78.

———. 1999b. 'Poverty; Caste and Child Labour: Plight of Scheduled Caste and Tribal Childrens', in Klues Voll (ed.), *Against Child Labour in India*, pp. 80–90, 2004–05. Delhi: F.E.S Foundation.

———. 1999c. 'Social Security in Unorganized Sector; How Secure are the Scheduled Caste?' *Indian Journal of Labour Economics*. Special Issue.

———. 1999d. *Rural Wage Labour—Magnitute; Employment and Wage Rate: A Comparative Analysis of Scheduled Caste, Scheduled Tribe and Others in India*. Chennai: Ambedkar Centre for Economics Studies, University of Madras.

———. 2001. *Dalit NGOs— Approaches to Dalit Empowerment*. A study for EED, With Bernward Casusemann, Boon, Germany.

———. 2002a. 'Oppressions and Denial: Dalit Discrimination in the 1990s', *Economic and Political Weekly*, xx(9 February): 21–26.

———. 2002b. 'Caste and Economic Discrimination, Reflections on Theory, Concept and Consequences', Conference paper, Goa University, Panaji.

———. 2003a. 'Will Strategy of Disincentive and Targeting Help to Control Population? Limitation of 2001 Population Policy', *Ambedkar Journal of Social Sciences*, special volume (January): 20–35.

———. 2003b. Planning Commission Delhi, Tenth Five Year Plan, Chapter 4.1, Socially Disadvantage Group.

———. 2004. 'Annual Report of National Commission for Scheduled Castes and Scheduled Tribes'1999–2000 & 2000–2001.

Thurow, Lester C. 1969. *Poverty and Discrimination*. Washington, D.C.: The Brookings Institution.

Tripathy, R.B. 1990. *Dalit: A Sub-human Society*. Delhi: Ashish Publisher.

Tripathy, Ram Niranjan. 1985. 'Cluster Planning for Production and Employment: A Project Approach to IRD Programme Planning', National Institute of Rural Development, Jatni Block, Puri (District), Orissa.

Venkateswarlu, D. 1990. *Harijan—Upper Class Conflict*. Delhi: Discovery Publisher.

2
Education in a Globalizing Era: Implications for Disabled Girls*

Anita Ghai

INTRODUCTION

One of the casualties of the ever increasing forces of globalization has been education, often understood as instrumental in providing an entry into the social, economic, and political world. Globalization, by definition, is broadly understood as 'a stretching of social, political and economic activities across frontiers such that events, decisions and activities that take place in one region can have significance for people in other regions' (Held and McGrew 2003: 54). While maintaining that globalization offers immense possibilities in enhancing trade, communication, interaction, travel as well as culture, there is agreement about its selective and uneven nature.

As Alison Symington (2002: 3) says, 'Its impact is felt in innumerable ways by various groups of people in different regions of the world; the process of globalisation is exacerbating existing inequalities and at the same time they produce all new divisions and asymmetries.' While it may take different forms, the dominant pattern is that of neoliberal capitalist ideals. Structural adjustment policies, which aim to balance budgets and increase competitiveness through trade and price liberalization, include reduction of the public sector expenditure and growth of the private sector, privatization of social services. The increasing privatization and a recasting of citizens as consumers result in the state losing power

*Reprinted from permission from *Social Change* (Volume 36, No. 3, September 2006).

because the locus of control shifts from the public domain of politics to an individualized and privatized world of economic cost and benefit analysis. This privileges the paradigm of profit over humanity which then pervades all aspects of life. Access to capital and markets is controlled by relatively small elites, primarily male-centric and mostly based in rich countries. For the developing countries like China and India, this leads to an ever increasing estrangement with the socialist ideals that they were identified with. The most devastating impact of the neoliberal policies is that they restrict the revenue of the state for use for welfare purposes. Consequently, governments find themselves unable to finance education. The pious intent of governments thus remains only in theory. For instance, in the National Policy of Education (NPE) (1986: Para 11.4), it was stated that 'the investment on education be gradually increased to reach a level of 6 per cent of the National Income as early as possible.' However, these commitments never became a reality. Now with the government's increasing dependence on external sources for financing a priority sector such as elementary education, the picture is extremely dismal.

Regardless of the initial reluctance to accept external funding in the education sector, the government policy changed drastically in the last 15 years. The result was that it was now not independent in drafting the education policy as the funding agencies demanded their pound of flesh in the form of the World Bank-sponsored District Primary Education Programme (DPEP). The programme, according to many researchers, meant 'the roll-back of the state, of contracting commitments for formal education, of the dismantling of existing structures of formal education, proliferation of 'teach anyhow' strategies, a thrust on publicity management, and a neo-conservative reliance on the community' (GOI 2000: 61; Kumar et al. 2001).

The compulsion to reduce spending on education was thus imperative, delimiting access to education for a vast segment of the population who live on the margins of society. In fact, their struggles have demonstrated that right to education rather than being a universal right represents 'a terrain of struggle over forms of knowledge, social practices, and values that constitute the critical elements of tradition' (Giroux 1988: 5). While every child is implicated in such attempts, the worst affected are the so-called vulnerable groups that were in any case marginalized in the education process. This marginalization can be caused by class, caste, gender, rural/urban divide, and ability/disability. While it is true that almost half the children in the age group of 5–14 are out of school (Sadgopal 2000: 251), the fantasy that there will be space for children with disabilities, especially if segregated schooling is advocated for them is really far-fetched.

Notwithstanding the fact that girls, poor, and tribal/backward are out of school, the education of the disabled still remains a contested site. The twin forces of globalization as well as the politics of normative hegemony make life of disabled girls traumatic. As Susan Peters (1999: 104) observes, 'The disabled students are relegated to a silent and silenced world where they become what they are perceived as being: incapable, illiterate, dysfunctional, and non-productive members of school and society.' To understand this politics of silencing, it is important to understand disability.

WHAT IS DISABILITY?

Within the dominant Indian cultural ethos the fate of the disabled is sealed with labels such as *langra* (crippled), *aandha* or *surdas* (blind), *behra* (deaf), and *pagal* (mad). The assumption of the labels' 'naturalness' is unquestioned. The assumption has its roots in the ideology that conceives disability as inherent in the mind or body. Deficiency and lack of ability are associated with these mental representations of disabled. In a culture that valorises perfection, all deviations from the perfect body or mind signify abnormality, defect, and distortion. Conveying feelings of inability and uselessness, disability epitomises 'failure', and gets conceived of as a personal tragedy. Destiny is seen as the culprit, and disabled people are accorded the 'victim status' with a clear enunciation that posits disability as a retribution for past *karmas* (actions) from which there can be no reprieve. Disability is thus constructed as an essential characteristic of the individual. The popular images in mythology attest to extreme negativity associated with disability in India. While there are different strands in the historical rendering of the myths, the associations that are conveyed construct the disabled as objects of pity and charity coupled with images of deviance, treachery, evil behaviour, and villainy. As I have pointed out in *(Dis) Embodied Form: Issues of Disabled Women*, another set of images portrays the disabled as capable of heroic efforts that result in overcoming the disability, setting an exemplary standard for others to follow. Needless to add, the objective of all these images is to posit disability as an oppositional category of normality.

A paradigmatic shift in disability and related issues came in the form of recognition that social oppression transforms 'impairment' into 'disability'. It highlights the tendency of the medical constructions that encourage cure/overcoming theories. The naturalness of disability thus gains further sanction from the overarching medical model. While the intervention of global agencies such as the World Health Organization (WHO) and the United Nations has brought in a change in the terminology used to define disabling conditions, these men, women, and children continue to be excluded and marginalized in every walk of life. Notwithstanding the neglect and associated negativity, the disabled have in the last three decades advocated their cause to reach a position where society is beginning to engage with the issues that concern their lives in some concerted way. One of the principal safeguards that have the potential to contest marginalization is education which has not been an easy endeavour for the disabled. To understand the marginalization it is necessary to comprehend the political economy of disability.

POLITICAL ECONOMY OF DISABILITY

If we consider the fact that even in the forward thinking movements such as feminism, disability is understood more as an individual's medical impairment, it will be easy to comprehend that the difficult interaction between the disabled individual's capacity to produce (labour) and the means of production, is rooted in the shackles imposed by the capitalist system. What needs to be articulated and understood is that the responsibility for turning the impairment into disability lies with the economic system. Although work is the central tenet of any capitalist system, the way it has evolved will clarify its effect on the disabled. It isn't as if the disabled had a carefree life before capitalism; they however, did have spaces in family-based work as well as local units that would absorb them in a dignified way. However, a shift came with capitalism as both the social organization and the concept of human labour changed (Stewart and Russell 2001: 61–75) with increasing assembly lines as well as precise mechanization of factory work; the disabled workers were not seen as having any value. They were excluded because they were not in a position to keep pace with the factory-based system of production. As Ernest Mandel (1962) noted, capitalism throws out of the production process a section of the proletariat: unemployed, old people, disabled persons, the sick, and so on. Consequently they were coded as 'needy'. In a capitalist society, disability according to Oliver (1990) became a marker through which people were categorized as belonging to either the work-based or needs-based system of distribution. In such a categorization, disabled people are excluded from the wage labour system as they do not fulfil the demands of the capitalist society. Commenting upon both the categorization and the medicalisation of the issue of disability, Oliver (1990) further states that:

It is possible to argue that the formal rationality underpinning the disability category makes it the ascription of privilege, in that it offers legitimate social status to those unable to work. But the substantive rationality, enshrined in the experience of disability, is much more concerned with the processes of stigmatisation and oppression.

This tendency gains impetus resulting in an increasing marginalization of the disabled thereby having a direct impact on the educational system which becomes a collaborator in keeping the disabled unskilled, further adding to their anguish. An employee who is significantly disabled is not likely to become an employee at all. It is not uncommon to find disabled people who have been impaired on a job and yet have to lead a marginal life thereafter because of the disabled-unfriendly environment. Thus, disabled people are disempowered because bodies which do not fit or require additional resources to become a part of the production are rejected in the system which emphasizes profit. Factors such as the reluctance to provide disabled-friendly environment, non-availability of materials in alternative formats for visually impaired people, and the mammoth task of acquiring even the disability certification are all geared towards keeping the employment rates for the disabled abysmally low. However, these low rates were not seen as having any relationship with the structural and attitudinal barriers in the capitalist society. It is worth noticing that the multinational corporations that abide by the legislations regarding accessibility both built and augmentative communication change drastically as they stepped into developing countries such as India. As Marta Russell (1998: 203) writes, 'do not act on the basis of what is good for the society, but on what will maximise profits'. Most dangerously, corporations acting in their own interests 'lull citizens into a false sense of security'. Therefore, employers will never think of social justice as a highly prioritized option. The revival and resurgence (not that it was ever dead) of capitalism in a globalizing world where global markets determine the policies results in rendering of disability purely in medical and labelling terms. Capitalism requires that greater value is placed upon individuals who make a productive contribution to the market economy. This image of not being able to contribute to production has serious implications on all walks of life, including education which is seen more in instrumentalist terms rather than genuine empowerment. Consequently, training offered to the disabled often has little or no meaning outside the special school classroom. As the national focus group points out:

With these so-called vocational skills that we impart, the disabled will never be able to catch up with their peers or transfer the skills taught in school to the real world, because society has no jobs for them. Thus, we deny most of the disabled a real chance of becoming gainfully employed and living a healthy life.[1]

A move away from construction of deficiency mandates that we provide skills that focus on full and equal citizenship rather than a bare minimum. It would be in order to understand the existing educational scenario.

EXISTING SCENARIO

While educational and rehabilitative services were launched as early as 1880 (Chauhan 1998: 46), it was not till 1992 that a statuary body called Rehabilitation Council of India (RCI) started functioning to recognize the need for systemic efforts in the rehabilitation of the disabled. The intervening period saw sporadic attempts aimed at rehabilitation both by disabled people and by non-governmental organizations (NGOs). It was with the declaration of the year 1981, as the International Year of the Disabled Persons that renewed efforts to rehabilitate disability gained impetus. That the dominant political discourse is neither concerned with the absolute number of disabled people nor with their social relevance and validity can be judged from the initial reluctance of census 2001 to exclude them from a preliminary head count. This was despite the fact that the first legislation advocating equal rights for disabled people became a living reality in 1996. Though disability can be conceptualized in numerous ways, namely, as an identity, as a symbol of oppression, as a marginal social status, as membership in a minority group, as an embodied experience, and as something distinct from impairment, the dominant bio-medical discourse looks at it as a disease. However, even developments within the social model of disability that have understood disability as an oppression tend to negate the experience of impairment, as they too tend to essentialize society as the root cause. It is important to understand that there are many key players involved and unless a holistic understanding of disability is evolved things are not likely to change much.

Notwithstanding the fact that the discourse in the developed world has progressed from the issues of service delivery and rehabilitation to an engagement with these multiple nuances/meanings/facets of disabled existence, the developing world continues to agonize over the very basic of survival needs. There are approximately 30 million disabled children in the age range of 4–14 years (Ghai 2001: 26–37). While statistical figures may lie or belie, the fact is that the majority of disabled children are denied educational opportunities to develop the knowledge and skills required for survival in a changing world. There were some indications in the form of the NPE of 1986, which advocated integrated education in general school for locomotor-impaired children and the mildly disabled children, and special education to the severely handicapped children. It also recommended orientation and pre-service training for general teachers on disability management and provision of vocational training. The policy document says that the objective should be to integrate the physically and the mentally handicapped with the general community as equal partners to prepare them to face life with courage and confidence. However in 1992, the government admitted that:

> The evaluation of special schools and the scheme of IEDC have revealed some grey areas. The general education system is not yet so mobilised to a noticeable extent for the education of the handicapped either at central or state level. The goal of UEE for this disadvantaged group would remain an unachievable dream unless concerted and urgent measures are taken. (Ghai 1999)

However, there was no reflection on the fact that the government has perpetuated this discrimination by having two separate systems. Whereas the general educational needs come under the purview of Human Resource Development (HRD), the responsibility for special education is discharged by the Ministry of Social Justice and Empowerment, thereby sandwiching the disabled children between the two ministries. The result is that though various schemes were launched in the country to promote education of children with special needs, the vision of true inclusion seems to be lacking. In principle, Integrated Education of Disabled Children (IEDC) launched in 1974 and revised in 1992; District Primary Education Programme (DPEP); Janshala, the joint programme of the Government of India and five UN agencies; and the newly launched scheme of Sarva Shiksha Abhiyan (SSA) reiterate the need for a just inclusion of disabled children in regular schools. Further by virtue of the Persons with Disabilities Act (Equal Opportunities, Protection of Rights, and Full Participation), 1995, better known as PWD Act, the central and state governments and local authorities are legally bound to provide access to free education to all the disabled children till the age of 18 years within integrated school settings.

The Act envisages a comprehensive education scheme to provide transport facilities; remove architectural barriers; supply free books, uniforms, and other materials; grant scholarships; restructure curriculum; and modify the examination system for the benefit of children with special needs, but is quick to point out that this can be accomplished as and when resources permit. However, even a cursory glance at suggestions in the Act such as part-time classes, non-formal education, open schools, and open universities for children with special needs belie the thrust on inclusion. Before 2002, the Articles 41, 45, 46 and all the Directive Principles of the Constitution of India were the only articles pertaining directly to the right of education. While the Constitution was ratified over 56 years ago, the goal of Article 45 was nowhere near attainment. In 1992, two Supreme Court rulings, namely, Mohini Jain versus State of Karnataka and Unni Krishnan versus State of Andhra Pradesh declared that right of education as directly connected to the fundamental right to life, namely, Article 21. Citing both the Universal Declaration of Human Rights as well as the International Covenant on Economic Social and Cultural Rights in support of the judgement, education was considered a fundamental right. One of the measures for achieving the goal of Education for All (EFA) was the 86th Amendment of the Constitution passed in the Lok Sabha (the Lower House of the Indian Parliament) on 28 November 2001, to make the right to free and compulsory education for children from 6 to 14 years of age a Fundamental Right. Parents were named as the agents responsible for providing opportunities for education for children in the age group of 6–14 years.

Notwithstanding the fact that this is an impossible task for most parents, the government continues to encourage privatization efforts that require a considerable investment on the part of people who are also fighting the stigma of disability. While experts lament over the fact that there has been a dilution of elementary education of eight years—the idea of what was the acceptable minimum-level of schooling, the disabled children do not even get that. The suggested alternatives of non-formal education, minimum levels of learning, and multi-grade teaching do not spell hope for the disabled. It is worthwhile to take note that whereas the disability act seeks to provide education till 18 years of age, most of the educational policy documents stop at 14. Also, the issue of early childhood care, which is essential for every child has been overlooked. As I have argued elsewhere, disabled children do not find representation in the Integrated Child Development Services (ICDS) thus reinforcing exclusion (Ghai 2001: 26–37). The observation of the National Policy on Education Review Committee (1990) that ICDS had come to acquire rigidity, bureaucratization, low performance, lack of community participation, and insensitivity to local needs, patterns, and socio-cultural conditions are worth remembering. As a result, disabled children were not included in the ICDS programmes. This meant that 4–5 million children with special needs, in dire need of services, at the critical age of 0–5, were denied the services. While the ICDS have now been mandated to include all children with special needs, the battle is far from over, as there is no fiscal allocation. My contention is that under a globalized economy such commitments will remain more an exercise in rhetoric rather than real change. This becomes even more significant when one realizes that the Government of India had reconstituted the Central Advisory Board of Education (CABE) vide Resolution dated 6 July 2004. Though initially not considered within its frame of reference, the government did include inclusive education at the behest of the Public Study group. Taking a cue from the disability movement's slogan of 'Nothing for us without us' the government nominated Javed Abidi, the Executive Director of the National Centre for Promotion of Employment for Disabled People (NCPEDP) and Mithu Alur, Convener of All India Regional Alliance for Inclusion (AIRA) to CABE. While it is definitely a step that needs to be applauded, the disability sector would do well to adopt a critical attitude towards such gestures for their token value. Notwithstanding the creative potential of Alur and Abidi, one cannot fail to ask why the government has not opened the issue for a more serious discourse. The ratification of National Mission of the Sarva Shiksha Abhiyan by the disability sector reflects the fact that the serious educational realities have not been negotiated. Within the stipulations made there are some serious contradictions. While on one hand there is a directive that as far as possible, every child with special needs should be placed in regular schools with needed support services, only a little later it says that wherever necessary, special schools may be strengthened to obtain their resource support, in convergence with departments and agencies working in that area. However, the boundary line that will separate the possible from the impossible is not clear. The listed support services which include physical access (if only it was that simple!), resource rooms at cluster level, special equipment, reading material, special educational techniques, remedial teaching, curricular adaptation or adapted teaching strategies can be made possible only when there is funding support. In an annual grant of Rs 1,200 per disabled child to be incurred in a financial year, these stipulations are nothing more than rhetorical statements. The fact that the ceiling on expenditure per disabled child will apply at the district level does not really make life easy.

Further, the government formed a core group to prepare a Draft Action Plan. The members included the two joint secretaries from the Human Resource Development Ministry, the joint secretary of the Social Justice and Empowerment Ministry, the Chief Commissioner of People with Disabilities, a representative from National Council of Educational Research and Training (NCERT), and Javed Abidi. The Action Plan (2005), announced by the HRD Minister, Arjun Singh stated that 'It should and will be our objective to make mainstream education not just available but accessible, affordable and appropriate for students with disabilities.' However, in reality no financial allocation was made.

> ...unfortunately the Ministry of HRD seems to have not been able to put their act together and put this on the back burner forgetting the commitment made by their Minister in Parliament and not worked out the financial allocation needed. No policy can be operationalised without fiscal support and it is likely that the Minister's Statement in Parliament will remain a policy without teeth ... just a statement of pious intent yet another policy which is rhetoric not going to be operationalised, with perhaps no intention of operationalising it. (Alur 2006)

One cannot fail to notice that this Action Plan is announced at a time before the CABE committee decisions became public. The all important question that begs an answer is whether the state which is abdicating the responsibilities is in actuality serious about such committees, as the piecemeal results in rhetorical statements and not in meaningful change. Advocates in any movement have to be sensitive to the dangers of co-option. It is a well known fact that despite the mobilization and lobbying efforts of civil social groups in the course of drafting the 86th Amendment, very little of what they suggested was reflected in the final amendment(Gopalan 2002). The disability movement thus has to be cautious of gestures which ultimately may prove to be an exercise in tokenism.

It is revealing that justification of the government's action plan is vested in the literacy figures obtained for the disabled rather than the absolute number of disabled being educated. It notes that compared to a national literacy figure of around 65 per cent the percentage of literacy levels of the disabled population is only 49 per cent. According to the National Sample Survey Organisation (NSSO), 2002 figures, of the literate disabled population only 9 per cent completed secondary and above education. The question which begs an answer is whether the government wants to provide formal education or just literacy skills that will aid the move towards consumerism. The focus on 'social training', 'general life skills', and specialist disability skills such as lip-reading and Braille rather than work-related skills would ultimately work against the disabled, resulting in lack of formal qualifications, higher unemployment, and social isolation. A report in *The Times of India* dated 20 April 2006 indicates that *out of the total of 44,000 available* seats in the University of Delhi, 1,320 seats are reserved for the *physically disadvantaged*. However, in 2001, only 250 such disabled students gained admission under this quota. What could be the reason? Is it because none of the disabled students qualify or is it because of the structural amnesia and attitudinal conservatism? One can well imagine that if this is the reality when the higher education is financed by the state, what would happen if the resources were to get transferred to the private sector as suggested by the *Ambani Birla Report* (GOI 2000). The corporate world's intention is too minimize costs, as the disabled people require the disabled-friendly infrastructure. Consequently the corporate exercises the sinister control by excluding the disabled people as the rationalization is that the disabled are not up to the mark.

My contention is that unless the holistic picture is visualized and participation of community living with disabilities is sought, these anomalies would be more a rule rather than exception. Unless we question the philosophical position of education vis-à-vis education of the disabled which posits the disabled children as distinctly different from 'normal children', we cannot usher in change. The option of keeping special school legitimizes the negative imagery associated with disability. From the vantage point of a traditional 'functionalist' perspective, disabled children need 'special' support for which the mainstream sector is not geared appropriately. Evidence-based research has demonstrated the practicability of inclusive education by setting up inclusive *anganwadi*s in the slums of Mumbai leading to the inclusion of over 3,000 children and families into mainstream education (Alur 2006). The prestigious CABE committee report states, 'Schools have a duty to try to include children with disabilities in regular classes unless the nature and severity of disability is such that education in regular classes with the use of supplementary aids and services cannot be achieved satisfactorily.' However, unless the expert committees interrogate as to what exactly is the meaning of 'nature' or 'severity', the state of affairs cannot change. It is mandatory that the certification process should be examined especially from the vantage point of those who are further marginalized because of caste, class, and gender among various other factors.

It has to be remembered that the 'special' status is a little more than an insidious system of social control. This view has been widely echoed by disability theorists, who argued that the special education system is the key element in the creation and perpetuation of social oppression of disabled people. In effect it is one of the main channels for disseminating the so-called able-bodied/able-minded perceptions of the world and ensuring that disabled school leavers are socially immature and isolated. The fact that this isolation results in passive acceptance of social discrimination, lack of skill in facing the tasks of adulthood, and ignorance about social issues of our times is often overlooked. Despite the humanitarian rhetoric, there is compelling evidence that the educational attainment of disabled children in separate school environments is inferior to that of the general population in mainstream schools. A narrower curriculum coupled with other factors such as low expectations of teachers result in constraining their performance. Very often the disabled children leave school with fewer academic qualifications and skills than their peers. However, in a state which is not willing to pay for education in general, how these special schools will be maintained remains a puzzle.

The move towards inclusive schooling cannot be successful, if we do not contextualize it in the present educational system, though living with the rhetoric of valuing diversity, has not really been very successful. Diversity is not just a reality to be tolerated, accepted, and accommodated... it is a reality to be treasured. If the furore caused by the recent order of taking the poor children into the public schools is any indication, it is not difficult to see that in a divided society, inclusive school will remain a pipedream, more by design than by default. For a state which follows the dictates of the World Bank, inclusion becomes a 'token' rather than a genuine attempt to create an environment in which differences are respected.

In comprehending the educational issues of the disabled children, the most serious danger arises when inclusion is presented as a means of alleviating oppression and subordination in much the same way as 'progress' of modernization is presented within capitalism. Thus, disabled children and adults, who are defined by reference to their lack of power which is seen as a natural outcome of their generalized low position within the hegemony of normality, often have to learn to live with the benevolence of the state and the civil society. Consequently, when the state backs out, their condition becomes worse, leaving them in a position in which it is not possible to interrogate what they are subjected to. Thus, the only hope that disabled people have is to coexist, but only in so far as it does not mean conflict potential in terms of resources. The alteration of built environment, translation of material into sign language and Braille, or providing computer technology for the visually impaired has severe resource implications for the state and are therefore high on conflict potential. This kind of inclusion then becomes a meaningless and often accidental by-product, albeit one which has tremendous ideological potential.

DISABILITY IN THE CONTEXT OF THE GIRL CHILD/ DISABILITY AND GENDER

The twin pressures of globalization and disability are much more difficult for girls. It does not require any creative effort to realize that in the world that we live in, gendered education is seen as a central factor that affects socio-economic change. While some of the boundaries are being blurred, the space that the girl child occupies in the educational system is at best marginal. As I argue elsewhere, penetrating the veneer of resistance that disabled women confront in a society where the dominant norm that operates is that of a perfect/unimpaired body is a very difficult endeavour. Without education and employment, disability is a burden women can do without. It produces lamentations such as one father in a remote village of Bihar exclaimed, '[W]asn't it enough that we are poor. Why did *kismat* (fate) have to add to our burden further by giving us a *pagal* (term used for developmentally disability) daughter?' (Ghai 2001: 26–37). The situation of physically disabled girls is identical as being a girl and being disabled are both considered as a curse. When the birth is an unwelcome happening, the life course is a denial against humanity itself. Within the advocacy movement, the domination of men and male concerns is clearly evident. Any index, whether it is education, employment, marriage, and so on, will clearly show that disabled men are featured more than the disabled women. Without undermining the emphasis placed on issues, such as inclusion in the census, discounted rates in the hotels, voting rights, tax exemptions, one can clearly see the middle class, male-centric concerns that are guiding the development of the disability movement in India. Major conferences organized at cultural centres such as India International Centre (IIC) or India Habitat Centre (IHC) while providing some visibility for the disabled do marginalize the more vulnerable (read) disabled women. It also makes the poor disabled invisible as they remain outside the discourse and the issues of poverty, gender, and so on, which compounds their problems escapes attention.

Disability is not a singular marker as disability intersects with factors such as caste, class, religion, urban/rural divide, and most importantly gender. Though the oppressed groups can establish the authenticity of their victimization, a danger vested in such identity politics is that both difference and identity are often organized into hierarchies. Such hierarchies do not lead to an equitable society. Setting up hierarchies of oppression does not lead to an equitable society. Inclusion of the disabled thus can only be possible in a system that does not marginalize *difference* of any kind. The most important and identifiable characteristic of inclusive education today is partisanship. Any student who belongs to a marginalized category should be first seen as a child. The approach is to provide 'bare minimum' to the marginalized. Rather it should be to educate each and every child notwithstanding the category that the child may belong to. The report of the National Focus Group on Gender Issues on Education and Teaching on Science set up by NCERT is perhaps the only official document which mentions the disabled girls. While it does privilege the issue, the language that it uses is that of 'double discrimination'. As I argue elsewhere, the double disadvantage theory does not really help disabled women. To say that disabled women must deal with the two-fold but separate oppressions of being a woman in a sexist society and being disabled in an ableist society implies that once each oppression has been charted out, one can then 'add' the two together to understand the disabled women's oppression. It is true that both the identities are similar in that both are social constructions derived from two biological facts—one of impairment, the other of sex. Moreover, as Alexa Schriempf (2001) says, 'both identities are similar in that neither impairment nor sex in and of themselves are problematic or difficult—that is, they become a problem only when placed in a social context that is designed to be unwelcoming to those biological characteristics'. So, if the reality of disabled women's lives is to be comprehended, the negativity associated with both sex and impairment needs to be visualized. Consequently, thinking which is marked by an 'additive' framework in which the attempt is to understand separate oppressions and then adds them back together as if that would explain the whole experience is to be avoided at all costs. An implicit assumption of this model is that gender, disability, impairment, and sex are binaries. As a result, disabled women are theorized only by adding the two 'biological foundations' of sex and impairment together to conclude that disabled women are oppressed along the twin axes of gender and disability. In a system where despite the fact that the girl's educational issues have been debated ad nauseam, the picture remains dismal. It is hard to imagine how the girls who live with additional marginalization will find space.

Real inclusion is a profound and deeper challenge to our schooling system. It is becoming unattainable in the profit paradigm that is predominant these days. It can be possible only when every student, irrespective of the nature or degree of their marginalization, should have the right to belong to their local school and their local community, with meaningful and appropriate support, enabling them to participate and contribute to the society. The approach that there is 'nothing problematic' with children would work against a host of professionals such as school counsellors who in a privatized context would squeeze anyone who is unfortunate to come under their care. For them to ask for a reflection that problems lie with the schooling system would be unthinkable. Some private schools in Delhi, which offer 'integrated' education, do so at a cost which is phenomenal even for those who can afford their services. What they get in return are cheaper alternatives to education, such as minimal literacy or vocational education.

CONCLUSION

In conclusion, efforts have to be made so that the definition of globalization can be challenged. Human agency has the potentiality to engage with the forces that treat it as unchangeable if we can (re)assert, (re) conceive and (re)construct globalization in a way in which we do take in the positive aspect of globalization while keeping the human rights of the marginalized intact. Given that the cultures of normativity and patriarchy are deeply rooted, attempts to demystify disability are essential and critical. Developing a political analysis of disability, influencing public opinion and evolving policies that do not have spaces which are to be filled or have been left unsaid will definitely go a long way in reaching the unreached. As a senior advocate of the disability movement, Oliver (1990: 142) writes:

> it is not disabled people who need to be examined but able-bodied society; it is not a case of educating disabled and able-bodied people for integration, but of fighting institutional disablism; it is not disability relations which should be the field for study but disablism.

NOTE

1. The focus group on work and education was chaired by Prof. Anil Sadgopal, a senior fellow, Nehru Memorial Museum and Library, New Delhi. The reports can be accessed from the NCERT website. (http://www.ncert.nic.in/html/pdf/schoolcurriculum/position_papers/work&education.pd)

BIBLIOGRAPHY

Alur, Mithu. 2006. 'Education for the Disabled: Wither Budgetary Support?' *India-Infoline News Service*.
Chauhan, R. S. 1998. 'Legislative Support for Education and Economic Rehabilitation of Persons with Disabilities in India', *Asia Pacific Disability Rehabilitation Journal*, 1(2): 46–52.
Ghai, A. 1999. 'Education of Disabled: An Excluded Agenda', paper presented at conference on Education in South Asian Context: Issues and Challenges, November 14–18, Central Institute of Education, University of Delhi, New Delhi.
———. 2001. 'Marginalisation and Disability: Experiences from the Third World', in M. Priestley (ed.), *Disability and the Life Course: Global Perspectives*, pp. 26–37. Cambridge: Cambridge University Press.
———. 2002. 'Disabled Women: An Excluded Agenda of Indian Feminism', *Hypatia*, 17(3) Summer: 49–66.
———. 2003. *(Dis)Embodied Form: Issues of Disabled Women*. New Delhi: Har-Anand.
Giroux, H. A. 1988. *Schooling and the Struggle for Public Life: Critical Pedagogy in the Modern Age*. Minneapolis: University of Minnesota Press.
Gopalan, Sarala. 2002. *Towards Equality—The Unfinished Agenda—Status of Women in India*. New Delhi: National Commission for Women.
GOI (Government of India). 2000. *A Policy Framework for Reforms in Education*. Mukesh Ambani and Kumaramanglam Birla. Prime Minister's Council on Trade and Industry, Government of India.
Held, D. and A. McGrew (eds). 2003. *The Global Transformations Reader: An Introduction to the Globalization Debate*. Cambridge: Polity Press.
Kumar, K., M. Priyam, and S. Saxena. 2001. 'Looking Beyond the Smoke Screen: DPEP and Primary Education in India', *Economic and Political Weekly*, XXXIV(7): 560–68.
Mandel, Ernest. 1962. *Marxist Economic Theory*, vol. 1. London: Merlin Press. p. 51.
National Sample Survey Organisation (NSSO). 2002. *Disabled Persons in India, July–December 2002*. Report no. 485. A Report of Disabled Persons, 58th Round, Ministry of Statistics and Programme Implementation, Government of India.
NPE (National Policy of Education). 1986. University Grants Commission (UGC). New Delhi.
Oliver, M. 1990. *The Politics of Disablement*. Basingstoke: Macmillan.
———. 1996. *Understanding Disability: From Theory to Practice*. London: Macmillan.
Peters, Susan. 1999. 'Transforming Disability Identity through Critical Literacy and the Cultural Politics of Language', in M. Corker and S. French (eds), *Disability Discourse*, pp. 103–15. Buckingham and Philadelphia: Open University Press.

Sadgopal, Anil. 2000. *Shiksha Mein Badlav Ka Sawal.* New Delhi: Granth Shilpi India Pvt. Ltd.

Schriempf, Alexa. 2001. '(Re)fusing the Amputated Body: An Interactionist Bridge for Feminism and Disability', *Hypatia,* 16(4): 53–79.

Stewart, J. and M. Russell. 2001. 'Disablement: Prison and Historical Segregation', *Monthly Review,* 53(3): 61–75.

Symington, Alison. 2002. *Re-inventing Globalisation for Women's Rights and Development.* Conference Report of Ninth International Forum on the theme of Reinventing Globalisation, Guadalajara, Mexico, October 3–6.

The Times of India. 2006. 'Right to Information', *The Times of India,* 20 April, New Delhi.

PART II

FROM RIO TO INDIGENOUS CULTURAL RESOURCES: EDUCATION FOR SUSTAINABLE DEVELOPMENT

3
Education for Sustainable Development: The Concept and Its Connection to Tolerance and Democracy

Michael J. Scoullos

INTRODUCTION—THE HISTORICAL BACKGROUND

The concept of Environmental Education (EE) emerged in the late 1960s. In 1972, during the Stockholm UN Conference on the Human Environment, it was recognized as an important tool to promote the protection of the environment and, later was acknowledged as the pre-requisite for any development. Principle 19 of the 'Stockholm Declaration' called for EE from grade school through adulthood to 'broaden the basis for enlightened opinions and responsible conduct by individuals, enterprises, and communities in protecting and improving the environment in its full human dimension'. The Belgrade (1975) and Tbilisi (1977) meetings described the principles of EE in a broad and generous way. The International Workshop on EE in Belgrade was convened by United Nations Educational, Scientific and Cultural Organization (UNESCO) in collaboration with the Centre for International Studies of Belgrade University and was attended by 96 participants from around 60 countries. The 'Belgrade Charter: A Global Framework for Environmental Education' was adopted unanimously at the close of this 10-day workshop at Belgrade, subject to modification by subsequent regional meetings, providing the framework and guiding principles for global EE. During the meeting, the UNESCO-UNEP (United Nations Environment Programme) International Environmental Education Programme (IEEP) was initiated. It has provided the global educational community with an important work in the field of publication for EE, the so-called UNESC-UNEP IEEP Environmental Educational Series. Two years later, the world's first Intergovernmental Conference on EE was held in Tbilisi, Georgia (former USSR), in October 1977. The 'Tbilisi Declaration', adopted at the close of the conference, together with two of the recommendations of the Conference, provided the inclusive framework, principles, and guidelines for EE at all levels—local, national, regional, and international—for all age groups, both inside and outside the formal school system. They have had great influence on all the evolutions in the field of EE.

In the late 1970s and 1980s, EE underwent a series of changes in countries with varying socio-economic and cultural conditions. It focused primarily on natural resource conservation and environmental pollution, though in many cases more critical and often controversial socio-economic aspects were also included. The UN Conference on Environment and Development (Rio de Janeiro, 3–14 June 1992) often referred to as the 'Earth Summit', devoted its Chapter 36 to Education as the basis of Sustainable Development. The Earth Summit marked the 20th anniversary of the UN Conference on the Human Environment. This major conference was attended by 178 countries, (100 at the level of head of state), more than 1,000 non-governmental organizations (NGOs), and tens of thousands of journalists. The participating world leaders signed five major instruments: The Rio Declaration; Agenda 21; the Framework Convention on Climate Change; the Framework Convention on Biological Diversity; and the Statement of Principles on Forests. The Chapter 36 of the 'famous' Agenda 21 focus on education, public awareness, and training.

Similarly, the international conference 'Environment and Society: Education and Public Awareness for Sustainability' held in Thessaloniki in 1997 recognized Education for Environment and Sustainability (EfES) as the basis of Sustainable Development. Because sustainable development is a very dynamic and new concept, for it to be understood and promoted, the entire education and learning system will require serious reorientation. The Thessaloniki Conference was organized by UNESCO with the support of the Greek government. The 1,400 participants included representatives from 84 countries, including governmental, intergovernmental, and NGOs. The conference declaration noted that 'Insufficient progress has been made five years after the Earth Summit in Rio as it has been recognized by the international community'. The declaration also demonstrated its commitment to 'reduce poverty' and utilize education in the best possible way 'to exercise personal choice and responsibility, to learn throughout life without frontiers, be they geographical, political, cultural, religious, linguistic, or gender'. Sustainable development requires a vision, a series of operational guidelines, and a strategy to be implemented, if possible, throughout the world.

The present chapter will focus on recent developments in the conceptualization of EE and its relevance for Education for Sustainable Development (ESD). This will be further linked to the UN Decade of ESD (2005–14) and will also focus on the United Nations Economic Commission for Europe (UNECE) Strategy for Education for Sustainable Development. The UNECE Region covers 55 countries: all the former Soviet Republics of Central Asia, the East and Central European countries, the European Union (EU), the USA, Canada, and a large part of the Mediterranean.

EDUCATION AND SUSTAINABLE DEVELOPMENT: THE RECENT DEVELOPMENTS (2001–05)

Several initiatives were launched during the World Summit for Sustainable Development (WSSD) held in Johannesburg, August–September 2002, demanding a stronger link between education and sustainable development. Among them was Education Reaffirmation for the 21st Century, the ERA 21 Campaign by MIO-ECSDE. The main target of the campaign was the promotion of the vital role of education in building sustainable development. The ERA 21 appeal was sent to governments, international organizations, social partners, and all major groups related to education that met during the WSSD. Thousands of signatures were collected and presented at a special event at the WSSD.

The UNECE Regional Ministerial Meeting for the WSSD (24–25 September 2001, Geneva) called for initiatives in the area of education. Specifically, the Ministers 'agreed to improve education systems and the design of learning programmes on sustainable development to increase the general understanding of how to implement and promote sustainable development in practice' (UNECE 2001).

Also, during the 4th Preparatory Meeting for the WSSD (Bali, 25 May–7 June 2002) a formal proposal for a Decade on Education for Sustainable

Development was made. Particularly, during the elaboration of the Draft Plan of Implementation for the WSSD that was a major objective of the Preparatory Meeting, in the section 'Means of Implementation'. A specific paragraph in the draft plan recognized the importance of education in the implementation of Sustainable Development (SD). The participants agreed on various major issues regarding education, namely, financial assistance and support to education; promotion of research; public awareness programmes and developmental institutions; the Millennium Declaration goal of achieving universal primary education; the impact of HIV/AIDS on the educational system; the allocation of national and international resources for basic education; integration of sustainable development into education systems; provision of a wide range of formal and non-formal continuing educational opportunities; integration of information and communication technologies (ICTs) in school curriculum; and affordable and increased access to programmes for students, researchers, and engineers from developing countries in the universities and research institutions of developed countries.

The 5th UNECE Ministerial Conference 'Environment for Europe', in August 2002, endorsed the drafting of a strategy on education for SD. A first draft was prepared by the lead countries of the initiative (Sweden and Russia). It was further developed by the 'Drafting Group' of governmental representatives and NGO representatives. The Drafting Group met in Geneva (February 2004), London (March 2004), The Hague (April 2004), and Rome (July 2004). The final text of the UNECE Strategy for ESD was adopted in Vilnius (Lithouania) in the year 2005 during the respective environment and education ministries meeting.

PUTTING THE HISTORICAL PIECES TOGETHER: THE CONCEPTUAL EVOLUTION FROM ENVIRONMENTAL EDUCATION TO EDUCATION FOR SUSTAINABLE DEVELOPMENT

In Tbilisi (1977), EE focused on raising awareness and protecting the environment and natural resources as pre-requisites for the economic development. Economic development was considered as being limited by the scarcity of natural resources and population trends. The implementation of EE was suggested as 'in', 'about', and 'for' the Environment. However, mainly due to political, ideological, and practical obstacles in many countries, EE was treated as a marginal or luxury issue or was reduced

Education for Sustainable Development

to covering only few aspects such as outdoors or nature education. At Rio in 1992, the concept of SD was developed on three pillars: the enviroment-ecology, economy, and society (Figure 3.1).

Figure 3.1 The 'Classical' Representation of Sustainable Development with Its Three Pillars

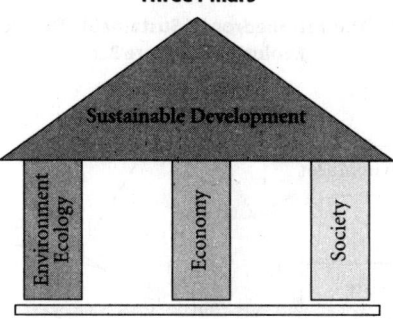

Source: Author.

However, one might ask, using the Rio formulation, whether EE is only useful to support the environment or whether it has a wider potential and scope. At Thessaloniki (1997), the question of whether the three pillars of SD are independent and separate was thoroughly discussed. The consensus was that EE should be the basis for the module of SD and should be expressed as 'Education for Environment and Sustainability (EfES)' (Figure 3.2).

Figure 3.2 The International Conference of Thessaloniki (1947) Suggested the Position of Education as Basis of the Three Pillars

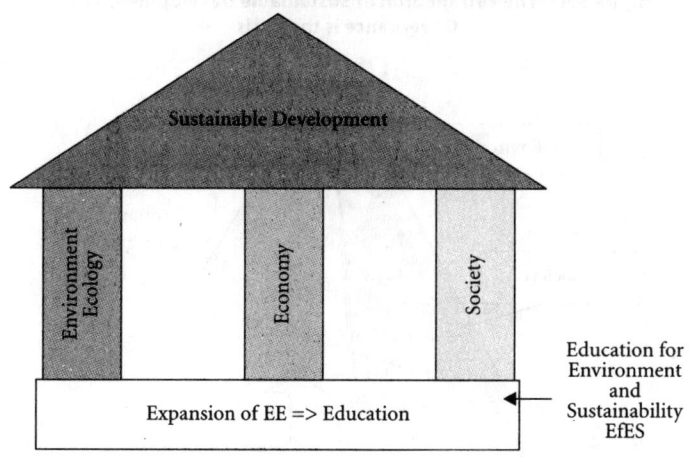

Source: Author.

Therefore, the SD module should be revised in order to convey the interdependence and interrelationships between its three pillars. The SD module could be represented three dimensionally as a pyramid whose facets are 'Environment', 'Society', 'Economy', and 'Education' (Figure 3.3).

Figure 3.3   The Tetrahedron of Sustainable Development as Evolution of Figure 3.2

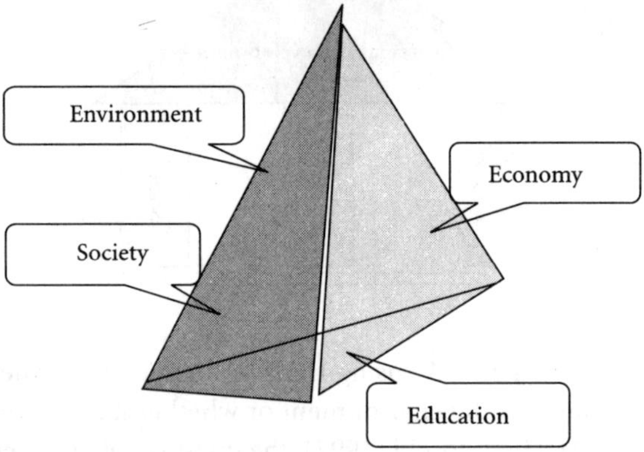

Source: Author.

Nevertheless, focusing only on education will not lead to sustainable development. Education is one of the components of the overall 'Governance' needed. To this end, the basis of the SD pyramid has become now Governance (Figure 3.4).

Figure 3.4   The Tetrahedron of Sustainable Development Where Governance is the Basis

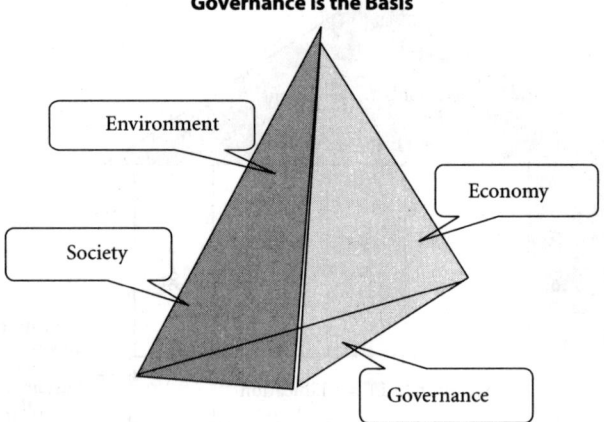

Source: Author.

Education for Sustainable Development

Exploring the role of governance in the implementation of SD, it should be mentioned that governance is the basis in the appropriate structure for approaching SD, where Institutions, Technology, and Education are the components, as represented in Figure 3.5.

Figure 3.5 **The Analysis of Governance and the Direct Connection between Democracy and Tolerance to Some of Its Components**

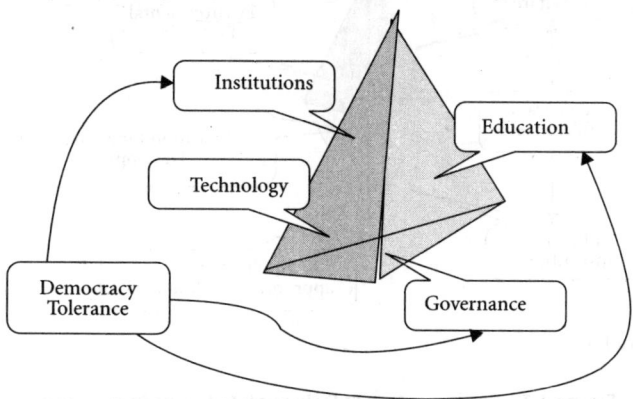

Source: Author.

Democracy and Tolerance should permeate the functions of governance and all its functions. Combining Figures 3.4 and 3.5, sustainable development can be visualized as a 'double pyramid' (Figure 3.6); so, in order to obtain SD we need: social cohesion and welfare, responsible economy, environmental protection, effective institutions, application of innovative technology, and ESD. From this updated and enriched module of SD, the components of ESD are becoming obvious as well. Therefore, in order to implement ESD, we should create the appropriate learning environments and teach the various topics through all relevant perspectives: environmental, social and cultural, economic, technological, governance, and institutional perspectives (Figure 3.7).

The role of 'tolerance' is imperative in order to address the cultural challenges of ESD, that are mainly focusing to allow learners to overcome the tensions and find a balance between:

1. Global and local.
2. Universal and individual.
3. Tradition and modernity.
4. The need for competition and equality of opportunity.
5. The extraordinary expression of knowledge and human beings' capacity to assimilate.
6. The spiritual and the material.

Figure 3.6 Components of Sustainable Development and the Means to Approach it (combination of Figure 3.4 and Figure 3.5)

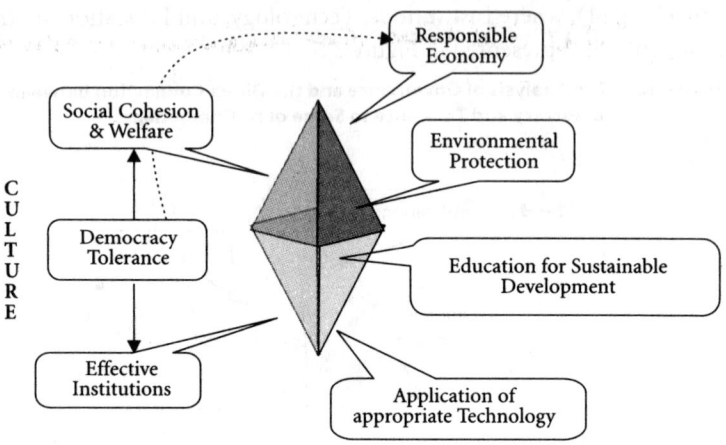

Source: Author.

Figure 3.7 Implementing ESD through Relevant Perspectives

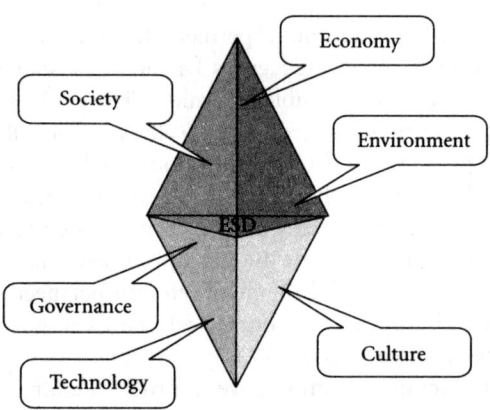

Source: Author.

Furthermore, ESD is fundamentally about values and respect for future and past generations, for difference and diversity, for the environment, and for natural resources. Education should enable people to understand themselves and others and their links with the natural and social environment. It should encourage and stimulate them to adopt behaviours and attitudes based on justice, responsibility, and dialogue. The role of ESD in promoting tolerance and democracy is also revealed through ESD's basic characteristics as they are declared, *inter alia*, in the International Implementation Scheme of the UN Decade of ESD (2005–14). (UNESCO 2005).

THE UN DECADE ON ESD

The United Nations (UN) General Assembly on 20 December 2002 adopted, by consensus, a resolution establishing a United Nations Decade of Education for Sustainable Development (DESD). The resolution designates the 10 year period as 2005–14, and proclaims UNESCO as the lead agency to promote the Decade. The Decade aims to promote education as the basis for a sustainable human society and to strengthen international cooperation towards the development of innovative policies, programmes, and practices of ESD. The five basic objectives of the United Nations Decade of Education for Sustainable Development (UNDESD) are to:

1. Give an enhanced profile to the critical role of education and learning in the common pursuit of SD.
2. Facilitate the links and networking between already existing initiatives and partnerships (Scoullos and Malotidi 2004) and to encourage exchange and interaction among stakeholders.
3. Provide a space and opportunity for refining and promoting the vision of and transition to sustainable development through all forms of learning (formal, non-formal, and informal) and public awareness.
4. Foster increased quality of teaching and learning in the field of ESD.
5. Develop strategies at every level to strengthen capacity in ESD (see UNECE Strategy on ESD).

THE UNECE STRATEGY FOR ESD

The basic aim of the UNECE Strategy for ESD, adopted at the High-level Meeting of Environment and Education Ministries (Vilnius, March 2005) is to encourage developing and developed countries of the UNECE region to develop and incorporate ESD into their formal education systems, in all relevant subjects and in non-formal and informal education. This will equip people with knowledge of and skills in sustainable development, making them more competent and confident and increasing their opportunities for acting for a healthy and productive life in harmony with nature and with concern for social values, gender equity, and cultural diversity. More particular, the objectives of the Strategy are the following:

1. Ensure that regulatory and operational frameworks support ESD.
2. Promote SD through formal, non-formal, and informal learning.
3. Equip educators with the competence to include SD in their teaching.
4. Ensure that adequate tools and materials for ESD are accessible.
5. Promote research on and development of ESD.
6. Strengthen cooperation on ESD at all levels within the region.

The Strategy is open to all UNECE member states and beyond. The Strategy is addressed to governments, motivating and advising them on how to develop policies and practices that incorporate SD into education and learning with the involvement of educators and other stakeholders. Moreover, the Strategy encourages interdepartmental, multi-stakeholder cooperation and partnerships, and encompasses the basic provisions of Education for All: Meeting our Collective Commitments. Furthermore, it supports the implementation of the implementation of Principle 10 of the Rio Declaration and the Aarhus Convention by promoting transparent, inclusive, and accountable decision making.

The basic principles of the Strategy are the following:

1. The concept of Sustainable Development is an 'evolving' one.
2. ESD: a lifelong process from early childhood to adult education—permeating *inter alia* learning programmes at all levels, including vocational education, educators' training, and so on.
3. Basic themes of ESD are: poverty, citizenship, peace, democracy, security, human rights, social and economic development, health, gender equity, cultural diversity, environmental protection, natural resource management, rural and urban development, production and consumption patterns, and corporate responsibility.
4. Fostering respect for and understanding of different cultures.
5. Developing critical and creative thinking of learners.
6. ESD should take into account diverse local, national, and regional circumstances as well as the global context, seeking a balance between global and local interests.

7. Providing opportunity for education to overcome its isolation vis-à-vis society: involving civil society, local community, and authorities. To this end, the role of educators for facilitating the process is critical.
8. ESD requires multi-stakeholder cooperation and partnership among authorities, education and science communities, the private sector, NGO, local community, international organizations, and so on.

The Implications for Education. In order to be effective, ESD should enable:

1. *(a)* Integration of ESD themes across all relevant subjects, programmes, and courses; *(b)* The provision of specific subject programmes and courses.
2. Meaningful learning experiences that foster 'sustainable behaviour'.
3. Learning activities in close relation with society adding to learners' practical experience.
4. An insight into global, regional, national, and local environmental problems; explaining them by means of a life-cycle approach and focusing not only on the environmental impact, but also on the economic and social implications, addressing both the natural environment and that modified by humans.
5. A wide range of participatory, student-centred and solution-oriented educational methods, including discussions, conceptual and perceptual mapping, philosophical inquiry, value clarification, simulations, scenarios, modelling, role playing, information and communication technology (ICT), surveys, case studies, learner-driven projects, good practice analyses, workplace experience, and problem solving.
6. All pupils and students should acquire appropriate knowledge of SD and become aware of the impact of decisions that do not support SD.
7. Appropriate training and re-training of educators.
8. Support of the non-formal and informal ESD activities, as essential complements to formal education.

Non-formal ESD has a special role as it is often more learner-oriented, participatory, and promotes lifelong learning. Informal learning in the workplace adds value for both employers and employees.

The UNECE strategy also provides an inclusive framework for implementing and analyzing major topics such as: national state implementation, areas for actions, international cooperation, roles and responsibilities, financial matters and evaluation. These topics are presented below in brief:

National State Implementation

Each country should translate the Strategy, distribute it to the relevant authorities, and designate a focal point.

1. A scheme of 'National ESD platform' could bring together experts from the different sectors, in order to coordinate the mechanisms for implementing the Strategy.
2. Cooperation and shared responsibility among all relevant State bodies, encouraging and coordinating the further integration of sustainable development concerns into formal education policies, programmes and curricula at all levels, and assessing the implementation of the Strategy.

Areas for Actions

1. Ensure that regulatory and operational frameworks support the promotion of ESD.
2. Promote sustainable development through formal, non-formal, and informal learning.
3. Develop competence within the education sector to engage in ESD.
4. Ensure that adequate tools and materials for ESD are accessible.
5. Promote research on and development of ESD.

International Cooperation

1. Need for a regional framework to review and facilitate the implementation of the Strategy, taking into account other developments that take place such as the UN Decade on ESD so that the Strategy comes to be seen as a contribution to the global initiatives on ESD.
2. Relevant international actors should be invited to work in partnership to implement the Strategy.

Education for Sustainable Development

3. Using the region's important experience in international cooperation on education: A number of national and sub-regional networks, education, working groups, networks, and associations of universities have started work on the development of multidisciplinary forms of education to devise solutions to the problems linked to SD.
4. Challenges to be addressed are: Solving the main problems in EE and in ESD in sub-regions such as Eastern Europe, EECCA, and south-eastern Europe, for example, lack of adequate instruction materials, inefficient use of the capacity of higher education and research institutions, shortage of skilled educators, lack of interdepartmental and multi-stakeholder cooperation on ESD, poor quality of education for children living in rural areas, and lack of financial and human resources to develop ESD.
5. Key actions could be: Strengthening existing regional and sub-regional alliances and networks on ESD, encouraging twinning programmes; using international legally binding instruments, such as the Aarhus Convention to raise awareness of SD; facilitating sharing of good practices, innovations, and national experiences and projects in development cooperation on ESD related issues (by using ICT tools, developing a website hosted by UNECE); integrating ESD in relevant bilateral and multilateral programmes; encouraging the participation of NGOs and other major groups in international cooperation on ESD; encouraging and coordinating international events for SD awareness raising.
6. Establishment of ESD focal points in all UNECE member states and in relevant international organizations.
7. The 'Environment for Europe' process could be used as a partnership platform for regional cooperation on ESD, and the UNECE Committee on Environmental Policy as a body to review progress in the Strategy's implementation in accordance with the Committee's work programme.
8. The 'Environment for Europe' Conferences could provide the opportunity for ministers to discuss progress in the Strategy's implementation based on national and other relevant reports.
9. Environmental performance reviews could also include an assessment of the reviewed country's efforts on ESD.
10. A joint session of the Committee on Environmental Policy and representatives from Education Ministries or equivalent state

bodies responsible for education in UNECE member states might be organized every third year to discuss progress on the Strategy's implementation.

Roles and Responsibilities

1. Governments: Proactive role in promoting and facilitating the Strategy's implementation; assessing and regularly following up the implementation at all levels of governance.
2. Local educational authorities and institutions of formal education: Responsible for implementing the relevant provisions of the strategy and monitoring.
3. All relevant stakeholders, including the education and science communities, the health sector, the private sector, transport and industry, trade and labour unions, local authorities, the mass media, non-governmental organizations, local communities, indigenous peoples, and international organizations should be invited to define their priorities and take responsibility for implementing and following up the Strategy.

Financial Matters

Education should be seen as an investment that will pay off in the long term:

1. Governments should ensure that appropriate resources are available: For example, considering using budgets and economic incentives to finance ESD for all forms of education, including for capacity-building in educational institutions.
2. Efforts should be made to integrate ESD components in relevant bilateral and multilateral programmes; partnerships may be formed and should be encouraged to seek support, including in kind contributions from international funding agencies and the private sector.
3. At the first stage of the Strategy's implementation, financial assistance to some parts of the region, in particular EECCA and countries of south-eastern Europe, is crucial to help those countries to start the process.

Evaluation: Contains Three Phases

1. Phase I (by 2007): Each country should identify what it is already doing that would fit within the remit of the Strategy. This would include: review of current policies, legal and operational frameworks, financial mechanisms, educational activities, identification of any obstacles or gaps; remedial actions to overcome weaknesses; drafting of a national implementation plan; development of evaluation methods (qualitative) and of indicators for the ESD implementation. At 'Environment for Europe' Conference, Ministers can share issues and concerns and report on progress of their National/State strategies.
2. Phase II (by 2010): Countries should review progress made in the implementation of their respective National/State strategies and revise them, if necessary.
3. Phase III (by 2015 and beyond): Countries should have made considerable progress in implementing ESD.

Evaluation: Issues To Be Measured In Order To Assess The Strategy's Implementation

1. Adoption of a legal and operational framework to support the Strategy.
2. Establishment of a framework for interdepartmental and multi-stakeholder cooperation and partnerships.
3. Allocation of leadership responsibility to coordinate and drive the Strategy.
4. Development of a communication strategy with key messages on SD.
5. Agreeing on a timetable for reporting and on a mechanism for monitoring and evaluation.
6. Ensuring the relevance of formal curricula and of learning programmes to key themes of SD.
7. Providing initial and continuing training on SD-related issues for educators, professionals, and decision makers.
8. Making adequate tools and materials for ESD accessible.
9. Availability of competent educators with a knowledge of SD and application of ESD.
10. Carrying out research and development on SD.

11. Making formal education, NGOs, and society work together: encouraging networking and sharing good practice to achieve SD.
12. Ensuring coherence of formal, non-formal, and informal ESD activities.
13. Encouraging the media to highlight SD.
14. Recognition and understanding of SD by professionals and the general public.
15. Competence of learners in SD.

BIBLIOGRAPHY

Delors, Jacques, In'am Al Mufti, Isao Amagi, Roberto Carneiro, Fay Chung, Bronislaw Geremek, William Gorham, Aleksandra Kornhauser, Michael Manley, Marisela Padron Quero, Marie-Angelique Savane, Karan Singh, Rodolfo Stavenhagen, Myong Won Suhr, and Zhou Nanzhao. 1996. *Learning: The Treasure Within*. The Delores Report submitted to UNESCO International Commission on Education for the 21st century.

UNESCO in Co-operation with UNEP. 1975. *Final Report of the International Workshop of Experts on Environmental Education*. Belgrade (October): 13–22. Paris.

UN (United Nations). 1973. *Report of the UN Conference on the Human Environment*. Stockholm A/CONF/4/8/14/Rev.1.1973. (June 1972: 5–16), New York.

———. 1992. *Promoting Education, Public Awareness and Training*, Chapter 36, Agenda 21, UN Conference on Environment and Development, Rio de Janeiro.

Scoullos. M. (ed.) 1997. 'Environment and Society: Education and Public Awareness for Sustainability', proceedings of the Thessaloniki International Conference. Athens: UNESCO and Government of Greece.

Scoullos, M. and V. Malotidi. 2004. *Handbook on Methodology used in Environmental Education and Education for Sustainable Development*. Athens: MIO-ECSDE.

Mediterranean Information Office for Environment, Culture, and Sustainable Development. 2005. 'The Mediterranean and ESD: A First Response to the UN Decade of ESD (2005–2014)', *Sustainable Mediterranean*. Issue No. 39. Athens: MIO-ECSDE, with the support of the EC, UNEP/MAP, and the Italian Ministry for Environment and Territory.

UNECE. (United Nations Economic Commission for Europe). 2001. Ministerial Statement for the World Summit on Sustainable Development.

———. 2005. *Strategy for Education for Sustainable Development*. Adopted at the High-level meeting of Ministers of Environment and Education of UNECE Member States, Vilnius (Lithuania), March 17. Available online at www.unece.org.

UNESCO. (United Nations Educational, Scientific and Cultural Organization). 1980. *Environmental Education in light of Tbilisi Conference*. Paris.

———. 2005. *International Implementation Scheme of the UN Decade on Education for Sustainable Development*, (January 2005–December 2014), Paris. Available online at http://portal.unesco.org/education/.

Education for Sustainable Development

UNESCO. (United Nations Educational, Scientific and Cultural Organization). 2006. *Highlights on Progress to Date*. UN Decade of Education for Sustainable Development. Available online at http://portal.unesco.org/education/.

World Commission on Environment and Development. 1987. *Our Common Future*. Oxford: Oxford University Press.

4

Education for Sustainable Tribal Development

Archana Prasad

The concept of Sustainable Development (SD) has acquired great currency after the Rio Summit of 1992. The recent Johannesburg Summit has also stressed on the fact that education can be a useful tool to achieve the aim of conserving the environment and using it in a sustainable way. But, if we have to relate the issue of sustainability to the most marginalized section of the society in India, then the definition of both 'education' and 'sustainable development' has to be applied in the broadest possible sense. For us, education must mean lifelong education, an opportunity to learn both within and outside the formal structures of school. However, it must also mean that issues of free and compulsory education and the extension of the educational infrastructure should also take place in these areas. The form and content of this education should however be defined by the needs of the tribal society and by a vision of creating a tribal citizen who can contribute to the wider society. In other words, the tribals must be educated not only for themselves but also for the fact that their integration into the larger political economy should take place at a more egalitarian level. In order to achieve this goal, it is important to have a holistic view of sustainable tribal development.[1]

Tribals have been described by many scholars as 'eco-system' people, that is, people who live close to their habitats and conserve their habitat because their lifestyle is intimately dependent on it by the ideologues of the environmental movement. The traditional lifestyle of tribal people is thus seen as socially, economically, ecologically, and culturally sustainable in the pre-colonial period. In fact, colonial capitalism and modern development are seen as two forces that disrupted this sustainable lifestyle and production system. The Indian Environmental Movement thus projects the revival of these traditional systems as a sustainable alternative to the current forms of unsustainable and destructive resource use patterns. While it is true that colonialism, the first phase of globalization in tribal areas, succeeded in destroying the productive base of almost all tribal economies, evidence from the past also suggests that pre-colonial tribal subsistence and resource use patterns were very precarious in nature. This means that the delicate balance between forest- and agriculture-based livelihoods followed by most tribal people in central and eastern India was never enough to either sustain the tribal society or ensure that the natural resource base of the tribal society could withstand any calamity or risk without incurring a substantial economic or social cost. It follows from this that any idea of sustainable tribal development has to be based on a vision of the future and not the past. Its core principles should include:

1. Restoring access to productive resources within and outside the tribal economy;
2. Ensuring that the tribal economy and society develop into an egalitarian system where the most disadvantaged sections get access to primary, technical and higher education, technology, and a fair share in all different levels of governance; and
3. Having a long-term vision and strategy to restore the surplus generating capacity of the tribal local economy that can correct the unequal balance between the tribal economy and the rest of the political economy.

But in order to achieve these goals our path of development must change and the innovations required within educational and research institutions should take place in a way that facilitates the achievement of these goals. The status of education and educational infrastructure in the colonial and post-colonial times must be evaluated from this point of view in order to gauge the impact of different 'civilizing forces' on the tribal people.

Archana Prasad

THE COLONIAL PHILOSOPHY OF TRIBAL DEVELOPMENT AND EDUCATION

The current politics of tribal development, and the social and economic underdevelopment of the tribal areas is a legacy from the colonial times. The visible impact of neoliberal globalization on agriculture and artisanal economies today was seen in the tribal economies of Central India from the late 19th century onwards. Their annexation by the British in the middle of the 19th century in effect signalled the first phase of colonialism and neoliberal globalization in the tribal areas. Tribal people were not only divested off their rights in natural resources but also engaged in a systematic incorporation of tribal labour into the global capitalist system. This was done through processes that transformed the tribal economy from a vibrant multi-occupational society to a servile adjunct economy to industrial capitalism in the 19th century. The consequent impact of measures like land settlements, forest laws, and segregation of tribal people from their local economy succeeded in converting these people from producers to cheap providers of labour and raw materials. It simultaneously generated a discourse and an ideology where the tribals were first seen as 'unruly' and 'wild' in the pre-annexation period, and 'timid, docile, innocent, and backward' in the post-annexation period. This change in perception also saw the beginning of a social project to set up a paternalistic 'civilizing mission' that would offset the detrimental impact of capitalist and imperialist incorporation. Thus, the Christian Missions started their work in the late 19th century and were also the first social reformers and educators of the tribal people in this region.

The missionaries saw the process of tribal transformation as a process of gradual evolution where moral upliftment and education would form the basis of material and cultural change. This, they believed, could be done by conversion of tribal people to Christianity, as this religion was a harbinger of superior social and moral values of the civilized modern world. All missionaries believed that education would play an important part in this modernizing project and used education as a mechanism to project Christianity as a vehicle of a secular, modern, and enlightened civilization. But what did this civilization mean in missionary terms? An ideologue of the Free Scotland Church, Dr William Miller, provided the answer to this question. He said that the Free Scottish Church should establish schools and colleges with the express aim of preparing the population of India for Christianity. These establishments should fulfil the dual aims of introducing moral and rationalist education (Miller 1893). Thus, moral change was a pre-requisite for the building of a rational and enlightened society that had the attributes of the Western civilization. In keeping with this line of thinking, the Churches in the Central Provinces saw a tenuous relationship between moral change and secular education and blamed the British government for not facilitating Christian education in the country. The missionaries asserted that secular education would be meaningless without the moral upliftment of the society. Within this broad perspective, the Methodist missionaries and Anglican missionaries continued to be one of the sole harbingers of social and educational enterprises in the Gond and Baiga areas. Almost every mission society in India started its work with the setting up of orphanages, primary schools, and doing industrial work. In each of these settings different types of education was imparted to the students. In orphanages children were taught the basics of a good Christian and modern life. They were taught how to cook and sweep, polish their shoes, and do their own homework. In this way they were taught how to cultivate an austere and self-reliant daily routine—the essential attributes of a 'Christian life' (Pumphery 1900: 75). In formal schools students were initiated into a model life through education provided by prescribed government standards. The third type of missionary work aimed at introducing students to practical work in the local 'craft' of the region. It also trained students in better techniques of agriculture. Agricultural education was of a specialized nature. It taught children how to propagate seeds and improve their variety and the theory of plant life and made them experiment with various types of fertilizers for the improvement of the crop. Along with these, a training in mathematics, science, and geography which was essential to any kind of farming was provided. But the most important part of this programme was the experimental farm where all students were given one acre of land to practice what they studied. One such farm school existed in Powarkheda in Hoshangabad. Students were sent up from mission schools in all parts of the province once they became proficient in agriculture (Meliesh 1921: 41–45). By 1921 the Methodist Church *Report of the Commission on Village Education* stressed the need to develop village schools as community centres since village education was integrally linked to the economic conditions. It thus stressed the need for basic education and vocational training as a means to help the tribals in coping with their growing penury.

But these measures had little success as they did not result in the massive spread of missionary activity in the region. By the 1930s

British government and social reformers like Elwin, Thakkar, and others started intervening in the process of the social, cultural, and economic transformation of the tribal people and a debate ensued on the nature of education and future of tribal societies. This in turn resulted in several attacks on missionary education and the conversions of tribals to Christianity. In fact education became a site for competing ideologies debating the future of tribal societies. Benevolent officials and anthropologists like Verrier Elwin argued that the needs of the tribal people were special and could not be fulfilled through literary education of a regular school. Such education alienated the tribal people from their own community and left them psychologically inept to handle any form of transformation. Thus, the formulation of an alternative educational project was an integral part of Verrier Elwin's recommendations that also involved a critique of existing methods of learning. In his inquiry into the conditions of forest communities, Grigson argued that the aims of 'aboriginal education' should be to conserve and develop 'tribal culture', religion, and institutions. It should also equip tribals to defend themselves against the destructive elements of civilization and improve their economic condition. He contended that such education was to be a specialized branch focused on selecting the right curriculum and teachers. These branches were to be controlled by local community institutions (Grigson 1944: 3). This view was clearly embedded in the idea that the tribals should be helped to cope with the impact of industrial capitalism. They should further be allowed to develop along their particular social and cultural path as they were 'different from the rest of the society'. Therefore, this idea of education was compatible with the idea of 'exclusion' and Elwin's proposal to form a National Park for the protection of tribal people.

However, the nationalists of the period had other ideas and believed that education should be used to forge a strong nationalist identity amongst tribal people. Foremost amongst these was A.V. Thakkar, an eminent Gandhian, who attempted to reinstate the position of these communities as the 'original inhabitants of India'. However, in doing so he also asserted that the present conditions of poverty and ignorance in which tribal people lived had to be changed. This transformation could not be brought about through a policy of isolationism or exclusion. Thakkar argued that the spirit of provincial government of national responsibility could only be inculcated into these communities through a policy of 'assimilation', an essential part of the process of development. Education was crucial to this process and would aim to build a 'common national identity'.

The nationalists contended that this required proper mental and physical training. The committee thought that craftwork would provide the necessary balance between intellectual and practical activity and asserted the importance of the 'literacy of the whole personality'. Thus, the Vidya Mandir Scheme was started by the first nationalist government in 1937. The introduction of such education was expected to break down the existing barriers between mental and physical labour. Economically, the productive capacity of the workers would be enhanced and their leisure time better utilized (Grigson 1944: 9–10). Though this scheme was meant for all schools, even pro-exclusionists like Elwin noted that the proposed scheme was particularly useful to forested regions. Neither Baiga nor Gond children were capable of completing the curriculum of regular school. Craft education afforded a good alternative to regular school and trained children to cope with the changes in their society without getting alienated from it. In this way it helped in the development of a nationalist identity and also helped the community to preserve its customary crafts (ibid.: 1).

The discussion above shows that none of the educational programmes were aimed at providing social or economic security to the tribal people in the wake of the assault of industrial capitalism on their lives. Rather these programmes were aimed at influencing their thinking so that they could adjust better to the existing realities. Further, the promotion of crafts as a survival tactic was rather unrealistic as it did not take into account the relationship of exploitation between the tribals and their rulers. Rather it was aimed at a process of adjustment where the tribals would get their own marginal space and the rest of the economy would be occupied by their exploiters. Within this marginal space, the tribals would be allowed to develop in the best possible way and preserve their 'culture' without really changing the productive relations that had brought about their penury.

NEHRUVIAN VISION AND TRIBAL EDUCATION

Independence saw the beginning of a new era in tribal development where Verrier Elwin and Jawaharlal Nehru emerged as two of the major ideologues for the policy of integration of the tribal people into the larger society. However, this integration was to be done in a manner that was to be gradual and did not bring about any dislocation in their life. Nehru himself stated that laws needed to be enacted to protect the tribal economies from the market economy which was alien to them and elaborated upon his plans for tribal development (Nehru 1958: 458–461).[2] He emphasized that these rights should be restored and implied that self-reliant development of the tribal economy could only take place if they were protected from exploitation and their legitimate rights were restored on natural resources. This could only be done if tribals were modernized gradually by allowing new modern ideas to permeate the institutions of everyday life through programmes of education and employment of tribal people. In keeping with these ideals, a separate Tribal Welfare Department was set up and all tribal areas were divided into Special Tribal Multipurpose Blocks for promoting welfare measures like education, public health, and income-generation activities. Ironically the question of rights over the rich natural resources that existed in these blocks was ignored by the policy makers. The tribals remained divested of their rights on natural resources and state monopoly over the ownership of land, biodiversity, and mineral resources continued and also represented the underdevelopment of the tribal areas. This was reflected in the Verrier Elwin Committee (Elwin 1969) that advocated for the integrated development of tribal people and was an attempt to reconcile tribal rights on land and forests with the policy of protectionism that came into being with the Scheduled Areas Act.

In this context, the mantle of educating the tribals was taken up by the state and the paternalistic attitude adopted by the Indian state was translated into several programmes for the socialization of tribal people into the mainstream Indian society. Of these, the spread of a network of formal education structures was only one strategy. Other programmes included special development projects that would help to expand 'plough cultivation' and horticulture that would give tribal people gainful employment. But migration, agricultural, and forest labour still seemed to form a major portion of the livelihood strategies of the tribals of the region. In the wake of this stagnation of the tribal economy, formal education structures, became more a mechanism to disseminate bourgeoisie ideas rather than being methods of upgrading tribal livelihood and lifestyles so as to properly integrate tribal people with the larger society. It is for this reason that the highest percentage of expenditure incurred in the Special Tribal Multipurpose Blocks was either on project administration or the social education that involved the dissemination of bourgeois ideas and the penetration of the service class into the tribal areas. This meant that the ruling classes of the country viewed the socialization of tribals into modern ideas of progress and development as essential for the advancement of these areas. This is why the little money that was spent on agriculture and allied activities was in supporting practices like settled cultivation and sowing of high yielding crops that were not suited for marginal areas. In this connection Verrier Elwin rightly opined that if this trend was not reversed then 'there may one day be few to educate and none to house' (Elwin 1969: 9).

The severing of links between the process of formal education and livelihood needs and practices was a relatively new trend in Nehru's India. The period before this, as seen in the earlier section, had visualized a programme of integrated tribal development and basic education which was not followed in the first decades after independence. Thus, there was an even greater divorce between formalization of the education process and the rest of the socio-economic development of tribal people. This resulted in further disparities and uneven development of the tribal society, which was unable to resist both state capitalism and private capital over its natural resource base.

STATUS OF INTEGRATION THROUGH FORMAL EDUCATION

School Education

The lack of synergy between the ways of learning and the positive reordering of a livelihood system has led to not only educational deprivation but also lack of gainful employment of tribal people in any productive activity. This in turn has had a negative impact on the tribal children's participation in the formal schooling system. The first indicator for this seems to be the drop-out rates of the school children which is seen for the decade of the 1980s (Table 4.1). The high drop-out rates at the primary stage itself suggest that the number of children completing schooling was very small and those reaching the technical and higher education stage even smaller. This problem seems to have worsened in the post-reforms era where the enrolment rates themselves seem to have registered a declining trend since the mid-1990s (Table 4.2). Three periods can be detected in the rise and fall of the enrolment of tribal students in schools. Between 1986 and 1992 there seems to have been a substantial rise in the enrolment rates while the rate of rise decreased between 1993–96. However, the steady declining trend from 1996 to 2000, which is a clear indicator of an emerging new crisis in tribal societies has prompted the setting up of educational guarantee and alternative school schemes in these areas under the Sarva Shiksha Abhiyan. The enrolment drive (which is reflected in the figures of the last two years) has been carried out with an aim of creating a partnership between the local community and seeks functional decentralization right down to the school level in order to improve community participation. Besides involving the Panchayati Raj institutions/tribal councils in schedule areas, the states would be encouraged to strengthen the accountability in implementation of the Programme by involving non-governmental organization (NGOs), teachers, activists, and women's organizations. Thus, the enrolment of tribal students is more indicative of the participation of children in the informal education system rather than an expansion of the formal education system to tribal areas.

Table 4.1 Drop-out Rates of Tribal Students

Year	Primary	Middle	Secondary
1980–81	75.66	86.71	91.18
1984–85	69.4	82.86	88.38
1988–89	64.53	78.08	86.72
1989–90	63.81	79.35	86.28
1990–91	62.52	78.57	85.01

Source: National Commission for Scheduled Castes and Scheduled Tribes, *Fifth Report of National Commission for Schedule Caste and Schedule Tribes*, 2002.

Table 4.2 Enrolment Rates of Scheduled Tribes at Different Levels

Year	Primary (I–V)	Upper Primary (VI–VIII)	Elementary (I–VIII)
1986–87	90.1	34.1	69.6
1987–88	96.7	35.4	75
1988–89	81	30.4	77.9
1989–90	100.9	39.2	79.5
1990–91	104	40.7	80.4
1991–92	104.7	41	81.6
1992–93	108.2	45.6	85.4
1993–94	107	48	85.6
1994–95	93.6	45.7	88.5
1995–96	96.9	46.5	90.9
1996–97	91.2	52.3	74.8
1997–98*	90.7	43.2	73.9
1998–99*	85.1	52.2	74.9
1999–2000*	97.7	58	85.2
2000–01*	101.1	60.2	88
2001–02*	96.3	70.3	88.9

Source: Department of Education, Government of India, *Educational Statistics*, 2003, Compiled by Institute of Applied Manpower Research, New Delhi.
Note: *Denotes provisional figures.

Education for Sustainable Tribal Development

Further, the declining trend from the 1990s in primary and secondary school enrolment clearly shows that fewer students are starting school and even fewer finishing formal education as reflected in the *National Human Development Report, 2001*. The adjusted intensity of formal education, at national level, was estimated at 2.04 years in 1978 and 2.70 years in 1993. For boys, it increased from 2.61 to 3.10 years and for girls, the increase was from 1.42 to 2.26 years. Between the two years, while gender gap declined from 1.19 to 0.84 years, rural–urban difference remained stagnant at 1.5 years. In 1978 it was 1.68 and 3.20 years for rural and urban areas, respectively, and in 1993 the corresponding figures were 2.31 and 3.81 years. This intensity is measured for the whole population and not for tribes, in particular. Presumably, the intensity would be much lower for the tribal people given that their educational indicators are much worse than the rest of the population. Thus, the government's claim that dropout rates have decreased is only indicative of the fact that the tribal people are going to more informal schools under the Sarva Shiksha Abhiyan (SSA) than before.

The logic of this analysis is in tune with the decreasing government utilization of funds on physical school infrastructure, under the different schemes operationalized for the marginalized sections. The performance budget of 2003–04 reveals a startling picture (Table 4.3). The situation becomes clearer if we see the distribution of beneficiaries for different schemes since 2001 as shown in the Ministry's Annual Report 2003–04 (Table 4.4).

Table 4.3 Pattern of Expenditure on Education Schemes (in Rs Crore)

Name of scheme	Budget year 2002–03		Budget year 2003–04	
	Outlay	Expenditure	Outlay	Expenditure
Grant-in-Aid for NGOs in Coaching and Allied scheme	32.00	30.00	32.00	26.9030
Vocational Training in Tribal Areas	12.00	6.3044	8.00	5.1802
Educational Complex in Low Literacy Pockets	8.00	6.00	8.00	5.7482
PMS Book Bank Scheme and Merit upgradation of ST students	68.49	53.89	65.49	66.42
Schemes for Hostels for ST girls and boys	24.00	13.50	24.00	18.14
Establishment of Ashram Schools	14.00	9.50	14.00	6.47

Source: Ministry of Tribal Affairs, *Performance Budget*, 2004–05.

Table 4.4 Number of Beneficiaries for Different Schemes

Name of scheme	2001–2002 Outlay (in lakhs)	Beneficiaries/ seats/centres	2002–2003 Outlay (in lakhs)	Beneficiaries/ seats/centres	2003–2004 Outlay (in lakhs)	Beneficiaries/ seats/centres
Boys/Girls Hostels	1,607.5	13,699	1,350	9,835	1,814.5	5,841
Ashram Schools for STs	997.75	9,180	950	7,625	647	3,800
Book Banks	72	3,492	139.98	10,177	63.43	7,426
Post-metric Scholarships	667.8	6,01,759	515.8	6,37,241	657.9	7,35,019
Upgradation of Merit	33.9	226	92.05	734	76.88	512
Vocational Training Centres	300	32	399.99	65	400	45

Source: Ministry of Tribal Affairs, *Performance Budget*, 2004–05.

Table 4.4 shows the declining trend in the physical benefits in almost all schemes except the schemes involving post-matric scholarships and book banks. Both these schemes require no infrastructural investments and only require distribution of books or money. It is this factor that is reflected in the overall dismal state of school and technical education in the tribal areas. According to the latest figures for the drop-out rates of scheduled tribe (ST) students from schools, the primary school drop-out rates are 62.25, the middle school drop-out rates are at 78.57, and the rate of drop-outs at the secondary school level are 87.71 (1991 figures). The reasons for these high drop-out rates are not only a lack of proper infrastructure but also the need to work at an early age to make two ends meet and also get an education that will enable tribal people to get proper jobs. It is significant that the schemes for providing vocational and technical education and skill upgradation for tribal people have performed below par and the expenditure levels in these schemes are falling. This means that any access to technical education, even at the lowest possible level is quite minimal.

Technical Education and Government Employment

In fact, the limited access to employment opportunities and higher education is conditioned by these structural constraints. In 1979–80, the pattern of enrolment of tribal students in undergraduate and post-graduate courses was as shown in Table 4.5. The position has only changed

Table 4.5 Pattern of Enrolment of Scheduled Tribes in Undergraduate and Postgraduate Courses

Faculty	Enrolment rates	
	Undergraduate	Post-graduate
Arts	2.72	2.42
Science	0.77	1.03
Commerce	1.46	1,40
Education	1.46	2.30
Engg./Tech.	1.43	0.01
Medicine	1.92	0.71
Agriculture	1.19	0.53
Vet Science	1.68	–
Law	2.02	1.31
Others	NA	1.04

Source: National Commission for Scheduled Castes and Scheduled Tribes, *Fifth Report of National Commission for Schedule Caste and Schedule Tribes*, 2002.

marginally since then. The 1998–99 enrolment pattern of ST students as enumerated in the Fifth Report of the National Commission for Scheduled Castes (SCs) and STs is shown in Table 4.6. Table 4.6 is significant because it shows that the enrolment patterns of ST students in higher education are well below the desired levels and this is directly affected by the quality and nature of education provided to tribal people. While many movements have been arguing about improved methods of pedagogy in tribal areas, promotion of tribal languages in schools and tribal teachers for tribal areas, the links of this education system with the nature of employment and forms of self-employment of tribal people need to be seriously explored. Tribal students and professionals are unable to partake of the provision of reservation because of their lack of qualifications for white collar and technical jobs. This means that the integration of the tribal people into the larger political economy takes place at the lowest possible level even if they have received some education.

Constitutional provisions entitle the tribals to get a reservation of about 7.5 per cent in all government departments and public sector undertakings. The Fifth Report of the National Commission for SCs and STs gives the following figures, for employment of STs in public undertakings (Table 4.7). As we can see, the majority of the STs are employed in the lower echelons of government undertakings and departments. This is directly related to the lack of skilled persons within the STs. Because of this, most STs are employed as sub-staff or Class IV employees. There is also a backlog of about 65 per cent in filling the ST vacancies. Further, most of the STs in the higher echelons of government services belong to well groomed tribal

Table 4.6 Percentage of Scheduled Tribe Students Enrolled at Various Stages

Educational stages	Boys	Girls	Total
Primary (I–V)	8.47	8.26	8.38
Middle (VI–VIII)	7.94	5.92	6.33
Matric (IX–X)	5.72	5.10	5.48
Sr Secondary (XI–XII)	4.68	3.52	4.24
Pre-university and Pre-degree	3.96	3.21	3.70
BA, BA (hons)	5.31	3.06	4.31
BSc, BSc (hons)	1.87	1.49	1.73
BCom, BCom (hons)	1.71	1.17	1.54
B.E./BSc (Engg.)	2.53	1.74	2.38
BEd/B.T	5.15	2.99	2.23
MBBS	3.37	2.76	3.12
MA	4.66	2.74	3.81
MSc	1.87	2.93	2.29
Mcom	2.25	1.47	2.03
P.hd/ D.Phil	1.46	1.83	1.57
Enrolment in Teachers Training Schools	8.09	5.57	6.90
Enrolment in Polytechnics	2.98	2.86	2.96
Enrolment in Tech Indus, Arts and Crafts	5.59	4.38	5.43

Source: National Commission for Scheduled Castes and Scheduled Tribes. *Fifth Report of National Commission for Schedule Caste and Schedule Tribes*, 2002.

Table 4.7 Impact of Reservations on Scheduled Tribes (STs)

Year (percentage)	1992	1994–95	1995–96	1996–97
Employment Group				
Central Government				
A	2.9	2.92	2.89	3.37
B	2.4	2.81	2.68	2.64
C	3.2	5.38	5.69	5.63
D	6.7	6.15	6.48	6.05
Sweepers	3.4	6.9	6.91	7.27
Total	18.6	24.16	24.65	24.96
Public Sector				
A	1.66	2.17	2.27	2.5
B	2.95	3.3	3.52	3.7
C	8.13	8.72	8.72	8.62
D	9.71	9.85	10.68	10.82
Sweepers	4.04	3.94	3.25	3.09
Total	26.49	27.98	28.44	28.73
Public Sector Banks				
Officers	3.12	3.52	3.65	4.1
Clerks	4.55	4.64	4.71	4.81
Sub-staff	5.79	4.84	5.84	6.16
Sweepers	4.73	5.16	–	5.63
Total	18.19	18.16	14.2	20.7

Source: National Commission for Scheduled Castes and Scheduled Tribes, *Fifth Report of National Commission for Schedule Caste and Schedule Tribes*, 2002.

aristocracies from the north-east and central Indian regions. This means that even though access to jobs increases through education, the poorest of the poor tribals have access to neither education nor employment.

GLOBALIZATION OF TRIBAL LIVELIHOODS AND EDUCATION

The Emerging Structure of Tribal Livelihoods

The data presented above show that the tribal representation in mainstream jobs or in formal education has never been very high in the first place. But the situation is becoming more serious with the withdrawal of the state from the agricultural and social welfare sector through which allocations were made for most of the tribal areas. The situation with regard to work was particularly bad in the decade of the 1990s as shown in the census figures in Table 4.8. The most disturbing factor is the sharp decline in the number of main workers (that is, people who are required to have at least 180 days of paid or unpaid work). In contrast, the number of people who are getting marginal employment has increased sharply indicating that most of them are getting employment that is less than 100–180 days. The failure of employment generation schemes is also evident from the declining ratio of SC and ST beneficiaries in employment generation projects (Table 4.9). This decline is directly related to the non-utilization of funds and the declining allocations for programmes that can aid in rejuvenating the productive capacities of the tribal people. Thus, the emerging trends in the newly globalized world show that tribal livelihoods are becoming more precarious and the challenge of sustainability is becoming more and more difficult in the current era.

Table 4.8 Work Participation of Scheduled Tribes, 1991–2001

Category of worker	Census 1991	Census 2001
Total Workers	49.3	49.0
Non-workers	50.7	51.0
Main Workers	42.02	33.8
Marginal Workers	7.1	15.2
Cultivators	54.5	44.7
Agricultural labourers	32.69	36.9

Source: Census of India, 1991 and 2001.

Table 4.9 Performance of Schemes for Self Employment: Coverage of Scheduled Tribe Youth

	Percentage of ST coverage			
Scheme	1998–99	2000–01	2002–03	2003–04
Jawahar Rozgar Yojana	18.75	29*		
IRDP	12.73			
Employment Assurance Scheme	19.37	22		
SGSY			23.7	15.76	12.99

Source: Performance Budget 2004–05, Ministry of Rural Development. Also Fifth Report of National Commission For Schedule Caste and Schedule Tribes, 2002.
Note: *For both Scheduled Castes and Scheduled Tribes.

The Impact of Education: Can It Meet the Challenge?

The trends outlined above show that the vision of tribal sustainable development has received a severe blow in the era of globalization. The framework of education promoted by globalization under the SSA has shown the following trends:

1. An increasing informalisation of education and its consequent privatization through NGOs. The recent Draft National Policy for Tribals, 2004, lays stress on development in a 'participatory way' which is building partnerships with NGOs and voluntary agencies. It states that 'some well established NGOs are eager to take part in the development of Schedule Tribes in general and Primitive Tribal Groups in particular'. The policy seeks to 'enlist and encourage NGOs in tribal development activities' and these efforts are to concentrate on their role in the opening of 'schools, hostels, vocational training centres, promotion of awareness programmes, and capacity building'. It is well known that a substantial number of NGOs funded in the last five years were affiliates of the Sangh Parivar who furthered their communal agenda. In this light, surely the UPA government will not commit itself to accepting this framework which in fact is nothing but shirking state responsibility for the minimum tasks required to be fulfilled for tribal development.
2. This has also led to the communalization of the tribal areas with Sangh Parivar NGOs getting a bulk of the projects and grants for running schools. [Recent work by Nandini Sundar and others on the nature of Right Wing education in tribal areas shows the lack of a network of physical infrastructure of school education in

these areas.] Further in the era of globalization, the Central and State governments shirk from committing to an extended role and responsibility towards the development of tribal areas.
3. Increasingly, education in tribal areas is being done through a contract system of untrained teachers who work in an alternate school system. These teachers are usually local 10th class pass and are paid a sum of Rs 500–800 per month for a period of three years. They are either *Shiksha Karmi*s or *Guruji*s under the SSA and are provided a minimum infrastructure by the community. Through this process the state is thus absolved of its commitment to provide any basic education and skills to the people.

In this situation it is essential that the tribal areas are provided a network of educational infrastructure that is sensitive to their needs. While issues of pedagogy and curriculum need to be taken on board, it is also important to put the onus for providing quality education on the state. This should be accompanied by a positive change in their economy; a system of research and development that alters the productive relations in favour of the tribal people rather than against them. Clearly, an education system that does not facilitate this is detrimental to sustainable tribal development in India.

NOTES

1. Forest Department, Eastern Conservator, Commissioners Office, Jabalpur Case file No. XVI-M of 1940, 3.
2. Nehru Jawaharlal. 'Approach to the Tribes' in *Jawaharlal Nehru's Speeches 1953–57*, 458–461. See p. 460. But there was also another view that feared that the formation of tribal councils would lead to the formation of a separate identity that would harm the process of nation-building. Many members of the Congress believed that all tribal areas would be faced with a movement for a separate state as in the case of the demand for a separate Santhal state in Bihar.

BIBLIOGRAPHY

Census of India. 1991. Schedule Tribe Tables.
———. 2001. Schedule Tribe Tables.
Department of Education, GOI. 2003. *Educational Statistics*. Compiled by Institute of Applied Manpower Research, New Delhi.
Elwin, Verrier. 1969. *Report of Multipurpose Tribal Blocks Committee*.
Forest Department, Eastern Conservator, Commissioners Office, Jabalpur Case File No. XVI-M. 1940.

Grigson, W.V. 1944. *Aboriginal Problem in Central Provinces of India*. Delete C.P.'s.
Meliesh, Alex. 1921. 'Industrial and Agricultural Work', *Methodist Education*, 1(1): 41–45.
Methodist Church. 1921. *Report of the Commission on Village Education*. Methodist Church, Bombay.
Miller, William. 1893. *Educational Agencies in Missions*. Chicago: World Congress of Missions.
Ministry of Rural Development. 2004–05. *Performance Budget*. Ministry of Rural Development, Government of India.
Ministry of Tribal Affairs. 2004–05. *Performance Budget*. Ministry of Tribal Affairs, Government of India.
National Commission for Scheduled Castes and Scheduled Tribes. 2001. *National Human Development Report*.
———. 2002. *Fifth Report of National Commission for Schedule Caste and Schedule Tribes*.
Nehru, Jawaharlal. 1958. 'Approach to the Tribes', *Jawaharlal Nehru's Speeches 1953–57*. Delhi: Ministry of Information and Broadcasting.
Planning Commission. 1997–2002. *Ninth Five Year Plan*. Planning Commission, Government of India.
Pumphery, Caroline. 1900. *Samuel Baker of Hoshangabad: A Sketch of Friends Missions in India*. London: Headley Brothers.

5
Premodern Indigenous Practitioners' Dilemmas in a Postmodern Globalized World

Janet Chawla

THE CONTEXT

Interest in indigenous knowledge is increasing as the general public and the policy makers observe the onslaught of problems associated with modern life. Traditional medicine is explored for use in the treatment of HIV/AIDS; indigenous knowledge is utilized in the service of agriculture and biodiversity conservation; strategies for the validation and protection of indigenous knowledge systems are being developed.[1] It is finally being acknowledged that we have left behind valuable resources along this road to progress and 'development'. This chapter, in general, explores and reclaims indigenous childbirth knowledge, with specificity to the Indian subcontinent. First, I will briefly (and critically) address the current scenario of how the world is being born—and the problems associated with what has come to be called 'the medicalization' of childbirth.[2]

Within this scenario, the mode of women giving birth varies according to their class status. The mass medicalization of birth effectively constructs this female physiological process as a medical, rather than a womanly and human phenomenon. Medicalization has negatively impacted the poor and the well-off in different ways as well as displacing indigenous practitioners, skills, and knowledge systems.

Data from an Indian study on caesarean rates showed that interventions during labour are correlated to families' utilization of private sector institutions, indicating that the ability to pay actually compromises women's health. But, there is no evidence that the outcomes of utilization of private sector institutions are any better.

There is reason to believe that current rates are part of a rising trend. This cannot be attributed only to the rise in institutional deliveries because of the strong association between caesarean sections and private sector institutions.... In Andhra Pradesh, Bihar, Gujarat, Karnataka, Punjab, and Uttar Pradesh, the risk of undergoing caesarean section in private sector institutions is four or more times that of a public sector institution. (Mishra and Ramanathan 2002: 42–48)

From the heart of the globalized public health establishment, the World Health Organization (WHO), comes an observation that improvements in outcome (the well-being of the mother and the newborn) are not associated with high caesarean rates.

Continued increases in rates of obstetrical intervention are unlikely to lead to improvements in birth outcome and may result in a higher incidence of adverse outcome for mothers and their offspring. The risks associated with caesarean section include: damage to uterine blood vessels; accidental extension of the uterine incision; damage to the urinary bladder; anaesthesia accidents; wound infections; maternal mortality. Depressed Apgar score; higher rates of neonatal respiratory distress; shortened mean length gestation; and higher perinatal mortality in subsequent pregnancies are also indicated. (WHO 1992)

Interestingly, these statistics are not showcased in the current United Nations (UN) public health agencies' data and publications. Perhaps because Safe Motherhood policies are formulated by biomedical doctors and the public health establishment who would rather be perceived as rescuers of women in distress, rather than practitioners over-utilizing obstetrical interventions!

However, buried in medical and health policy journals, critical evaluations do exist—such as this reference to a caesarean 'epidemic' in developing countries. In 'Over-medicalisation of Maternal Care in Developing Countries', the author concludes: 'The epidemic of caesarean sections (C-sections) continues in Latin America and extends into Asia. In addition, there are signs of a worldwide epidemic of other interventions.

There is an urgent need to build strong strategies to promote evidence-based interventions' (Buekens 2001: 17–25).

Some health analysts advocate that medical institutions themselves should monitor caesarean rates performed by obstetricians practicing in their hospitals. J. Quilligan, MD, an editor of the *American Journal of Obstetrics and Gynecology* wrote:

> Every hospital that has an obstetric service should have some committee that examines every cesarean section that is performed in that hospital and determines whether it was indicated or not. If it was not indicated, then the physician who performed the section should be educated as to why it was not indicated. (Flamm and Quilligan 1995: 12–30)

Often the obstetricians performing surgeries are out of touch with the women's suffering caused by surgical interventions.

The lack of concern among many obstetricians about the after-effects of the rising caesarean rates may result from the fact that they spend little time post-natally with women who had had caesarean sections and are far removed from any physical or psychological ill-effects resulting from the operation. (Francome et al. 1993: 178–79)

On the other hand, some research confirms that within a supportive environment, the judicious interfacing of traditional practitioners and quality referral units in case of emergency (like birth at home) can be not only affordable but also relatively safe.

The Comprehensive Rural Health Project in Jamkhed, Ahmednagar District of Maharashtra was the site of a study involving 2,861 deliveries—85 per cent of these births were at home. Hospitalized patients with obstetric complications constituted only 11.4 per cent of all deliveries. The C-section rate for all deliveries was only 2.0 per cent (McCord et al. 2001). This is with poor and rural women where as in urban hospitals it is not uncommon for caesarean rates to reach 50 per cent!

The authors point out that their findings radically question these policies and assumptions—and proceed to make their own recommendations. Some assume that in developing countries, hospital service for the poor must be in government hospitals and that a large proportion of deliveries need to be in these hospitals to provide timely access to emergency care. This presents a major problem in countries like India, where almost all rural deliveries are at home and accessible government hospitals generally do not provide surgical treatment for obstetric emergencies.

The Comprehensive Rural Health Project has established a network of private clinics with a voluntary, low-cost hospital providing effective emergency obstetrical care in remote rural areas at a very low per capita cost in the absence of easily accessible government service and with only 15 per cent of deliveries in hospitals. Charges are minimal and low per capita cost is primarily due to intelligent self-selection of patients who need hospital care. Even though overall cost is low, cost is still an important barrier for many poor families. According to the authors of the article, improving the purchasing power of poor families through insurance or subsidy could be a more effective way to improve emergency obstetrical care than trying to improve inadequate government facilities.

Although there were maternal deaths in their project, there were only two (70 per 100,000 live births whereas the National Family Health Survey estimates the national average as 450 per 100,000 live births) and these, according to the authors, could have been avoided by earlier referral to hospital.

Socio-cultural phenomena are also implicated in high caesarean rates among the moneyed classes. The induction of labour, often leading to C-sections if the cervix does not dilate, is sought by mothers-to-be or their families for various reasons: in order to bring the mother and baby home by Diwali; to time the birth to be auspicious, according to astrological reckoning; and one interesting study asserted that the 90 per cent caesarean rates among the middle-class Calcutta women was due to patient-selected surgery as a means to avoid postpartum work in the mother's *sasural*! (Donner 2003).

INDIGENOUS KNOWLEDGE, INDIGENOUS LANGUAGE: THE *DAIS* AND *NARAK*

Look, sister, at the time of birth it's only the woman's *shakti*. She who gives birth, at that time, her one foot is in heaven and the other, in hell (*narak*). The woman's *shakti* is indeed a lot when she gives birth to a child. Before doing a delivery I get the woman to open all the trunks, doors, and so on. I pray to the One above to open the knot quickly. I take off the sari, open the hair, and take off the bangles or any jewellery. I put *atta* on a *thali* and ask the woman to divide it into two equal parts. Also, I get Rs.1.25 in the name of *sayyid* kept separately. But mostly I remember *Bemata*. Repeatedly, I pray to *Bemata* 'O mother! Please open the knot quickly'. (Shakina Dai—A Muslim midwife from Delhi)

Premodern Indigenous Practitioners' Dilemmas

Girls are considered holy before puberty. The marriage of a young girl, who has not had her periods, is performed with her sitting on her father's lap. After puberty, the woman is considered unclean, and is unholy, because she bleeds, and this is *narak*. (interview taken in Bihar)

On the *chhati* day the *narak* period ends. The *dai* checks if the umbilical cord has fallen off. Then she bathes the baby and beats a *thaali* (plate). After this, the mother is given bath and wears new clothes. The *dai* cleans the room where the delivery took place and where the woman was kept separately for six days. The dirty clothes of mother and child are washed. After this, the *dai* is given soap and oil for bathing. All this is on the sixth day after delivery. (interview taken in Bihar)

As a writer-researcher, I have studied traditional Indian midwifery—*dai*s and their knowledge of the female body, skills, and customs—for many years. While taking the Shatabdi train to Chandigarh some years ago, I met a public health professional of the United States Agency for International Development in charge of 'reproductive health and nutrition'. As we stood in the train chatting, he asked if I was still active in the research of *dai*s. I said 'yes.' He spoke the standard line, 'If a birth is normal, then *dai*s are fine, but if any complication arises, they are incapable of handling it.' I spontaneously responded to his statement, by sharing what we were learning about the use of the placenta, stimulating it by heat, to resuscitate a listless newborn.[3] The gentleman's eyes glazed over and he terminated the conversation politely by saying 'I hope your research goes well.' I got the impression that I could have quoted any set of health statistics, no matter how spurious, and we could have continued talking. But because I, as academics would say, 'shifted the terms of the discourse' and mentioned the lowly placenta, and what I had learned from some *dai*s, our communication could not proceed.

Safe Motherhood discourse in India speaks the language of statistics—how many mothers die and of what complications. But that interface between the mother's body and the growing fetus, the placenta, and its indigenous medical use by *dai*s, is outside the boundaries of professional public health interest and discourse. Equally unmentionable is the vast legacy of indigenous, hands-on and low-tech, body knowledge of *dai*s—because this healing and health modality has been totally rejected as unviable knowledge by 'modern' professionals. Yet if we, the powerful, moneyed, and English-educated segment of the Indian populace (including doctors and public health professionals) are serious about reducing maternal and infant mortality and reaching any kind of 'health for all by the year...' we must reach out to indigenous practitioners like the *dais* and the traditionally oriented women whom they serve, and make efforts to understand their ethnomedical expertise and religio-cultural knowledge systems. 'Participation', a much bandied about term in NGO circles, is meaningless unless such mutually respectful exchanges take place.

Too many health policy makers and biomedical institutions are frozen in their approaches to maternal-child health, in part because they presume that Western medicine is the only scientific and effective body-knowledge system and also because they consider the *dais* ignorant and superstitious. These presuppositions bias so many well-intentioned health care initiatives, rendering local knowledge invisible. An advertisement for a health guide for grassroots women, *Where Women Have No Doctor*, illustrates this perspective—'All over the world women rise to their daily work, care for their families, and participate in community life. Too often, women must face these challenges while struggling against illness—lacking even basic information about their health.'

It is truly shocking that people who mean well are so ignorant of the knowledge and skill resources of 'the other'. Thus, an indigenous, culturally appropriate, affordable, and sustainable body of knowledge is rendered invisible in the enterprise of 'development' and delivery of health services.

And this invisibility pervades the professional mindset. Scientific method seems to have culminated in a process in which validation of efficacy necessitates double-blind, randomized control trials. This methodology may be suitable for pharmaceuticals, but not for indigenous, holistic therapeutics which heal or restore balance in the body via multi-factoral interventions. The dominance of this research paradigm challenges researchers to describe, interpret, and value indigenous therapeutic methods. These health-and body-knowledge modalities utilize Asia-specific body mappings and draw upon human capacities alien to biomedical and public health approaches. Even qualitative research methodologies use biomedical assumptions as a starting point, enter the field armed with questionnaires and interview schedules, and neglect to contextualize their research in the grassroots realities of extreme poverty and radically different ontologies and epistemologies.

Furthermore, 'gender' becomes a whipping boy and health interventions fail to apprehend traditionally oriented women as subjects, knowers, and decision makers within their own contexts.

Linking modern with traditional understanding and practice can be a despairing task.... At times, we just cannot do it. This may be because we see something wrong—anti-woman—in a tradition being followed with devotion by many women. Or, we may feel we do not know enough or anything at all about a set of practices and the belief system behind them. (Dr Mohan Deshpande, Curriculum Revision and Development, Women and Health Programme)

It is essential that indigenous cultural resources be valued rather than denigrated as a stumbling block that detracts from the use of more appropriate biomedical treatment—especially in the case of childbirth, which is not a pathological state.

MATRIKA RESEARCH METHODOLOGY

In 1997, we set out to research *dais*' knowledge and practice—the indigenous heritage of women's body-knowledge encoded in religio-cultural forms. The ethnographic data contained in this chapter is drawn from three years of research by MATRIKA (Motherhood and Traditional Resources, Information, Knowledge and Action)—an NGO's efforts to document, interpret, and analyze traditional midwives' ethnomedical and religio-cultural traditions. The MATRIKA team learned of *dais*' practices and cosmo-visions in three years of workshops in Rajasthan, Bihar, Punjab, and slums on the outskirts of Delhi. Invaluable assistance was provided by local NGOs, particularly their health workers who were themselves from the communities and often had longstanding relationships with the *dai*s. Health workers, who are not a part of the professional cadre, or part of the NGO establishment, often have a 'feel' for the language and orientation of traditionally oriented women. When given permission from their superiors they can be an invaluable human resource in orienting organizations toward a respectful understanding of the 'client' communities. Unfortunately, being keenly aware of the power and attitudes of their supervisors, they usually remain quiet.

MATRIKA's methodology has been to reverse the common TBA (Traditional Birth Attendant) training model by asking groups of *dai*s to 'train us' by answering the question 'what does a woman need during pregnancy, labour, birth, and postpartum?' Role plays, ritual drawings, singing of birth songs, sharing of birth experiences (ours and theirs) as well as *dais*' life narratives were our workshop activities. We were able to access, and remain with, this alien (to us) information because we decided at the outset not to execute the common approach of limiting ourselves to the modern categories of 'medicine' and 'health'. Rather we chose to be receptive to diverse ways of facilitating birth, diagnosing, and healing—to ritual enactments, notions of deities and demons, *bhut-pret* (ghosts and spirits) and the *nazar* or evil eye.

We attempted to let the data speak for the categories rather than have the categories shape the data. At first, of course, *dais* seemed to want to impress us with their knowledge of the modern, biomedical approach. But especially after our own enactments of the loneliness and confusion of a woman labouring in a hospital, they were convinced of our critical evaluation of modern birth and began to trust and share what they really believed and practiced. Ours was a collective effort: a group of researcher–activists interacting with a group of *dais*. We ate, slept, talked, sang and danced, and produced drawings and plays together. Our workshop activities were a celebration of the fertile capacity of the female body and of the *dais*' cultural handling of the childbirth. Our goal was to generate data which would enable informed, interactive dialogues between indigenous and biomedical practitioners.

RETHINKING 'POLLUTION' AND REFORMULATION OF *NARAK*

Mediation between the ethnomedical and the biomedical, and retrieving valuable cultural resources, involves crossing boundaries and listening carefully—to the unspoken as well as spoken words. We learned that although the *dais* use some of the language of caste Hindu (and Sikh, Muslim, and Christian) orthodoxy, denoting the defiling nature of birth, older *dais* often maintain a healthy distance and ironic disdain for the attitudes which demean their work. Inheritors of the *dai* tradition see themselves primarily as servants of the life force and can't be bothered with rebutting Brahmanic theological and caste formulations—they are occupied with delivering babies, caring for their families, and agricultural and other work.

Although often translated as hell or demonic place, *narak* can be understood as the site or energy of the unseen inner world—of the earth and of the body.[4] *Narak* has the connotation 'filth' but also signifies the fertility or fruitful potential of the earth and the woman's body. So-called 'pollution taboos' are related to *narak*, in that the idea of the sacred is radically separated from the reproductive potential of the female body.

During menstruation and postpartum women are considered 'unclean'. However, the *dai* speaks with a very different voice than the pundit about *narak*. To her the placenta, the ultimate polluting substance to caste Hindus or the 'twice born', is spoken of reverently, as 'another mother'. It is no coincidence that *dais* are mainly from and outcaste communities. Both caste and gender are involved in concepts of *narak*. (Ayurvedic and naturopathic practitioners often employ low caste people to apply the hands-on therapies they prescribe). And interestingly in our MATRIKA team's analysis of birth time (which in obstetrical terminology is referred to as 'labour', 'birth', and 'postpartum'), we adopted some of the *dais*' language of 'the opening body', 'the open body', and 'the closing body'. Thus, *narak* can be viewed as representing 'the open body'. This is the time when what is normally closed (literally the cervix) is open, and that is the liminal and dangerous time/space of generative, female bodily processes.

Narak also functions as a basic ethnomedical idea, providing a conceptual framework for a host of non-invasive therapeutic interventions. *Narak* signifies the inner world of the body, particularly the mysterious creative power of the female body (and simultaneously the earth), invisible to the human eye. This concept allows for a mode of understanding facilitating non-invasive diagnostics and therapeutics. *Dais* practice gentle techniques to negotiate and affect the inner body without violating the integrity of the skin/body/life force. And indeed the *dais*' holistic health modalities utilize touch (massage, pressure, manipulation), natural resources (mud, bath and fomentation, herbs), application of 'hot and cold' (in food and drink, fomentation, and so on), and behavioural changes (isolation and protection from domestic, maternal, and sexual obligations).

> After delivery a woman is not given any grain or heavy food. This is called *narak* fasting (*narak upwaas* or fasting during the time of *narak*). Grain is only given on the third day after all the dirty blood comes out. On first day, she eats biscuits with tea. She drinks warm water. Second day—heat-producing balls made out of ginger, pepper, turmeric, roasted rice, milk, and jaggery (*saunth laddos*). Third day rice, lentil soup, and vegetables. Rice is not given immediately after birth. First, we massage her. This relaxes her muscles, only after this she can digest her food. Turmeric lessens pain, dries the *shareer* (body, generally, and vagina/womb) and the *saunth* helps in forming milk. (Interview with Pairia Devi, Bihar)

> It is called dirty blood because it has collected over a period of nine months in the body. It is dark, smelly, and clotted. It comes out first and then fresh, clean blood comes out. With a little pressure and massage we take it out

completely, and when the colour of the blood becomes clear like monthly cycle, we believe that it is clean. (Interview with Swarn Kaur, Punjab)

Gola is baby's home. When the house becomes empty, only dirty blood is left. When this comes out there is pain. Hot brew (*ajwain, saunth, pipar,* and *gur*) is given. This drink cleans the belly. After the baby is born, the *gola* roams around. This *gola* has taken care of the baby, now it must leave. If the pain is intense then warm fomentation is done and *gola* melts away (*pighal jata hai*). This is dirty blood and needs cleaning up. (Kamala, Delhi)

On the 13th day after birth, the new mother is allowed to enter the kitchen (*Chauka Charhana*). Some do it on 7th or on the 11th day. Everybody celebrates. There is singing and dancing. On this day, the new mother and the baby bathe and wear new clothes. She comes out to get everyone's blessing. Friends and relatives are invited and eat food together. The *Dai* is given clothes, food, and grain. (Interview taken in Punjab)

On the day of the birth-ritual celebration (*Chhatti*—6th day), the women wears everything that was taken off at the time of the birth. She puts on *bindi*, bangles, henna, and nose ring. We make ritual drawings of *Swasthik*, put ritual drawing, worship *Bemata*, and light a lamp. We make a foot impression of the mother on the floor and then the woman enters the main house. Till the 5th day, *Bemata* roams around in the house. After the birth celebrations, *Bemata* leaves—she goes to another house. The *dai* also goes to serve others. (interview taken in Paana, Rajasthan)

CONCLUSION

Narak, as the unseen source of life and site of birth and death, provides a field for indigenous cultural reasoning to play. But this play is not simply fantasies of the imagination. It is an empirically grounded mapping of female physiological processes. And this mapping allows for the sophisticated indigenous reasoning system of diagnostics and therapeutics, as shown above. *Narak* provides space for intuition, imagination, other epistemologies, and other therapies. Female embodiment is known and respected. Dignity is bestowed on human qualities: the need for affectionate touch; processing and expressing emotion; and the reality of physical sensation. Conceptual categorization does not dominate and attempt to control female physiological processes. *Narak* and *Bemata* can hold both ethnomedical knowledge and the mysteries inherent in the birth process.

The challenge to biomedical practitioners and public health professionals as well as policy makers at all levels is the creation of a vital interface, a placenta—if you will, between themselves and the women who bear and deliver the majority of the babies born in India. We must learn to speak the languages of placenta and *narak*.

NOTES

1. World Bank, Washington, organized a videoconference seminar 'Using Indigenous Knowledge for Millennium Development Goals', addressing these topics from 28 March to 1 April 2005 at TERI Distance Learning Centre, New Delhi as a part of the Global Development Learning Network.
2. For an overview of the politics behind the medicalization of birth in the West and in India see Sagar (2005).
3. *Dais* from Punjab to Kanyakumari report this resuscitation technique. One *dai* in Rajasthan stated that doctors had drugs and machines, which they didn't have, but they had the placenta. This widespread practice has, to my knowledge, never been studied in order to understand how it is effective. However, it is congruent with Ayurvedic principles.
4. For a more extensive analysis of *narak* see Chawla, 2002.

BIBLIOGRAPHY

Buekens, Pierre. 2001. 'Over-medicalisation of Maternal Care in Developing Countries', *Studies in Health Services, Organization and Planning*, 17(3): 20–25.

Chawla, Janet. 2002. 'Negotiating Narak and Writing Destiny: The Theology of Bemata in Dais' Handling of Birth', in Nilima Chitkopetkar (ed.), *Invoking the Goddess: Gender Politics and Religion in India*, p. 132. Delhi: Har-Anand.

Donner, Henrike. 2003. 'The Place of Birth: Childbearing and Kinship in Calcutta Middle-class Families', *Medical Anthropology*, 22(4): 47.

Flamm B. L. and E. J. Quilligan (eds). 1995. *Cesarean Section: Guidelines for Appropriate Utilization*. New York: Springer-Verlag.

Francome, C., W. Savage, H. Churchill, and H. Lewison. 1993. *Caesarean Birth in Britain*. London, Middlesex: UP.

McCord, C., S. Arole, R. Premkumar, and R. Arole. 2001. 'Averting Maternal Death and Disability: Efficient and Effective Emergency Obstetric Care in a Rural Indian Community Where Most Deliveries Are at Home', *International Journal of Gynecology and Obstetrics*, 75(3): 297–307.

Mishra, U. S. and Mala Ramanathan. 2002. 'Delivery-related Complications and Determinants of Caesarean Rates in India', *Health Policy and Planning*, 17(1): 90–98.

Sagar, Alpana. 2005. 'Doctor's Business or Women's Business? Towards Making Childbirth Safer for Poor Women in India', in Janet Chawla (ed.), *Birth and Birth-givers: the Power behind the Shame*, p. 265. New Delhi: Har-Anand.

WHO (World Health Organization). 1992. *International Differences in the Use of Obstetrical Interventions*.

PART III

EMPOWERING THE HUMAN CAPITAL: CHALLENGES AND STRATEGIES IN INDIA

6
Market, Deprivation, and Education in the Age of Globalization*

Ravi Kumar

Mahatma Gandhi once said and we found it inscribed on the first page of every school textbook, until it was taken off, as a source of inspiration for the school children:

> I will give you a talisman. Whenever you are in doubt, or when the self becomes too much with you, apply the following test. Recall the face of the poorest and the weakest man [woman] whom you may have seen, and ask yourself, if the step you contemplate is going to be of any use to him [her]. Will he [she] gain anything by it? Will it restore him [her] to a control over his [her] own life and destiny? In other words, will it lead to swaraj [freedom] for the hungry and spiritually starving millions? Then you will find your doubts and your self melt away.

The poor and weak man/woman of Gandhiji seems to have got lost in the rapid strides that the Indian state took from 'welfarism' to 'neoliberalism'.[1] That lost person is never recalled though he/she is present at every nook and corner in the country. Now, even the textbooks do not have Gandhi's Talisman for the children. Located in this chapter is an effort to understand why the weak and poor of the country have been ignored in our policy decisions and commitment, education being an example in point.

A flurry of activities characterized the 'education sector'[2] in India recently. The 86th Constitutional Amendment making education a

---

*An expanded version of this chapter was published in *Social Change* (Vol. 36, Number 3, September 2006).

Fundamental Right was passed in 2002 (though it failed to clearly define the responsibilities of the state and also excluded children in the 0–6 age group (Sadgopal 2004a). Many versions of the Right to Education Bill [3] meant to operationalize the Amendment have come up (though with an increasing tendency to include clauses that free the government of its responsibilities and favour the private capital); and then came the constitution of the Central Advisory Board of Education (CABE), the highest *advisory* body on education after around a decade. Seven committees [4] were constituted within CABE to look at some of the most fundamental issues confronting education in contemporary India. At the same time, there have been a host of activities after loans for Sarva Shiksha Abhiyan (SSA) were sanctioned by the external financing agencies. Despite such efforts the problems of quality in Indian education persist and so does the task of making equal educational opportunities available to all children. This chapter makes an effort to understand the nature and extent of the problems.

Scholars, like Amartya Sen, caution that 'it would be a great mistake to see globalization primarily as a feature of imperialism. It is much bigger—much greater—than that' (Sen 2002). He contends that 'we cannot reverse the economic predicament of the poor across the world by withholding from them the great advantages of contemporary technology, the well-established efficiency of international trade and exchange, and the social as well as economic merits of living in an open society' (ibid.). What is important is to see whether the benefits of globalization are distributed across different sections of the society. Markets are not the culprits for inequality, he argues, because they have their own potential for development. 'Even though the operation of a given market economy can be significantly defective, there is no way of dispensing with the institution of markets in general as a powerful engine of economic progress' (ibid.).

Sen formulates his ideas about development within the context where there are multiple institutions and where there is a possibility to strike a balance of power among them such as the state institutions as well as the market. And within this framework the markets are not the single most important determining factor. However, what if the state policies are themselves determined by the market forces?

> The central issue of contention is not globalization itself, nor is it the use of the market as an institution, but the inequity in the overall balance of institutional arrangements which produces very unequal sharing of the benefits of globalization. The question is not just whether the poor, too,

gain something from globalization, but whether they get a fair share and a fair opportunity. (Sen 2002)

However, it is extremely difficult to state that the market would provide 'fair share and fair opportunity' to the poor. We also have evidence which indicates that in an economy where markets have an uncontrolled freedom it becomes difficult to control accumulation of wealth and ensure that the public expenditure on education, health, and so on, could be maintained. The recent developments in the education sector in USA (Farahmandpur 2006; Gibson 2006), in Britain (Hill 2006), and in Latin America show how markets have compelled the states to curb expenditure on education.

In the contemporary times, dominated by the neoliberal capital, it is extremely difficult for the phenomenon of globalization to arrive at the kind of institutional arrangements that Sen imagines. For instance, the framing of an education bill that provides leverage to private schools to operate as they wish to is just another example of a system where market is allowed to function without controls. In fact, it results in the sharpening of educational inequalities.

Multinational firms can exert their influence on the priorities of public expenditure in less secure third-world countries by giving preference to the safety and convenience of the managerial classes and of privileged workers over the removal of widespread illiteracy, medical deprivation, and other adversities of the poor. (Sen 2002)

Not exactly on the other side of the spectrum in the debate on globalization is placed the argument of Stiglitz, who does not oppose the current phase of globalization as such because he believes that 'in many countries, globalization has brought huge benefits to a few with few benefits to the many. But in the case of a few countries, it has brought enormous benefit to the many' (Stiglitz 2002). His analysis critiques the form of globalization that international financing agencies such as the International Monetary Fund (IMF) and the World Bank seek to push forward. And to support his argument he shows that 'the countries that have managed globalization on their own, such as those in East Asia, have, by and large, ensured that they reaped huge benefits and that those benefits were equitably shared'. These countries rejected the basic tenets of the 'Washington Consensus', which argued for a minimalist role for government, rapid privatization and liberalization, and engaged with the global economy on their own terms.

Contrarily, the countries whose globalization was managed by the terms and conditions of the IMF fared quite badly (Stiglitz 2002).

Globalization *per se* is not the problem because it 'can yield immense benefits' and has quite significantly encouraged the emergence of global civil society movements. With the programmes carried forward according to the IMF's guidelines problems of unemployment are bound to increase. No doubt what Stiglitz argues sounds true in the Indian context as we witness immiserization, manifested in different ways in the post-liberalization phase. If one looks at the urban sector, the post-liberalization phase has resulted in large scale casualisation of the work force and there has been a declining sense of economic security. A recent study by the United Nations Development Programme's (UNDP) Human Development Resource Centre estimates the percentages of informal employment among total workers at a whopping 91.7 per cent; 90.1 per cent in the case of males and 95.3 per cent among females (Sastry 2004: 28). Likewise, rural India, which has seen tremendous migration over the years as reflected in its population, is no better placed. Rural India represents a paradox wherein the causes of underdevelopment are lost in the commercialized vision of development which vests the agency of change with markets and logic of mindless profiteering. The responsibility of the state is considered secondary in this development paradigm.[5] Even small and marginal farmers now look forward to commercializing their agricultural production expecting to improve their economic plight, which has negative impacts on livelihood of people. Markets are everywhere and they function on the basic logic of profit-making. This has made the majority of Indians vulnerable.

The current phase of globalization (it needs to be mentioned emphatically) cannot be looked at as a phenomenon in isolation. It is characterized by the neoliberal capital's assault. It allows us to understand the current situation in context as well as posit certain bare facts about the growing anxiety of people concerning insecurity, survival, and death that is looming large today. It is also, at a macro-level, reflected in the worry of the masses who are getting 'excluded' from the basic facilities that they require for survival. With schooling getting privatized, the states fail to make any commitment to educate the children. Water, land, forests, and other resources are being thrown open for sale and purchase in the market. How will the issue of *accessibility* be addressed in a society and economy that is dominated by the market? How will the problems of *ownership* and *sharing* be resolved in a society where the collectives and collective symbols are being broken up into fragments? Neoliberalism has brought forth before us such pertinent questions. Unless education is located within this larger context of how the policies of the state change as per the desires and design of the capital, one will be at a loss to explain or understand why the state—which promised and saw Common School System as an equalizing instrument in education up to 1986—not only began a wholesale delegitimization process of the full-fledged government schools but also refuses to pass legislations to make elementary education free and compulsory. It also remains a challenge for those arguing wholeheartedly in defense of capitalism to explain why in a country where unemployment is rising, casualisation of labour force is taking place, education and health infrastructures are in shambles, and the emphasis on privatization under various nomenclatures continue to dominate the state policies.

The debate between the 'market fundamentalists' and the 'liberal-welfarist scholars', who want globalization with a human face, has the danger of getting our discourses trapped in the viciousness of a reproductive logic, which fails to transcend the 'given' context of capitalism. It does not try to critically evaluate the *role* and the *rule* of capital, which by its natural logic of evolution takes such a vicious form in the age of neoliberalism. To put it squarely, capital has always been on the look out for surplus generation, only the forms might change or the intensity might differ. Rather, historically one needs to look at the 'continuities in capitalist mentality and practices'(Tabb 1997), if one has to understand the dynamics of capitalism and the current phase of so-called globalization.

> The current offensive of capitalist logic into all realms of social life undermine many of the legitimation functions of the state which have provided citizen loyalty for the accumulation patterns of the capitalist system that demand that everything be done through the market (that college tution not be subsidized by the state, legal aid be abolished, public housing discontinued, and health care provided through the market) represent attacks on programs which have broad support. But the self confidence with which market ideologists attack any sense of public space, of solidaristic provision of services and shelter from the relentless individualistic values of the market, represents a measure of defeat of democracy. Similarly, devolution of service provision from the federal to the state to the local levels, and then to the individual procurement based on ability to pay, undermines the limited solidarities which hold society together. These processes have little to do with globalization, and a great deal to do with the victories of capital over labour, and the resulting damage to the rights of citizenship. (ibid.)

Ravi Kumar

EDUCATION AND NEOLIBERALISM, OR WHY DOES THE STATE NOT MANAGE EDUCATION AS A PRIORITY?

The current avatar of capital, in fact the current politics of capital, is manifested in neoliberalism and it becomes important for us to understand what it does to social sector and society at large because it has affected education adversely the world over and India is not an exception. Giroux (2004: 494) argues that,

> [N]neoliberalism attempts to eliminate an engaged critique about its most basic principles and social consequences by embracing the 'market as the arbiter of social destiny'. Not only does neo-liberalism bankrupt public funds, hollow out public services, limit the vocabulary and imagery available to recognize anti-democratic forms of power, and produce narrow models of individual agency, it also undermines the critical functions of any viable democracy by undercutting the ability of individuals to engage in the continuous translation between public considerations and private interests by collapsing the public into the realm of the private.

The experience unleashed has been such that even in the Western societies, leaving aside the Latin American experience (Saad-Filho and Johnston 2005: 222–29), serious thought has been given by social scientists such as Zygmut Bauman who argues that it is no longer the colonization of the 'private' by the 'public', rather it is the 'private' which is colonizing the 'public'.

Within this new space, defined by an ever increasing domination of a hegemonizing meta-discourse, that uses all possible instruments of state apparatus and the strength of capital to diminish the presence of alternative discourses, education has become one of the most significant sites of contest and struggle. It needs to be noted here that neoliberalism is different from the classic liberalism of the mid-19th century in the sense that the latter 'wanted to roll back the state, to let private enterprise make profits relatively unhindered by legislation', whereas the former 'demands a strong state to promote its interest' (Hill 2004). It is this difference that makes the activities of the state resemble the interests of private capital. What can explain the situation much better than the fact that the legislations which the Central Government formulates 'promote privatization and 'corporatisation' of school education' and franchises parts of the education infrastructure to corporate or religious bodies (Sadgopal 2004b: 38), leave aside the fact that it closes down its own schools, sells its assets, and deliberately allows the government schools to deteriorate, which then gets replaced by the fee-charging private schools (Kumar 2005a; Sadgopal 2006b: 23).

Today neoliberalism is creating a common sense that 'education should be divorced from politics and that politics should be removed from the imperatives of democracy' (Giroux 2004: 495). And if we try to locate this in the Indian context we find that education and health are seen largely as isolated governance issues which have no place in the political priorities of the state. Hence, questions such as finance crunch and feasibility/viability argument dominate the discourse on education though we have examples of countries poorer and/or bigger than India having tackled their educational issues in a much better way. The tragedy of this country has been that though great hullabaloo is created at the rising growth rate of Indian economy the state is not able to contribute anything substantial to the education sector. It is still 'strapped' of basic resources and remains in a perpetual state of neglect, which, lamentably, is now done as part of the state's formal decisions.

At another level, discourses have been constructed by the judicial system in favour of privatization and the once 'progressive' academia is now all-out to establish that students' politics is essentially harmful for the students, as they destroy the 'academic environment'.[6] The students' politics, which has the history of resisting the proposals of massive fee-hike in many universities like Jawaharlal Nehru University, has been curtailed and rebuffed as 'violent', 'indecent', and so on, even by the academics, leave aside banning elections to students' unions in many states. This has been going on together with the judiciary favouring the private capital. In August 2005 the Supreme Court of India through its judgement made it clear that *(a)* 'private presence in higher education is inevitable', *(b)* the 'private players' must be given the right to 'establish and administer', *(c)* hints at viability for a high-fee paying system, *(d)* 'appropriation' of seats by government is taken as nationalization, and *(e)* 'the right to regulate must be exercised in a manner that implies reasonable restriction, that does not question the foundation of private provision of educational services' (Chandrashekhar 2005: 99). Hence, what we come across is a situation where the campaign to promote privatization continues at different levels while dissent and protests are simultaneously discouraged and ruthlessly suppressed. No doubt, the larger conceived strategy is to delegitimize the voices of protest and resistance through all means—from mass media to bureaucracy and market.

Within such a situation we find the following aspects emerging out of the politics of neoliberalism:

1. It is wedded 'to the belief that the market should be the organizing principle for all political, social, and economic decisions' and conducts 'an incessant attack on democracy, public goods, the welfare state, and non-commodified values' (Giroux 2004: 495).
2. 'It has the dual task of using education to train workers for service sector jobs and producing life-long consumers' (ibid.: 495).
3. The state makes 'a grim alignment with corporate capital and transnational corporations' and pursues a wide range of deregulations, privatization and paves way for the participation of market even in the areas which are considered to be its responsibility (ibid.: 495).
4. 'Social relations between parents and children, doctors and patients, and teachers and students are reduced to those of supplier and customer....' (ibid.: 496).
5. 'In fact, as the state is being reconfigured, it is increasingly becoming a punitive state more concerned with punishing and policing than with nurturing and investing in the public good' (ibid.: 496).

The neoliberalism, as argued above has resulted in 'utter' privatization and

> offers absurd solutions to collective problems, such as suggesting that the problem of water pollution can be solved by buying bottled water. Thus, noncommodified public spheres are replaced by commercial spheres as the substance of critical democracy is emptied out and replaced by a democracy of goods available to those with purchasing power and the increasing expansion of the cultural and political power of corporations throughout the world. (ibid.: 497)

In the sphere of education in neoliberalism 'pedagogy both within and outside of schools increasingly becomes a powerful force for creating the ideological and effective regimes central to reproducing neoliberalism' (ibid.: 494).

WHY DOES THE STATE NOT MANAGE EDUCATION AS A PRIORITY?

Welfare has proven to be a tricky subject for the Indian masses. We had a welfare state with an economy that sought to operate, at least in rhetoric, on the principles of distributive justice so that the benefits of development could accrue to people in general. However, after half a century, questions at the nature of welfare state have been raised about who have benefited, how much, and in what way. The questions become furthermore complex once the variables of 'commodification' and 'ability to pay' are posited against each other. In other words, while education is today available in the marketplace like any other commodity for sale and purchase, the purchasing power is increasingly getting concentrated within a small section of population alienating the majority from the basic education[7] facilities. This alienation is reflected in the way the Indian state has been destroying the formal schooling system. Schooling facilities were already insufficient, now even that system of state run schools, over the years, has been delegitimized as low quality education centres. All these processes have been accelerated after economic reforms to liberalize the economy were started. The neoliberalism in India has resulted in the following:

1. It has commodified education at a much faster pace for it must be noted that education in the form of private and state-run schools were already present in India.
2. It has established, through mobilizing and creating new centres of knowledge, that the state cannot provide quality education of *comparable* quality to all children, hence, new forms.
3. It has reduced the role of state bodies such as CABE and has managed to mobilize the state to serve the interests of private capital directly.
4. It has managed to transform the nature of discourse on education and equated it with literacy, making its attainment the *only* goal of elementary education.
5. It has successfully tied the *alternative* discourses on education within a framework that inevitably turns to the state for concessions despite knowing that it caters more to private capital.
6. Even in the realm of research, very few ask as to why efforts were not being made to strengthen the formal government schooling system, through better facilities to teachers, improved training, better schooling infrastructure, and encouraging innovations instead of opening a variety of education centres. This would serve different clientele according to their purchasing capacity.
7. The possibilities of social movements of a larger scale have been diminished due to the boom in economy and the effective use of state apparatuses (though everyday resistances have increased over

the years but without the ability to take the shape of a larger political resistance).

Thus, the impact of neoliberalism has not been much different in India. It has gradually diminished the differences between the market and the state in the sense that both are pursuing similar kinds of policies/politics. The state withdraws in order to let the market flourish. There has been either a reduction in the amount spent on the social sector as a whole or there has been a very marginal increase which does not contribute much to salvage the situation.

One of the obvious developments due to the situation described above has been the burgeoning of private schools in urban as well as rural areas. Some studies have pointed out that 'access to school in urban areas is largely through private schools' and 'even in rural areas, poorly monitored government schools have created a good field for the new private schools. However, cost remains an excluding factor for private schooling. The very poor are dependent on government schools and in fact can generally access only the government primary schools which are seen to be the worst in the sector (Noronha and Samson 2001: 5235). What one comes across then is that students access private schools even in the rural areas though they are not only poor in infrastructure (poorer than the government schools in most of the cases) but even the teaching–learning is worse. In states such as Bihar one finds nearly every village having some sort of private school or 'tuition centres' where the students, who can afford to pay the fees (which is not very high compared to the urban private schools but is definitely higher than the local government schools), flock in great numbers.

Many analysts and scholars have treated these developments as indicator of a general 'hunger for education' among people. No doubt, everybody wants to send their children to school but the issue does not stop there. Thereafter emerges a host of issues that determine the nature and status of education in society. Education is seen primarily as a source of upward mobility and if it fails to deliver that (due to various reasons, such as bad quality of education or the larger logic of the capitalist economic system that flourishes on minimizing its costs of production, by employing less people and at lower costs to maximize profiteering), a sense of disenchantment seeps into the general psyche, which gets reflected in people relapsing in illiteracy among other things.

It is in this context that the emphasis on education as a source of enhancing the human capital, which is the dominant discourse in education today, needs to be seen. And from there emanates the ideas and the emphasis on 'skill-based education'.

Most human capital is built up through education or training that increases a person's economic productivity—that is, enables him or her to earn a higher income... Governments spend public funds on education because they believe that a better-educated population will contribute to faster development. Employers pay for employee training because they expect to cover their costs and gain additional profits from increased productivity. And individuals are often prepared to spend time and money to get education and training, since in most countries people with better education and skills earn more. Educated and skilled people are usually able to deliver more output or output that is more valuable in the marketplace, and their employers tend to recognize that fact with higher wages. (Soubbotina and Sheram 2000: 35)

Education, thus, is losing its critical edge as it becomes nothing more than a mechanistic process as well as an instrument for producing 'professional' beings geared to render their services (in other words, sell their labour) as required and whenever asked to. However, the idea of education as a tool to enhance productivity has its own inner contradictions such as what if the economy is not able to absorb the new productive workforce that is generated as shown by the increasing unemployment in the country?

The other repercussion of this tendency in education is that it would reproduce the existing social relations (which Bourdieu analyzed so appropriately) much more easily.[8] However, movements against the system emerge despite the efforts to mechanize and objectify the education process, as the recent example of movement by students in France illustrates, but what the neoliberal capital does, especially in the Indian context, is that it delays the emergence of a movement. It also becomes important to analyze the situation and look at it critically; we have to understand the rhetoric of decentralization and community participation, which tries to provide a democratic colour to the process and creates the illusion about the whole process.

At such a juncture, it becomes crucial to understand and conceptualize the reality which may appear to be located at two different levels but are in fact united as a part of the larger system. For our conceptual clarity, let us look at these two different levels taken in abstraction: *(a)* the discrimination within society reflected in the school and education system at large bears semblance of the unequal social relations such as in the case of the girl child (Chanana 2006); *(b)* the policies of the state, which, during the era of the welfare state were supposed to rectify many of such maladies, but have rather been perpetuating the inequality in education in the age of globalization dictated by the neoliberal capital. In fact, discrimination is being institutionalized, as Rama Paul and I have argued in 'Transforming Spaces or Refashioning Hierarchies?' Therefore, what one comes across is a system where the poor, Schedule Castes (SCs), Schedule Tribes (STs), and the girl child are deprived of education because they are the most marginalized in the larger society outside the school as well. Similarly, at the macro-level the policies of the state have very clearly spelt out that for the out-of-school children 'other' methods of education will be followed. Hence, comes the non-formal methods and the SSA. Why can't the formal schooling system that existed be strengthened so that every child gets education of comparable quality?

These two levels also unite because they are components of the same reality. If one brings down the abstracted conceptual categories to reality it becomes clear that the Indian state has always lacked interest in implementing the paradigm of equal educational opportunities of *comparable quality* for every child. Though scholars have tried to explain this failure as 'lack of political will', 'problem of financial crunch', 'low growth rate', and so on, what one finds is that many nations in the world, despite their low growth rate, effected laws of compulsory and free education for all. Second, 'lack of political will' is not something that is constituted in isolation but there are interests that constitute a 'strong' or a 'weak' will. Why does it happen that the central government takes half a century to enact education as a Fundamental Right and then decides not to pass a central legislation in Parliament for free and compulsory education, (Goswami 2006), but takes decisions about investments in construction of infrastructure for Asian Games or Commonwealth Games at the wink of an eye. Before liberalization the logic of resource crunch many a times emanated from the fact that the growth rate of Indian economy was too low but the same situation persists even now when the growth rate is being touted to be above 8 per cent.

HIGHER EDUCATION AND THE RULE OF THE PRIVATE CAPITAL

The university in its modern form [invented 200 years ago by German Idealists and Romantics for the University of Berlin] has traditionally been in very close relations with the state and in relatively distant relations with the market. Now, as the state/market relations get changed with the advent of globalization, the university is unexpectedly located in a different landscape in which the state [or 'government' in American tradition] is becoming—generally, with notable exceptions—weaker and the market is becoming stronger. (Kwiek 2003: 71)

While the withdrawal of the state from elementary education meant that the formal schooling system, which is more affordable, is destroyed and schemes are introduced for common masses, while those who can afford can go to private schools for higher education, the private capital has shown tremendous interest. Higher education is under tremendous pressure from the international as well as the domestic market, as Jandhyala Tilak has argued in 'Higher Education: A Public Good or a Commodity for Trade?' (2005). There are evidences of decline in public expenditure on higher education per student world over. It is part of the larger market logic and the way the private educational institutions of higher learning have expanded in India is an ample proof of the fact.

> The neoliberals view higher education institutions neither as centres of learning, nor as important social institutions. For them there is no distinction between higher education and production of cars and soaps. They treat universities as knowledge factories. For them investment in higher education is a venture capital; and equity in higher education means 'equity' in share markets relating to investment in higher education. (Tilak 2005)

The state is trying hard to get through options to ensure that the private capital has a field day in higher education. The Private Universities Bill, as a Central legislation, is pending in the Parliament and many believe that it is not because the government wants to delay privatization but because many of its clauses like free quotas and government control is not being liked by the private capital (Sharma 2005: 70). In absence of such legislation at the Centre, the state of Chattisgarh enacted Private University Act in 2002. One hundred and eight such universities came up in the state, with 94 in the state capital, Raipur, alone (Kapu and Mehta 2004). Other states would have done the same but certain belated regulations from the University Grants Commission (UGC) and the Supreme Court's judgement did put some brake on it. Because of these logistical reasons, there has been a rapid increase in the number of 'deemed universities' in the country, which are primarily private. Today, the private institutions dominate the 'professional' courses in engineering and medicine. They have exceeded the government institutions in a major way and that is one reason why it is called a case of *de facto* privatization.

AMIDST DEATH, DESTRUCTION AND DEVELOPMENT: WHO CAN AFFORD THIS EDUCATION?

The much touted above 8 per cent growth of the Indian economy has not resulted in any major benefits accruing to the majority. The landless agricultural labourers, the small and marginal farmers, and the daily wage workers as well as the section striving to meet their basic needs through employment in this age of globalized world order, none of them have gained from the new economy that has come into existence. The Government of India estimates that

> the unemployment rate went up between 1993–94 to 2004. On the basis of current daily status [unemployed on an average in the reference week], during the reference period, unemployment rate for males increased from 5.6 per cent to 9.0 per cent in rural areas, and from 6.7 per cent to 8.1 per cent in urban areas. Similarly, unemployment rate for females increased from 5.6 per cent in 1993–94 to 9.3 per cent in 2004, in rural areas and from 10.5 per cent to 11.7 per cent in urban areas. (GOI 2006a: 208)

On the other hand there has been tremendous commercialisation of the agriculture sector. The stress on growing cash crops led the farmers to opt for loans from a variety of moneylenders—from banks to the pesticide shopkeepers. However, it has had tragic consequences as the agricultural productivity did not match the amount invested in agriculture and the farmers were compelled to commit suicide. The investments in agriculture have substantially gone up while the rate of return has come down. For instance, in Andhra Pradesh, where thousands of farmers committed suicide, the share of agriculture in the gross state domestic product has come down from 53 per cent in 1960–61 to about 13 per cent in 2002–03 but the workforce in agriculture declined only marginally. Thus, the population has been sharing the declining income from agriculture. On the other hand, the area under cash crop cultivation has grown but the yield has gone down. 'With a high cost of cultivation, diminishing productivity and low returns, it becomes difficult for farmers to withstand crop failures'[9] (Rao and Suri 2006: 1547). The result has been suicides on a mass scale. However, they were not limited to only Andhra Pradesh as more or less similar problems—the market and its ethos invaded the countryside—confronted the farmers in Karnataka, Maharashtra, and Punjab. In South India,

> [A]round 75 per cent of the farmers who took their lives in 1995 died at the prime age of 35, with Karnataka accounting for one-fifth and Kerala

for one-eighth of the total suicides. Regional distribution of suicides in Andhra Pradesh shows that most of the victims were from Telangana [84.5 per cent] followed by coastal Andhra [14 per cent] and Rayalaseema [1.48 per cent]. Nearly half of the victims were below 40 years and around 63 per cent was small and marginal farmers. The percentage distribution of causes for suicide deaths of cotton farmers was as follows: credit and indebtedness 36 per cent; natural factors 23 per cent; government lapses 22 per cent; government policies 13 per cent; and lapses by farmers 6 per cent. (Devarajan 2004)

The ideal agricultural model of India post-Green Revolution has been Punjab. But even that model is proving to be a failure. By an estimate, the number of debt-related suicide by farmers in Lehra and Andana blocks of Sangrur District of the Malwa region [10] (between April 2001 and 31 March 2002) stood at 56 (Dhaliwal 2002). Village after village in Punjab is up for sale. Rural indebtedness has reached such alarming proportions that entire communities are being forced to 'distress-sell' their lands. For instance, Bhutal Kulan, a village in Sangrur District, comprising around 1,000 acres of land, is up for sale. Local farmers, heavily indebted to moneylenders and corporate banks, are selling their land holdings at a pittance. Similar is the story in the neighbouring Bhutal Khor which has over 1,200 acres of land. Practically the entire village is up for sale (Sehgal 2005). Cotton crop is predominantly grown in the Malwa region of Punjab, producing nearly 2,000 to 2,100 bales of lint every year in around 500 hectares of land out of a total of 4,200 hectares of cropped area. This amounts to nearly 5 per cent of the total cropped area in terms of crop intensity of 186 per cent in Punjab. But this 500 hectare cropped area consumes nearly 70 per cent of total pesticides and chemical inputs used in Punjab every year. An average farmer of the cotton belt spends nearly Rs 4,000 per acre on agro-chemicals; that means in total, the cotton farmers spend more than Rs 5,000 million on 1,250,000 acres of land (Sharma 2005). The tendency to invest in order to seek profits has been induced among farmers but these farmers invest at the cost of their lives, playing a gamble. If they fail, they die and if they win, which is not happening much now, they become examples for others, looking forward to live a better life, to invest.

The market is there, everywhere, meeting one in every nook and corner. Now, one need not go to the actual marketplace to experience it, it has penetrated deep inside every household. Education, considered to be the state's responsibility, is being thrown open to market. But can the majority of Indians buy it in contemporary India? The answer is obviously a big No! Given the condition that farmers have been committing suicide in the states of Maharashtra as Sainath argues, and in Andhra Pradesh, Punjab, and Karnataka specifically; workers are beaten mercilessly when they protest against their employers (Kumar 2005b: 4–5); *Economic Survey* (GOI 2006a) shows that the unemployment is rising; there are still a great number of people trapped in the viciousness of poverty; the Mushars in Bihar remain stagnantly trapped in the viciousness of their educational deprivation, as I have argued elsewhere; there is the ever serious problem of hunger staring the poor people (Pattnaik 2004); and the Dalits, the poor, and the girl child comprises the majority of those who drop out of school after class V, class VIII, or class X on account of various reasons (GOI 2006a). In this situation when the facts indicate unambiguously that it is the poor and the marginalized who remain deprived of education, it becomes difficult to imagine that the recent policies, as schemes, framed at the behest of private capital will contribute anything positive.

The state's role has been diminishing though the government has been claiming that education and health are its priority areas. Of late, not much development is happening except for figures of enrolment showing slight improvement. In the whole exercise of achieving target figures the aspects of quality have been lost, in fact they have been intentionally ignored as the new plans for education tell us. Quality education is no longer the thrust of the state, those who want it are 'free' to approach the fee-charging private schools, who will equip them in the art of serving the capital. After all, that is what education in capitalism needs to do.

Globalization today is essentially about neoliberal avatar of capital taking over the reins of state and, therefore, development. In such a milieu where the primary principle of survival is dependent on the capacity to buy, given the deprivation in Indian society, education will remain outside the reach of those who cannot pay for it. Those who stand in opposition to market and privatization of education are not able to locate the causes of such a system. It does not lie in globalization, it lies in the way capital puts forth its interests over and above the interests of the common mass in this neoliberal globalization. The opposition to the state's refusal to legislate a Central law, or implement Common School System must be understood in this context. It is the state driven by an ever powerful capital that produces such an education system. Hence, any effort to change the system entails: *(a)* understanding the transforming character of education and education policies in context of the changing forms, needs and requirements of the capital and *(b)* developing an understanding that such a system can be reformed (social transformation is a much longer and more political question) only if there is a strong resistance based on this understanding. The possibilities of 'entering the system' to bring about change are not only bleak but also inconceivable at the current juncture. However, one may go about it given that the interventions inside the system, in committees and ministries, are also formulated with this understanding. What is more important is a wider social movement that would pressurize the state as well as the representatives inside the system. Unless the two complement each other there are no chances of even reforms. Asking the state to go back to welfarism is too radical a demand when it is serving the neoliberal capital. That demand can be raised only if there is a strong mass resistance advocating such a demand.

Within this larger framework, as a counter resistance to the tendencies of objectification of knowledge and shrinking critical spaces of engagement, it is important to reclaim even the social and cultural politics as the site of 'dialogue, critique, and public engagement' so that in 'a democratically configured space of the social…the political is actually taken up and lived out through a variety of intimate relations and social formations'. Culture becomes even more important as a site of new pedagogical possibilities to create new spaces of resistance under neoliberalism, which destroys the ethos of dialogicity and therefore criticality by dissolving the 'public issues into utterly privatized and individualistic concerns' (Giroux 2004: 499). However, while culture becomes an important site of resistance it needs to be carefully treaded due to the fear of relapsing into the graveyard of *postmodern fantasmas*. This can be done if we locate different sites of struggle as components of a singular system, where the economic, social, political, and cultural coalesce into one singular mode of production.

NOTES

1. Neoliberalism emerged as an ideological response to the crisis of the 'Keynsian welfare state', which was precipitated by the generalized capitalist crisis associated with the end of the post-war reconstruction boom and was brought to a head by the escalating cost of the US war against Vietnam at the beginning of the 1970s. The crisis manifested itself in a slowing of the pace of global capitalist accumulation alongside escalating inflation and a growing difficulty of financing government budget deficits, which forced governments to impose restrictive monetary policies and cut state expenditure plans. What was seen as a mark of abject failure of Keynesianism was acclaimed as a positive virtue by neoliberals, who, amid the recession of the early 1980s, reasserted the traditional liberal dogma of purgative powers of the market, a reassertion that appeared to be justified by the subsequently resumed expansion

of global capital on the basis of the further liberalization of the world market. (Clarke 2005: 58)
2. The term 'sector' is used primarily in terms of a locale that has been assigned to education nowadays. It is relevant to recall that there are a host of players active in this locale now such as the government, non-governmental organizations (NGOs), independent academics, and some 'activists'. It is also important to mention that this locale also functions within a paradigmatic framework, which largely treats education as an agency capable of effecting radical changes on its own (which I have argued in 'Nationalism and Education in India') and does not link education to the larger framework of development (which largely excludes the critical engagements with the development plans and strategies) and thus education becomes, what the state wants, another field where the 'apparent' contests do not question its own policies and politics. It is interesting to note that such problems have been part of the international organizations as well as Katarina Tomasevski (2005) has shown.
3. The Right to Education Bill was first drafted by the Right-wing National Democratic Alliance but was never put to vote in Parliament. The United Progressive Alliance government constituted a committee under the aegis of the Central Advisory Board on Education to prepare a draft Bill, which was changed many a times in an undemocratic way, without the consent of the members of the committee. The Bill is yet to be tabled in the Parliament. Recently, *The Economic Times* reported that the government has decided, after looking at the financial commitments involved, to ask the different state governments to pass their own respective Bills. What can demonstrate a more blatant non-commitment to provide education to all children than this? The government's claim of 'no money' and therefore consequent withdrawal from its responsibilities proves to be a sham as glaring evidences are present that money is spent and invested for building infrastructure for Commonwealth Games, beautify the city of Delhi, or pay subsidies to the private power distribution companies so that their losses are compensated.
4. The following seven committees were constituted vide the Government of India notification dated 8 September 2004: *(a)* Free and Compulsory Education Bill and other issues related to Elementary Education, *(b)* Girls education and the Common School System, *(c)* Universalisation of Secondary Education, *(d)* Autonomy of Higher Education Institutions, *(e)* Integration of Culture Education in the School Curriculum, *(f)* Regulation Mechanism for the Text books and parallel text books taught in schools outside the Government system, and *(g)* Financing of Higher and Technical Education.
5. Bihar which is among the most backward states of India, in terms of poverty, insufficient (read 'no') industrialization, virtually absent health and other infrastructure, and so on, has also begun privatization. Recently, an alliance of the right wing came to power and began wholesale privatization of health sector among others.
6. Rajasthan High Court in 2005 directed the state government to ban elections to unions of students, teachers, and employees in educational institutions. It also expressed its concern over the declining academic standards because of campus politics (*The Telegraph*, 6 May 2005).
7. There is a need to differentiate between 'literacy' and 'education'. The arguments presented in the paper are concerned with comprehensive 'education'. It is also important to keep this in mind because the Indian state has consistently tried to

spread the confusion by substituting one for another. Hence, for the state, it is not the education in terms of completion of primary or upper primary or secondary stages that is taken as the measure of education; rather it is the literacy figure.
8. This does not imply that there is no alternative. We have seen in history that at different points of time, the discontentment does culminate in movements that transform the character of the state or at least compel the state to acknowledge the deficiencies of the capitalist system. What can be more immediate as example than the recent movements in France by students, or other popular movements in Latin America and many other places.
9. For a detailed account on the suicides in Andhra Pradesh and Maharashtra, please refer to the series of articles by P. Sainath that appeared in *The Hindu*. One may also look at them to understand the gendered dimension of the agrarian crisis (Sainath 2004c), the growing commercialization, and how the government relaxed rules and controls for the multi-national companies (MNCs). After such dropping of controls the rate of germination of seeds has gone down, farmers are made to sign papers by shopkeepers who also act as moneylenders when the farmers need loan for agriculture (seeds, pesticides, and so on) (Sainath 2004a, 2004b).
10. Cotton crop is predominantly grown in the Malwa region of Punjab, producing nearly 2,000 to 2,100 bales of lint every year in around 500 hectares of land out of a total of 4,200 hectares of cropped area. This amounts to nearly 5 per cent of the total cropped area in terms of crop intensity of 186 per cent in Punjab. But this 500 hectare cropped area consumes nearly 70 per cent of the total pesticides and chemical inputs used in Punjab every year. An average farmer of cotton belt spends nearly Rs 4,000 per acre on agro-chemicals; that means in total, the cotton farmers spend more than Rs 5,000 million on 12,50,000 acres of land. And it is this region which has been the centre of debt, destruction, and displacement, where over 3,000 farmers have committed suicide (Sharma 2005).

BIBLIOGRAPHY

Bourdieu, Pierre and Jean-Claude Passeron. 1990. *Reproduction in Education, Society and Culture*. London: Sage Publications.
Chanana, Karuna. 2006. 'Educate Girls, Prepare Them for Life', in Ravi Kumar (ed.), *The Crises of Elementary Education in India*, pp. 200–24. New Delhi: Sage Publications.
Chandrashekhar, C. P. 2005. 'Chipping at the Margin: Judicial Institutionalisation of the Privatisation of Higher Education in India', *Social Scientist*, 33(9–10): 90–99.
Clarke, Simon. 2005. 'The Neoliberal Theory of Society', in Alfredo Saad-Filho and Deborah Johnston (eds), *Neoliberalism: A Critical Reader*, pp. 50–59. London: Pluto Press.
De, Anuradha, Claire Noronha, and Meera Samson. 2002. 'Private Schools for Less Privileged: Some Insights from a Case Study', *Economic and Political Weekly*, XXXVII(13) 30 March–5 April : 5230–36.
Debroy, Bibek. 2005. 'In Defence of This Book', Foreword to Norberg, Johan, *In Defence of Global Capitalism*. New Delhi: Academic Foundation.

Devarajan, P. 2004. 'Lending a Helping Hand to the Farmer', *The Hindu BusinessLine,* 27 August. Available online at http://www.thehindubusinessline.com/2004/08/27/stories/2004082700362000.htm (accessed on 23 January 2006).
Dhaliwal, Sarbjit. 2002. 'Farmers Continue to Commit Suicide', *The Tribune,* 26 May. Available online at http://www.tribuneindia.com/2002/20020526/punjab1.htm (accessed on 13 June 2004).
Farahmandpur, Ramin. 2006. 'A Critical Pedagogy of Hope in Times of Despair: Teaching against Global Capitalism and the New Imperialism', *Social Change,* 36(3): 77–91.
Frankel, Francine R. 2005. *India's Political Economy 1947–2004.* New Delhi: Oxford University Press.
Gibson, Rich. 2006. 'The Rule of Capital, Imperialism, and its Opposition: Radical Education for Revolution and Justice', *Social Change,* 36(3): 92–120.
Giroux, Henry A. 2004. 'Public Pedagogy and the Politics of Neo-liberalism: Making the Political More Pedagogical', *Policy Futures in Education,* 2(3&4): 494–503.
Goswami, Urmi. 2006. 'Guaranteeing Right to Education: Centre to Pass the Bill to States', *The Economic Times,* New Delhi, 15 May.
GOI (Government of India). 1944. *Post-war Educational Development in India: Report by the Central Advisory Board of Education.* Simla: Government of India Press.
———. 1966. *Education and National Development: Report of the Education Commission.* New Delhi: Ministry of Education.
———. 1967. *Report of the Committee of Members of Parliament on Education.* New Delhi: Ministry of Education.
———. 1998. *One Hundred Sixty Fifth Report on Free and Compulsory Education for Children.* New Delhi: Law Commission of India.
———. 2006a. *Economic Survey 2005–2006.* New Delhi: Economic Division, Ministry of Finance.
———. 2006b. Educational *Statistics at a Glance 2003–04 (Provisional)* (As on 30 September 2003). New Delhi: Department of Secondary and Higher Education, Ministry of Human Resource Development.
———. n.d. *Sarva Shiksha Abhiyan: A Program for Universal Elementary Education.* New Delhi: Department of Elementary Education and Literacy, Ministry of Human Resource Development.
Hill, Dave. 2004. 'Educational Perversion and Global Neo-Liberalism: A Marxist Critique', *Cultural Logic,* Vol. 7. Available online at http://clogic.eserver.org/2004/hill.html (accessed on 14 July 2006).
———. 2006. 'Class, Neoliberal Global Capital, Education and Resistance', *Social Change,* 36(3): 47–76.
Kapu, Devesh and Pratap Bhanu Mehta. 2004. 'Indian Higher Education Reform: From Half-baked Socialism to Half-baked Capitalism', CID Working Paper no. 10, Centre for International Development (CID) at Harvard University.
Kumar, Ravi. 2004. 'Nationalism and Education in India: The Rise of the BJP', *Eurasia Bulletin,* pp. 6–8. Brussels: European Institute for Asian Studies.
———. 2005a. 'Education, State and Class in India: Towards a Critical Framework of Praxis', *Mainstream,* XLIII(39): 19–26.
———. 2005b. 'Farewell to Class Struggle in Name of Secularism', *Mainstream,* 4 (July–August): 4–5.

Kumar, Ravi. 2006a. 'Introduction: Equality, Quality and Quantity—Mapping the Challenges before Elementary Education in India', in Ravi Kumar, (ed.), *The Crisis of Elementary Education in India*, pp. 13–56. New Delhi: Sage Publications.

———.2006b. 'Educational Deprivation of the Marginalized: A Village Study of Mushar Community in Bihar,' in Ravi Kumar (ed.), *The Crisis of Elementary Education in India*, pp. 301–42. New Delhi: Sage Publications.

Kumar, Ravi and Paul Rama. 2006a. 'Transforming Spaces or Refashioning Hierarchies? Some Preliminary Reflections on Gender Relations, Media and Globalisation', in Sakarama Somayaji and Ganesha Somayaji (eds), *Sociology of Globalisation: Perspectives from India*, pp. 377–390. New Delhi and Jaipur: Rawat Publications.

———.2006b. 'Institutionalising Discrimination: Challenges of Educating Urban Poor in Neo-Liberal Era', in Sabir Ali (ed.), *Managing Urban Poverty*, pp. 253–289. New Delhi: Council for Social Development and Uppal Publishing House.

Kwiek, Marek. 2003. 'The State, the Market, and Higher Education: Challenges for the New Century,' in Marek Kwiek (ed.), *The University, Globalization, Central Europe*, pp. 71–114. New York: Peter Lang.

MacGregor, Susanne. 2005. 'The Welfare State and Neoliberalism', in Saad-Filho, Alfredo and Johnston, Deborah (eds), *Neoliberalism: A Critical Reader*, pp. 142–148. London: Pluto Press.

Nayyar, Deepak. 2006. 'Globalisation and Development in the Long Twentieth Century', in S. Jomo K. (ed.), *Globalisation Under Hegemony: The Changing World Economy*. New Delhi: Oxford University Press.

Norberg, Johan. 2005. *In Defence of Global Capitalism*. New Delhi: Academic Foundation.

Noronha, Claire and Meera Sampson. 2001. *Primary Schools and Universal Elementary Education*. India Education Team Report. Oxford University Press.

Pattnaik, Utsa. 2004. 'The Republic of Hunger', public lecture on the occasion of the 50th birthday of Safdar Hashmi, organized by SAHMAT (Safdar Hashmi Memorial Trust). New Delhi. Available online at http://www.macroscan.org/the/food/apr04/fod210404Republic_Hunger.htm (accessed on 17 July 2006).

Rao, Narasimha P. and K. C. Suri. 2006. 'Dimensions of Agrarian Distress in Andhra Pradesh', *Economic and Political Weekly*, XLI, 22 April(16): 1546–52.

Saad-Filho, Alfredo and Deborah Johnston. 2005. 'Introduction', in A. Saad and D. Johnston (eds), pp. 1–6, *Neoliberalism: A Critical Reader*. London: Pluto Press.

Sadgopal, Anil. 2004a. 'Globalisation: Demystifying Its Knowledge Agenda for India's Education Policy', *Durgabai Deshmukh Memorial Lecture*. New Delhi: Council for Social Development and India International Centre.

———. 2004b. 'Elementary, it's Education' in Bharat Jan Vigyan Jatha, *India's Education Policy: Creating Political Space for Social Intervention*. Ghaziabad: Bharat Jan Vigyan Jatha.

———. 2006a. 'Dilution, Distortion and Diversion: A Post-Jomtien Reflection on Education Policy', in Ravi Kumar (ed.), *The Crisis of Elementary Education in India*, pp. 92–136. New Delhi: Sage Publications.

———. 2006b. 'Privatisation of Education: An Agenda of the Global Market', *Combat Law*, 5(1): 22–27.

Sharma, Vijender. 2005. 'Commercialisation of Higher Education in India', *Social Scientist*, 33(9–10): 65–74.

Sainath, P. 2004a. 'Seeds of Suicide—I'. Available online at http://www.indiatogether.org/2004/jul/psa-seeds1.htm (accessed on 10 July 2006).
———. 2004b. 'Seeds of Suicide—II'. Available online at http://www.indiatogether.org/2004/jul/psa-seeds2.htm (accessed on 10 July 2006).
———. 2004c. 'How the Better Half Dies'. Available online at http://www.indiatogether.org/2004/aug/psa-womenfarm.htm (accessed on 10 July 2006).
———. 2005. 'The Swelling Register of Deaths', *The Hindu*, 29 December.
Sastry, N.S. 2004. 'Estimating Informal Employment and Poverty in India', Discussion Paper Series-7, Human Resource Development Centre, United Nations Development Programme, New Delhi.
Sehgal, Rashme. 2005. 'Whole Villages up for Sale in Punjab'. Available online at http://www.infochangeindia.org/features265.jsp# (accessed on 10 July 2006).
Sen, Amartya. 2002. 'How to Judge Globalism', *The American Prospect*, 13(1) January 1–14. Available online at http://www.prospect.org/print/V13/1/sen-a.html (accessed on 21June 2006).
Sharma, Ashok B. 2005. 'Organic Farming to Boost Punjab's Kharif Season'. *The Financial Express*. Available online at http://www.financialexpress.com/fe_full_story.php?content_id=92984 (accessed on 10 July 2006).
Soubbotina, Tatyana P. and Katherine A. Sheram. 2000. *Beyond Economic Growth: Meeting the Challenges of Global Development*. Washington: World Bank.
Stiglitz, Joseph E. 2002. 'Globalism's Discontents', *The American Prospect* 13(1), January 1–14. Available online at http://www.prospect.org/print/V13/1/stiglitz-j.html (accessed on 21 June 2006).
Tabb, William K. 1997. 'Globalisation Is *An* Issue, The Power of Capital Is *The* Issue', *Monthly Review*, 49(2). Available online at http://www.monthlyreview.org/697tabb.htm (accessed on 12 September 2006).
Tilak, Jandhyala B.G. 1996. 'How Free is 'Free' Primary Education in India?' *Economic and Political Weekly*, XXXI(4–5): 275–82.
———. 2003. 'Public Expenditure on Education in India: A Review of Trends & Emerging Issues', in J.B.G. Tilak (ed.), *Financing Education in India*. New Delhi: NIEPA (National Institute for Educational Planning and Administration) and Ravi Books.
———. 2005. 'Higher Education: A Public Good or a Commodity for Trade? Commitment *to* Higher Education or Commitment of Higher Education to Trade', keynote address at the 2nd Nobel Laureates Meeting, Barcelona, December 2.
Tomasevski, Katarina. 2005. 'Has the Right to Education a Future within the United Nations? A Behind-the-Scenes Account by the Special Rapporteur on the Right to Education 1998–2004', *Human Rights Law Review*, 5(2): 205–237.
UNESCO (United Nations Educational, Scientific and Cultural Organization). 1997. *Challenges of Education For All in Asia and the Pacific and the APPEAL Response*. Bangkok: Principle Regional Office for Asia and the Pacific.

7
Literacy Instruction in Indian Schools

Shobha Sinha

The nature of relationship between literacy and development is very complex and challenging. More so because defining either term is not easy. However, a direct causal link between the two has been assumed in the past. This assumption was the basis of mass literacy campaigns launched by the third world countries with the hope that economic development will be facilitated. The reason for this assumption could be that the developed countries have had high levels of literacy; hence a direct causal correlation was assumed (Daswani 1994: 279–90). Close examination reveals, however, that this assumption is too simplistic. Daswani (1994) describes this assumption as 'fallacious' and provides examples to demonstrate complex patterns of literacy and development. For example, even the Western model needs to be re-examined as economic development in the Western countries preceded mass literacy, not the other way around. Some Southeast Asian countries, for example, Thailand, have high levels of literacy, yet not corresponding economic development.

In theoretical terms too, the earlier notions of 'consequences' of literacy and its transformational abilities, in cognitive, social, and other sense received challenges. Earlier literacy was viewed as a cause of these changes. However, later this view was criticized for being too deterministic and its neglect of context of literacy usage. Therefore, now instead of focusing on the consequences of literacy the need is to focus on the uses of literacy, thus, differentiating between the causal and instrumental conceptions of literacy. Further, to understand the relationship between literacy and social development, as Olson and Torrance (2001) argue, we need to view literacy in broader terms regarding its forms and functions.

Right now an unqualified belief regarding the consequences of literacy has been replaced by a deeper understanding about its complexities. As Daswani (1994) points out, literacy related programmes have altered from simple literacy programmes to programmes dealing with a wider notion of literacy. This change was in response to issues such as poor response to campaigns, policies that disregarded the motivations of the participants, and inability to sustain literacy practice. This raises questions about the quality and context of the literacy programmes. One of the concerns that both the policy makers and scholars have had to contend with is the definition of literacy. It is clear that literacy is not a static, monolithic condition that will automatically transform the life of an individual or that of a society. Among other things, it is important to consider the level of literacy one is dealing with. A distinction is necessary between literacy that is 'embedded in a system of social functions and cultural processes whereas alphabetical competence is only a technical skill' (Triebel 2001: 21). This is an important distinction because in many literacy campaigns literacy was viewed in a very simplistic manner and the goals were to provide minimal skill of reading and writing without any concern about its usage and meaning in a person's life.

Despite the fact that literacy is no longer viewed as an unqualified path to economic and social development, it cannot be denied that it affords many possibilities and hence is an important concern in keeping with the theme of this volume. The possibilities need to be explored by educators as in itself some skill of decoding and encoding will not transform much of the social reality. Freire's contribution to the field of education was important as he went beyond viewing literacy as a mechanical skill and viewed it as a means to 'liberation' (Freire 1985). He emphasized not reading the word but also reading the world.

In this paper literacy will not be viewed merely in quantitative terms but also qualitatively. Thus, literacy is not defined merely as a technical, mechanical skill but rather as a practice that can empower a person. First, I will begin with a broad overview about literacy practices in India. Then, I will discuss the role of schooling followed by a discussion on the issues and problems in terms of school literacy in India.

LITERACY IN INDIA

The literacy rate in India has shown a steady increase from 18.33 per cent to 64.8 per cent from 1951 to 2001 (Census). However, this increasing rate conceals some depressing facts. One of the facts is that with the corresponding increase of the population the absolute number of illiterate people has not decreased. Also, there is a considerable disparity in terms of regions, gender, and between urban and rural populations. A further aspect of the grim story is that the ones who do qualify as literates do not necessarily have the quality of literacy which one deems necessary in the sense of realizing oneself or promoting critical consciousness in any degree. According to Kumar literacy in India has a 'restricted, rather enfeebled meaning' (2004: 121). The tendency is to define literacy in minimalistic terms. The extent of literacy knowledge includes, being able to display some basic ability to decode texts and write, for example, in terms of signing a document (Agnihotri 1997: 199–206). Thus, if literacy was to be defined as the 'ability to understand and produce written texts which in some sense would empower the individual and open up new areas of investigation, the literacy rate would drop dramatically, possibly to less than a quarter of the population aged seven and above' (ibid.: 199). It is evident that the percentage of literacy is actually inflated due to a very liberal criterion for literacy.

Agnihotri has traced the history of literacy teaching in India. Literacy was part of the agenda in many social reform movements and later on during the struggle for independence. Many national leaders, including Gandhi and Tagore recognized the importance of literacy in national reconstruction. However, later on, after the zeal associated with independence struggle was over, the adult literacy programmes assumed a more limited functional character. During the post-independence period, the literacy agenda was taken up by government and non-governmental organizations (NGOs). Unfortunately, meaningless and boring material, along with narrowly conceived understanding of literacy (such as reading and writing one's name and address), poor financial resources, and lack of vision contributed to the low success of these programmes.

In India discussions about literacy leave out almost entirely the role that schools play in making a person literate. The major problem is seen in terms of vast numbers of illiterates and the major response is in terms of adult literacy campaigns. Kumar (2004) points out that the term 'literacy' is completely appropriated by adult education in India and policy documents as well, as research journals are silent about literacy in the context of school and children's education. While one does not question the important role of adult literacy programmes, yet, one wonders why an obvious context where children acquire literacy is entirely disregarded. With very few exceptions the literature is silent about the kind of literacy experiences that children get in the school context.

This is a strange omission, considering the important roles schools play in literacy acquisition, especially in a country like India. Teale and Sulzby's (1986) research studies in children's early literacy development in countries with high levels of literacy reveal that children also acquire literacy in informal settings where they get opportunities to interact with literacy in meaningful ways and hence hypothesize about its nature. However, in India, most low socio-economic status children, especially from non-literate homes do not get opportunities to informally interact with print. Additionally, they may not get formal support in their homes in terms of coaching or tuitions, even though these may be of dubious educational quality. Hence, these children are entirely dependent on schools in acquiring literacy. Therefore, the role of schools in terms of acquiring literacy is all the more critical in India. If children do not get adequate help in school they are bound to remain illiterate unless they go to an adult literacy programme in their later years. Their survival in school becomes severely at risk if they do not successfully acquire literacy in early grades. They will suffer not only in the language classes but also across school subjects, for example, social studies and science. They might also be compelled to drop out because the subsequent years of schooling will demand more and more literacy knowledge for survival. It is clear that literacy is a basic requirement to continue in schools. In fact, N. Kumar (2000) has examined the relationship between the high drop-out rate and children's experiences with literacy in the school.

According to Olson and Torrance (2001: 10) 'schooling and literacy are essentially coterminous in modern societies' and the 'literacy levels in a nation are closely tied to years of schooling'. It is important to investigate the nature of reading instruction in Indian schools and the likely reason for it. It is a difficult task because as pointed out earlier very little scholarly work is available in this area.

LITERACY IN THE SCHOOL CONTEXT

The problem of the drop-out rate has plagued primary education in India. This problem has been investigated by many researchers. In the past, mostly the background of children was cited as the reason for dropping out

(K. Kumar 1993). K. Kumar (1992) pointed out the need to examine school related factors to fully understand the problems of drop outs. He contends that poor literacy pedagogy may account for it. The recent Annual Status of Education Report conducted by NGOs reports lesser drop-out rate in rural areas. However, the figures related to reading are far from heartening. According to this national level survey, reading tasks were classified as reading at a paragraph level (at Standard I level of reading difficulty), reading a simple story (Standard II level of reading difficulty), reading words, and reading letters. Some of the findings are that 35 per cent of all children could not read a simple paragraph and 52 per cent of children could not read a story. With younger children (7–10) age group the number is even higher: 48.2 per cent could not read level I paragraph and 68 per cent were unable to read level II stories. Forty-four per cent of the children could not read simple Standard II level paragraphs. There are wide variations across regions. The figures are based merely on children's decoding ability and do not take comprehension into account. Yet children performed very poorly. Many systematic studies are not available on comprehension. However, some studies that are available reveal poor performance in reading comprehension. Thorndike (1973) in his study of 15 countries found that Indian students performed poorly in comprehension. Even though this study was conducted a while ago, there is no reason to believe that the situation has changed. Recent studies do not show great improvement. For example, Narasimhan (2004) conducted language comprehension tests for children from the elite schools of Mumbai. The test included narrative, expository, and instructional texts. He found the results 'unexpected' since the children belonged to elite schools of Mumbai, yet their performance displayed a wide spread and the average was poorer than what they achieved in public exams. He explained that the public schools coached children to perform successfully in the examinations but failed to prepare them to negotiate unfamiliar texts and tasks.

LITERACY PEDAGOGY IN INDIA

To understand this type of performance by Indian children it is important to examine literacy instruction in the classroom, particularly in the early years. One has to mainly rely on textbooks to get ideas about the nature of pedagogy. Teachers heavily depend on textbooks for teaching so it is a good indicator of what happens in the classrooms.

In India, literacy pedagogy is primarily traditional. The focus is overwhelmingly on sounds rather than meaning. Again, even though much descriptive study of classrooms is not available, yet some conclusions about literacy pedagogy can be drawn by analyzing primers since instruction in India is heavily dependent on textbooks. In a study where 10 Hindi primers were analyzed to understand the nature of early reading instruction (Sinha 2000: 38–43), the analysis revealed a total absorption with graphophonics. Lessons were constructed around particular sounds, not themes. So, generally they began with a list of words featuring a target sound. For example, in a lesson the following words were listed: car, rice, government, asthma, evening, sword, year, and black. This puzzling collection of words were featured together because in Hindi they have a common sound 'a' (rhyming with the sound 'a' in car). Thus, in Hindi the words are: car, *bhat, sagar, sarcar, dama, sham, talwar, sal, kala*. The list of thematically unconnected words is followed by sentences where maximum words are used with the target sounds. For example, in a lesson with 'o', the sentences are as following:

> *Dhol bajao. Chor bhagao. Shor na machao. Paathshala chalo. Kitab kholo. Bolkar padho. Dekhkar likho. Tote ko ram ram ratne do.* (Beat the drum. Scare the thief. Don't make noise. Go to school. Open the book. Read aloud. Look and write. Let the parrot say ram ram.)

Due to their obsession with sounds to the exclusion of everything else, the texts are unfocused and at times blatantly absurd. For example, *aam par chadh* (climb on a mango), *gilas sir par mat rakh* (don't keep the glass on your head).

These texts actually teach 'not' to seek meaning while reading. If one reads these texts for comprehension, then the experience will be very bizarre because there is no coherent text to comprehend in the first place. If a child depends on these texts exclusively to learn to read, she will get the message that reading is a very meaningless, mysterious, and rather absurd process. Occasionally, when the texts even paid attention to the theme, the style was not very readable or interesting. It lacked flow and the content though coherent was not interesting.

In another study, Kaushik (2004) examines first grade teachers' assumptions about early literacy. She found that the views of the teacher corresponded to the views presented in the textbooks. They focused on the sequential learning of letters, blending of letters to form words. Decoding was conceptualized as the main goal of reading and practice of each sound was to be the focus of each lesson. Teachers were tenacious in their beliefs about the sequential nature of literacy. They were primarily concerned with correct pronunciation and correct formation of letters while writing. Any deviation from the print was viewed as an error.

THEORY AND RESEARCH ON READING

Traditionally, reading was viewed narrowly as a decoding process, that is, of finding oral equivalent of written language. Thus, the graphophonics (letter–sound correspondence) aspect of reading was emphasized in literacy instruction. The early literacy instruction consisted of teaching children to sequentially master the sub-skills of reading. Thus, children were expected to master the letter–sound correspondence and learn about blending to decode words. There was also a tendency, as Teale and Sulzby (1986) suggest, to focus on the formal and not the functional aspects of language while learning to read.

This approach to reading was criticized on several grounds. The behaviouristic view of learning, with its emphasis on sequential mastery of sub-skills and drilling fragmented language into meaningless units. Consequently, learning to read ended up being a tedious and mechanical process which was uninteresting and irrelevant for children (Goodman 1986). The other problem with this approach was that it excluded any functional use of language. Unlike oral language development where children acquire and use the language simultaneously, here they were expected to wait to use it till they fully acquired the formal aspects of the written language.

During the 1960s and the decades following it, breakthrough work was done on reading which questioned the belief that reading was merely decoding (Pearson and Stevens 1994: 22–42). The powerful influence of Noam Chomsky in language influenced the field of reading as well. Initially psycholinguistics, and then other disciplines such as cognitive psychology questioned the bottom-up approach of reading which constituted adding letters to form words, adding words to form sentences, and so on. Reading came to be viewed as not merely a mechanical activity of decoding but a sense making activity. Literacy was not confined to phonics but encompassed the whole act of reading, including comprehension. According to Smith (1971) too much attention to letters was seen as detrimental to the comprehension process.

In terms of learning to read, a developmental perspective, emergent literacy, based on a different and broader conceptualization of reading gained prominence. Right from the beginning reading was seen as a sense making activity. Children became literate by actively generating hypotheses about print around them. A child's early attempts at reading and writing, for example, scribbling, invented spelling, or pretend reading were seen as legitimate literacy engagements and were not rejected as being different from conventional reading (Teale and Sulzby 1986: vii–xxv). The instructional implications of this approach were not drill and sequential mastery of phonics but engagement with literacy in a meaningful and holistic manner. Authentic tasks were recommended to promote literacy development in children. According to Hiebert (1994: 391), authentic tasks 'involve children in immediate use of literacy for enjoyment and communication. They are not tasks that have typified school literacy instruction, in which pieces of literacy…have been practiced for some undefined future use'. Additionally, Goodman (1986) argues that literacy learning would be considered easier if it was sensible, interesting, and relevant to the life of children.

This type of theory building and research was developed primarily in literacy rich environments such as North America and New Zealand. A recent review of research in various countries shows the constant concern about process by which children learn. If we look at this type of research, what we see in terms of pedagogy in India appears disheartening. It is clear that what goes on in the name of early reading instruction in India is closer to the more traditional model of teaching reading and is unaffected by the research based on constructivist approaches to reading. Apart from the meaninglessness, the literacy instruction suffers by not giving legitimacy to children's early engagement with literacy. Children's activities such as pretend reading and invented spelling are subject to correction. The problem is that teachers do not have the theoretical tools to assess the developmental nature of children's literacy. This problem is not confined to teachers. Children's early attempts to writing were accepted but labeled as 'crude' while describing a major literacy programme in India (Bannerji et al. 2004: 62–69). Another problem with these pedagogical practices is that they are totally based on formal aspects of writing and ignore the functional aspects of literacy altogether. Children who have literacy at home get to see how literacy impacts life continuously. However, a child from a non-literate home does not get a chance to see its functional aspect. He/she may have heard that literacy will be useful to them in some future date but at the moment the school fails to reveal to them what one can do with literacy.

One can safely conclude that the contact with literacy in the school context is dull and boring. The exercises are sheer drudgery. The consequences for children who depend on schools to acquire literacy are serious.

They really have to be more than willing to suspend the disbelief about literacy and its merits in order to survive schooling. Mostly children and their background get blamed for not providing literacy experiences at home. However, instead of blaming illiterate parents it is important for the schools to realize their responsibility towards these children and provide support in the form of print-rich environment, meaningful interactions with literacy, and opportunities for using literacy in rewarding ways. It is important to find how these goals can be realized in Indian classrooms.

LITERACY RESEARCH IN INDIA

Often it has been argued that one cannot just lift ideas or pedagogical practices of the developed countries and apply it to different contexts. This is certainly true. One can easily argue about high levels of literacy in these countries and the print-rich environment that is readily available for exploration to children. But on the basis of these arguments it is still not appropriate to dismiss this body of research, especially when this area has not been explored at all in educational literature.

In India a major part of the problem is that the focus on processes and pedagogy of reading is absolutely negligible. Part of this situation can be explained as a general problem with Indian education. N. Kumar (2000), while describing the educational projects in Banaras claims that most failed due to 'pedagogic inefficiency'. She further goes on to state that:

> [T]his taking-for-granted of children's responses and assumptions of their passivity has cost the adults dear. The educators assumed that their intentions were going to be executed once they had broadcast their intentions. How these intentions got translated into children's experiences and, further what they meant to children in terms of learning interested no educator... (Ibid.: 2000: 23)

It seems that in India the lack of concern about actual pedagogic practices is nothing new barring some notable exceptions, for example, the science programmes in Hoshangabad. Literacy pedagogy has not occupied the mind of the educators or institutions in any significant way. A look at course structures in the universities bears out this neglect.

Here, it is important to note that in the recent *Handbook of Reading Research*, Volume III, there was difference in the way reading process and pedagogy were focused on in countries like the United States, United Kingdom, Australia, and New Zealand on one hand, and Latin America on the other. In the former, there were discussions of research on processes and instructional strategies, whereas the latter did not focus as much on it. Santana (2000: 41–52) noted that the nature of educational research in developing countries differs ideologically from the research in industrialized nations since research is also a form of social practice and hence sensitive to the context. In fact, when the research draws too much from the industrialized nation then it might be guilty of ignoring the context. India has some interesting parallels with Latin America. For instance, research is not a priority here as well. However, it is not enough to dismiss the lack of instructional research on the grounds that we obviously differ from the industrialized nations. It is critical to understand how children read in the Indian context, what type of instruction goes on in the classroom, what does innovative ideas mean in terms of classroom practice, and so on. These are questions that educators deal with on a daily basis. Ignoring them on the basis of contextual difference is not good enough.

In this context, it will be pertinent to discuss the role of the education department in the universities. Unfortunately, they are so preoccupied with teacher education that they do not find it necessary to contribute to the research. In fact, to some degree, commitment to research is seen as being detrimental to teaching. There is some quality work in policy studies and textbook analysis but classroom studies and instructional studies are either negligible or of low quality. The problem is that even teacher education suffers due to a lack of substantial material to refer to. This situation is due to many problems: A mindset which does not permit the teacher educators to see the value of research, the poor structure of these programmes which does not allow the faculty to participate in ongoing research in schools. This is a serious gap because universities do have a critical role to play in building knowledge in this field.

TEACHER EDUCATION AND LITERACY PEDAGOGY

Lately, the notion that children drop out of schools and perform poorly due to low motivation and lack of parental support has been challenged and school factors are examined as a cause of failure for students to remain in schools. This shift is welcome because it identifies a very important factor in children's performance in education. However, the implication may be seen as blaming the teachers. This is not appropriate because one has to examine the knowledge and expertise that teachers bring to the field of reading. In India, the situation is very unfortunate. There is hardly any separate course for teaching reading and even the innovative Bachelor of Elementary Education (B.El.Ed.) programme does not adequately address the needs. One cannot condemn teachers for not trying out ideas that they themselves are unfamiliar with. Further, as discussed earlier, there is not much instructional theory-building and research. Students deal with theories in a broader sense and are supposed to find classroom applications on their own. That gap is not easy to cover so they mostly end up relying on familiar traditional practices. It is important to explore thoroughly what these theories mean in the context of the classroom. Thus, more discussions on the knowledge that teacher training helps acquire needs to be given important consideration. The discussion has not even started yet.

CONCLUSION

It is clear from the preceding discussion that the situation related to literacy learning in India is very bleak due to poor pedagogical practices and research, among other factors. These areas have been ignored for too long even though there is a lot of concern about literacy in India. It is clear from the discussion at the beginning of this paper that mechanical knowledge about literacy does not translate into empowerment or development. As Narasimhan (2004) points out, literacy needs to go beyond social service and needs to develop a body of worthwhile professional knowledge. Therefore, it is important to engage with the process of acquiring literacy in a significant way and developing culturally sensitive and informed pedagogical practices.

BIBLIOGRAPHY

Agnihotri, R. K. 1997. 'Literacy Teaching in India', in V. Edwards and D. Corson (eds), *Encyclopedia of Language and Education*, pp. 199–206. Netherlands: Kluwer Academic Publishers.
Bannerji, R., M. Chavan, and U. Rane. 2004. 'Learning to Read', *Seminar,* 536, April (536): 62–69.
Daswani, C. 2001. 'Issues of Literacy Development in the Indian Context', in D.R. Olson and N.Torrance (eds), *The Making of Literate Docieties*, pp. 284–95. Oxford: Blackwell.
Daswani, C. J. 1994. 'Literacy and Development in South-east Asia', in L. Verhoeven (ed.), *Functional Literacy: Theoretical Issues and Educational Implications*, pp. 279–90. Amsterdam: John Benjamins.

Freire, P. 1985. *The Politics of Education*. Massachusetts: Bergin & Garvey.
Goodman, K. 1986. *What's Whole about Whole Language?* Portsmouth, NH: Heinemann.
Hiebert, E. H. 1994. 'Becoming Literate through Authentic Tasks: Evidence and Adaptations', in R. B. Ruddell, M. R. Ruddell, and H. Singer (eds), *Theoretical Models and Processes of Reading*, pp. 391–413. Newark: IRA.
Kaushik, S. 2004. 'Teachers' Assumptions about Early Reading', M.Ed. dissertation, University of Delhi, New Delhi.
Kumar, K. 1992. *What is Worth Teaching?* 3rd edition. New Delhi: Orient Longman.
———. 1993. 'Literacy and Primary Education in India', in P. Freebody and A. R. Welch (eds), *Knowledge, Culture, and Power: International Perspective on Literacy as Policy and Practice*, pp. 102–13. Pittsburgh: University of Pittsburgh Press.
———. 2004. 'Literacy, Socialization and the Social Order', in T. Nunes and P. Bryant (eds), *Handbook of Children's Literacy*, pp. 711–20. Great Britain: Klewer Academic Publishers.
Kumar, N. 2000. *Lessons from Schools: The History of Education in Banaras*. New Delhi: Sage Publications.
Narasimhan, R. 2004. *Characterizing Literacy*. New Delhi: Sage Publications.
Olson, D. R. and N. Torrance. 2001. 'Conceptualizing Literacy as a Personal Skill and as a Social Practice', in D. R. Olson and N. Torrance (eds), *The Making of Literate Societies*, pp. 3–18. Oxford: Blackwell.
Pearson, P. D. and D. Stevens. 1994. 'Learning about Literacy: A 30-year Journey', in R. B. Ruddell, M. R. Ruddell, and H. Singer (eds), *Theoretical Models and Processes of Reading*, pp. 22–42. Newark: IRA.
Pratham Resource Center. 2005. *Annual Status of Educational Report*. Mumbai: Pratham Resource Center.
Santana, I. S. 2000. 'Literacy Research in Latin America', in M. Kamil, P. B. Mosenthal, P. D. Pearson, and R. Barr (eds), *Handbook of Reading Research*, pp. 41–52. Mahwah, NJ: Lawrence Erlbaum Associates.
Sinha, S. 2000. 'Acquiring Literacy in Indian Schools', *Seminar*, September (493): 38–42.
Smith, Frank. 1971. *Understanding Reading: A Psycholinguistic Analysis of Reading and Learning to Read*. New York: Holt, Rinehart & Winston.
Teale, W. and E. Sulzby. 1986. 'Introduction: Emergent Literacy as a Perspective for Examining How Young Children become Readers and Writers', in W. Teale and E. Sulzby (eds), *Emergent Literacy: Writing and Reading*, pp. vii–xxv. Norwood, NJ: Ablex.
Thorndike, R. L. 1973. *Reading Comprehension in Fifteen Countries: An Empirical Study*. Stockholm: Almquist &Wiksell.
Triebel, A. 2001. 'The Roles of Literacy Practices in the Activities and Institutions of Developed and Developing Countries', in D. R. Olson and N. Torrance (eds), *The Making of Literate Societies*, pp. 19–53. Oxford: Blackwell.

8
Empowering Pedagogy: Potentials and Limitations

Sadhna Saxena

In this chapter, I share my experiences of a literacy programme, Jan Shikshan Abhiyan (JSA, hereafter), which was carried out in 25 villages of Bankhedi block of Hoshangabad district (Madhya Pradesh) in the late 1980s. Though the classes at each centre were primarily meant for children who had no access to formal education, a few adults also attended the night classes. Involvement of adults was very heartening as they contributed actively in running the centres in a variety of ways.

By and large, literacy work adheres to the behaviourist paradigm of learning that requires drilling and rote memorization as opposed to engaging process of meaning construction. Indifference to the research findings of the past many decades, in the field of socio-linguistics and psycho-linguistics and its incorporation in teaching methods, especially in the formal system, is disconcerting and puzzling. The major challenge for the JSA team was to apply this understanding of literacy process in a predominantly oral rural milieu, among the first generation learners. These children had little or no access to written resources that are taken for granted in most of the research studies. The challenge was compounded as the programme was funded by the Ministry of Human Resource Development (MHRD), and the six monthly installments of meager grant that JSA received were either released late or not released at all. Ironically, it was easier to mobilize government grant for large literacy projects that ran on conventional understanding and claimed high rate of literacy achievement (with little comprehension) than to run a small, pilot-level project that was struggling to weave in the research understanding and addressing the issue of lack of comprehension prevalent among learners.

This chapter is divided into two main sections. The first section briefly discusses the social context of the learners, and the second deals with the pedagogical issues. Evolution of the literacy pedagogy used by JSA was based on and informed by the research in the psycholinguistics and sociolinguistics. Though at the first instance, the two sections may seem disjointed or unconnected, the issues of cognition and learning and pedagogy are as important as the reality of the learners in which the programme is embedded. On one hand, research informs us that the rich, oral traditions of the first generation learners and the literate environment, which these learners are deprived of, play a significant role in facilitating literacy acquisition. On the other hand, as I have argued in 'Nellore Revisited' (Saxena 2002), the power that deprived acquires through literacy or through spaces created by literacy process brings them in direct conflict with the state and the powerful elites. Therefore, through the two seemingly disjointed sections, I am trying to build a nuanced picture of the complex relationship between literacy, power, and pedagogy.

THE CONTEXT

After the closure of Kishore Bharati (KB)[1] in 1989, a group of young volunteer teachers, trained by KB, decided to continue the educational work among the non-school going children of that area. These teachers, as I discuss in 'Education of the Poor' (Saxena 1998) and *Shiksha* (Saxena 2000), were also active in a people's organization called Kisan Majdoor Sangathan (Sangathan, here after) that was struggling for the rights of small farmers and the landless labourers. Their active participation in Sangathan had created an awareness and 'demand' for children's education among the landless labourers and small farmers. This demand was however unsatiated by the abysmally dysfunctional primary school system. Many of the villages, where JSA ran its centres, did not have even primary schools, while elsewhere schools existed but children saw their teacher only on rare occasions.

Various innovative education programmes developed in KB preceded the JSA's work. While it had drawn upon the experiences of intervention in the formal schools through the Hoshangabad Science Teaching Programme (HSTP), KB's interventions with non-schoolgoing children and illiterate adults, particularly women, had formed the enriched basis for trying new methods in JSA. Of all these efforts, the preceding Children's Activity Programme (CAP, hereafter)[2] was instrumental in evolving insights into how children in these environs learn (CAP 1991). One of the important legacies of CAP was a rich collection of children's literature. CAP had also published the *bundeli* versions of some of the English and Hindi children's books. All of this formed the rich reading resource for the JSA activities. The efficacy of cycle-borne mobile libraries and publication of cyclostyled newsletter of children's writings, *Bal Chiraiya*,[3] had also been well established by the earlier efforts. In fact, publication of *Bal Chiraiya* created such a stir among the children, who were at various stages of writing, that for them a separate newsletter called *Gulgula* had to be launched. *Gulgula* contained oral narratives of these children that the mobile library volunteer wrote for them. The JSA tried to build upon these experiences by adapting to the gradually evolving context of organization and struggle in the region. Clearly, group's focus was the youth and children who had either been left out or dropped out of the formal school system.

THE CONFLICT

During the second year of the programme, one day, a Local Intelligence Bureau (LIB) person visited one of the JSA education centre situated in a forest village, Kamti-Murgidhana, miles away from road, near the foothills of the Satpura ranges. His seniors had ordered him to investigate JSA's activities and file a report. Some of the centres in that vicinity were not functional for quite a while as five members of the JSA team were in jail on fake charges of attempt to murder and Kamti-Murgidhana was one such centre. The Sangathan had organized struggles on the issues of people's rights to forests, land for the landless, for setting up agro-based production centres for employment of the rural landless, and against corruption and repression of the local police, forest, and revenue functionaries. This had naturally brought them in conflict with the feudal-vested interests and the local bureaucracy. Due to their active support to the Sangathan activities, the local police had implicated many villagers in criminal charges and the JSA activists were also among them.

Therefore, the LIB man was sent for an investigation on JSA's activities. Of all the centres that he visited, it was at the Kamti-Murgidhana centre he took photographs of the handwritten posters displayed on the four walls of the ram shackled makeshift classroom. He targeted certain poetry posters that he was particularly perturbed by. He took photographs of the posters that had poems of famous poets such as Sarveshwar Dayal Saxena, Nirankar Dev Sevak, Rameshchandra Shah, Prayag Shukla, Chandralal Yadav, Sohan Lal Diwedi, Dharam Pal Shastri, Naveen Sagar, Sudha Chauhan, and Rabindra Nath Tagore written on them. Also, he copied the text of many poems in his diary. Interestingly, the following two poems 'confirmed' LIB man's suspicion that JSA had a subversive agenda:

> *Phone uthakar kutta bola*
> Picking up the phone the dog said
> *suneiye thaanedaar*
> listen O' police officer
> *ghar mein chor ghuse hain*
> inside the house thieves have entered
> *bahar soya chawkidaar*
> outside sleeps the watchman

This children's poem was written by Vishnukant Pande, a renowned Hindi writer, and was published in *Bal Sakha*, a popular children's Hindi magazine published from Allahabad till the 1950s. 'This is what you teach' he said sarcastically to the villagers who had gathered at the centre. Apparently, he was upset with this poem because its content lowers the dignity of a police officer (a dog calling the police officer) and its hidden message is to undermine the authority. Therefore, it had the potential of instigating the people against the police force. The second poem was:

> *Tapper tapper ghume re naakedaar thaanedaar*
> Hovel to hovel they roam O' forest guard police officer
> *Daaru murgaa maange re naakedaar thaanedaar*
> Liquor chicken they demand O' forest guard police officer
> *Ballhar bhuttaa mange re naakedaar thaanedaar*
> Beans and corn they demand O' forest guard police officer
> *Rupiya paisa lootey re naakedaar thaanedaar*
> Money they rob O' forest guard police officer
> *Hukkaa-paani mange re naakedaar thaanedaar*
> Hookah-water (or bribe) they demand O' forest guard police officer
> *Jhonpri hamaari tore re naakedaar thaanedaar*
> Raze down our huts O' forest guard police officer

This song emerged during an agitation following a raid by the forest department functionaries in nearby Junetha village a couple of years ago when people's houses were searched and pulled down on the pretext of seizing stolen timber. They beat up the people and arrested a few villagers who resisted, later implicating them in false cases. These events were issues of discussion at the centre among the children who witnessed and suffered the highhandedness and brutalities of the forest department. The lyrics as well as the tune of this song, which is borrowed from a folk song, made it very popular among the villagers. The song had traveled through activists of a similar organization from western Madhya Pradesh and Rajasthan and was spontaneously adapted and sung lustily in subsequent marches and demonstrations. It is not difficult to see how effectively it expresses the sentiments and tribulations of tribal inhabitants of the forest regions sprawling across central India.

The LIB officer tore down these two posters in front of the villagers. Later, he told a local 'journalist' that he had documentary evidence to establish JSA's involvement in subversive activities—its role in instigating the villagers against the state. He strongly recommended a complete halt to JSA's activities instantaneously. Interestingly, these were the most popular or 'successful' 'chapters' of the JSA 'curriculum', as children and adults learnt to 'read' these, the fastest. Following are examples of two more popular poems, which were used in JSA classes. These examples would help in understanding the relevance of such written materials, sometimes based on oral forms, as a pedagogically useful resource for literacy work among the children from the marginalized sections.

> *Mindobai paani de, kodo kutki dhani de*
> Queen frog, give rain, give millets and paddy
> *Sabhe galla paani de, dhor bacheroo saani de*
> Give all grain and water, give cattle and calves fodder
> *Chahe jitno paani de, bachbe chappar channi de*
> Give as much water as you like, but spare our thatched roofs
> *Raja de naa raani de*
> For neither the king nor the queen give anything
> *Hamein to kainon nani de*
> Whatever meagre we get is from our grandmother.

Based on a popular children's rhyme game, usually rendered during rainy season, this poem was composed by a JSA team member in his classes. Another popular poem has been taken from a collection written by Nirankar Dev Sewak, well known for his contribution to Hindi literature for children. It goes as follows:

> *Nehru chaachaa gir pade*
> Nehru chaachaa had a fall

Ek din wo din dhale
One day at dusk
Ghode per chad ker chale
As he went horse riding
Nehru chaachaa gir pade

Children enjoy these two poems immensely. Adults reciting them invariably resulted in heated and polarized debate on the content. There was agreement on the disappointment with the authority; that is, neither the king nor the queen is bothered and only our own people care for us. A few, however, expressed reservations. Criticizing and defying the authority did make some uncomfortable. There was agreement that the poem depicts the reality yet, 'this should not be expressed openly as there is no choice except depending on them'.

The pupils in JSA, both adults and children, had access to carefully selected poems and songs from various sources, including their own resource. There is ample research and field-based evidence that shows that meaningless text acts as a dampener in literacy efforts. Beginning with familiar content not only generated interest but also inspired and helped in building confidence to engage with unfamiliar and interesting text. Also, considering that working with the marginalized children and adults may lead to conflict with the authority, the often asked question was, 'Does literacy takes a back seat in such situations?' There are no clear answers as I have shown in 'Nellore Revisited'(Saxena 2002), on the Nellore Total Literacy Campaign experience. However, those are no reasons to let literacy for the underprivileged remain a didactic and meaningless exercise.

SECTION II

Reading without comprehension was one of the major problems that we encountered in the 1970s when we started working with the middle school children. Much of this was due to meaningless and alien content of the books used. Also, the difference between their spoken language and the chaste and Sanskritized version of Hindi used in their textbooks did not facilitate learning. Spoken language in that region is either *bundeli* or 'nimadi', with influence of tribal languages like 'gondi' and 'korku'. In classrooms, there was no appreciation of children's own language resource. On the contrary, their culture and language was considered a sign of backwardness, which was often ridiculed and undervalued. The understanding of children's alienation and their silence in the formal schools, arrived at by the CAP's and other KB's experiences, was sharpened further by the writings on politics of language, although there is little documentation of these in the context of classroom transactions.

Research establishes, beyond doubt, that all normal children, no matter where and under what conditions they are raised, have full command of the grammatical system of their own language by the age of five. And children who are silent and unresponsive in formal classes and are assumed to be lacking in verbal ability are extraordinarily skilled communicators out of the school, in peer group situations (Gumperz 1985: 47–67). Hence, it is not the linguistic deprivation that is an explanation for the literacy failure. Rather, it is the misunderstanding of their discourse practices and undervaluing of their culture and language. 'Schools that do not understand the real nature of language differences are likely to underestimate the difficulties that the children face in adapting to the classroom environment' (ibid.: 46).

In addition to undervaluing the culture and language of the learner, lack of/wrong understanding of the cognitive aspects of reading process among the teachers and the resource persons also have long-term consequences for literacy. For instance, it was revealing to learn about the literacy process in the classrooms at the primary school levels in Hoshangabad district. During the first year of their schooling (6–7 years of age), children learnt only by sequential word and alphabet identification method with little or no adult guidance and this method did not create any opportunity for engagement with the text. At the same time, the process was mechanical and confined to singing of alphabets in the lower classes and often without being introduced to any printed matter. In the textbooks, introduction of each new vowel was accompanied by small, unimaginative, meaningless, sterile, and often, ridiculous sentences. Children read these sentences by spelling out each alphabet and vowel of the each word, and then synthesizing these to pronounce the word. Thus a sentence, *Madan ghar jaa* (Madan go home), is read as follows:

> *Ma khali* (without *matra* or a vowel), *da khali, na khali, – madan;*
> *Gha khali, ra khali, – ghar;*
> *Ja mein aa ki matra – jaa;*
> *Madan ghar jaa.*

This was their entry into the world of literacy—boring, unchallenging, and much of it meaningless too.

UNDERLYING PRINCIPLES

Generally, two significant principles guide the literacy work at the school levels. First, that literacy is simply a skill that is acquired, not constructed. And second, that there is a particular stage termed as 'reading readiness', before which introducing reading is stressful. This stage could be at a different age in different countries and also differs within a country. Mason and Sinha (1993: 137–50) cite ample research evidence that contests this 'reading readiness' paradigm. 'Reading readiness, with its emphasis on waiting until the child is ready to learn to read, also appears to be attractive to scholars concerned with childhood stress' (ibid.: 139). Thus, it is assumed that no reading should be introduced prior to school, and in school, it should begin from 'simple' to 'difficult' words, however abstract or meaningless they may be. This is when children are already negotiating the linguistic complexities—written and oral—depending on their environment. The research and writings by cognitive psychologists in the 1950s and 1960s provided evidence that early childhood was crucial in the cognitive development of an individual, emphasizes Mason and Sinha. This conclusion called into question the notion of waiting for the child to mature. Commenting on the stress factor, Mason and Sinha say that 'Formal instruction with reading readiness lessons includes rote memorization, sequential drills, and repetitive practices thus could be more stressful' (ibid.: 139).

Also, very importantly, Mason and Sinha (1993) critique the understanding of reading that has long been viewed in a dichotomous manner, with 'all-or-none' implying that children can either read or they cannot. Consequently, reading is narrowly defined in terms of ability to decode. This implies that a child who knows other aspects that are associated with reading, for instance, pretend reading, guessing by understanding the context, and remembering printed words to understand the strategies he/she could use, and so on, but cannot decode is viewed as a non-reader. In this paradigm, assert Mason and Sinha (1993),

> [T]ransfer was assumed between skills, without necessarily any scientific basis. For instance, even skills like crawl, hop, and skip were supposed to indicate reading readiness. This suggests that maturation in sensorimotor skills is assumed to transfer to reading skills. Moreover, it was assumed that general cognitive skills transfer to reading skills: if children were trained in the general cognitive skills, they would acquire the reading readiness constructs. (ibid.: 140)

Mason and Sinha say that there is little evidence to show that reading capabilities of children develop from general cognitive and motor skills though there is much evidence to establish that children who experience reading, even informally, do develop reading skills. Which means that, 'they learn to read in part through involvement in the act of reading' (Mason and Sinha 1993: 140). Based on intensive field work, CAP also found that 'children learn to read only by reading, just as they learn to speak only by speaking' and 'that they lose touch with meaning if they are forced to spell out each word and are forced to master the alphabet before being allowed to read' (ibid.: 8). In fact, research in cognitive psychology shows that children can, very early in life, form ideas about reading.

According to Mason and Sinha (1993), Vygotsky believed that development of children occurs in two interactive but qualitatively different lines; elementary processes that were biological in origin and higher psychological functions that were socio-cultural in origin. The latter was not 'biologically given' but culturally acquired (Vygotsky, cited in Mason and Sinha 1993: 141). And reading, in reality, is a very sophisticated and culturally acquired skill and cannot be explained on the basis of simplistic biological model of development.

Reading readiness paradigm was accepted more or less uncritically from the beginning of 20th century and it was not until the 1970s that 'readiness' was really presented with a 'unified challenge'. After this however, as Mason and Sinha emphasize, 'There appeared a proliferation of studies challenging both behaviourist theories and the notion of neural ripening' (ibid.: 141). All these studies shared the following perspective on reading:

> Literacy emerges before children are formally taught to read. Literacy is defined to encompass the whole act of reading, not merely decoding. The child's point of view and active involvement with emerging literacy constructs is featured. The social setting for literacy learning is not ignored. (ibid.: 141)

The term applied to this kind of research is 'emergent literacy' which gives legitimacy to children's literacy behaviour but still indicates a difference from conventional reading behaviour and provides a way to broaden its focus. That is, although decoding is a necessary component of learning to read, it should not be the only measure of gauging the ability to read. Thus, emergent literacy could be understood as knowledge about directionality, reading print in context, the ability to distinguish print from other graphic forms, understanding the function of print and its meaning, pretend or invented reading and writing, and shared reading and writing, all of which constitute early literacy development of children that needs to be considered as well. Vygotsky described children as active constructors of language and literacy, which he says, do not develop in vacuum. Although several researchers emphasized on the 'natural' way in which children learn reading, a close examination of natural way reveals a plethora of activities, including informal interactions that use literacy concepts, involvement in reading and writing, and staged opportunities for exploration of literacy materials that go on at home with parents or other siblings.

Emphasizing the roles of emergent literacy, researchers discuss the crucial role of 'read aloud' or story reading by adults/teachers to children. The adult acts as 'mediator' between the child and the text in the areas where the child cannot function alone and needs guidance. So all the prereading experience such as, interest in books, exposure to print, observing people read, pretending to read, reading to peers, reading to children, repeated reading, dramatization, and writing all of which happens 'naturally' in a literate environment contributes to literacy.

For almost all the children in a literate society, learning to read and write begins very early in life say Teale and Sulzby (1986). Further, literacy is not regarded simply a cognitive skill to be learnt, but a complex sociopsycholinguistic activity. As the social aspects of literacy play a significant role, literacy learning is not just investigated in researcher's laboratory, but also in home and in community settings. Also, children's oral language proficiency is related to their growth in reading and to the ways in which they write. Educators have long seen that a strong oral language base facilitates literacy learning, though this is generally ignored in formal education. Storytelling traditions are therefore a treasure for acquiring reading and writing abilities.

When children encounter written language, they try to figure out how it works. In trying to do this, they form hypotheses and test them, try to distinguish between drawings and written forms, and attempt to sort out relationships between these forms and oral language. That is, young children are active learners as constructors of meaning of written language and this is central to emergent literacy. Discussing the research findings with five year olds, Teale and Sulzby (1986: xv) write, 'This early research showed that young children could engage in important reading behaviours, such as visual sensitivity to letter and word forms, appropriate directional movements, self correction, and synchronized matching of spoken word units with written word units.'

In conclusion, therefore we could say that literacy development begins long before children start formal instruction. Literacy develops in real life settings from real life activities. Children learn written language through active engagement with their world. They interact socially with adults in writing and reading situations; they explore print on their own, and they profit from modeling of literacy of significant adults, particularly their parents. The reading is viewed as a process in which the reader deals with information and constructs meanings continuously. As Teale and Sulzby argue, the reading process involves readers in making predictions, confirming or disconfirming these predictions while reading, and integrating information from the text with their background knowledge to form solid, holistic interpretation of texts.

PATTERN RECOGNITION AND GUESSING

Crucial aspects of understanding of the process of reading, guessing, and predicting, evolved in Psycholinguistics, were reported in Scientific American in the early 1970s. Here, Kolers wrote in the context of a reading experiment in which all the words were written backwards and the students were able to read the abnormal sentences:

> [P]artly because in reading, one's concern is not so much with letters and words as it is with the meaning. The letters and words are symbols; it is meaning that you are after, and even if familiar symbols are altered, you can ascertain the meaning quickly once your visual system has found the clue that reveals the patterns of the symbols'. (Kolers 1972: 84)
>
> It is just this process of generating coherent messages from patterns of marks on a page that the skilled reader is engaged in. He is not, as one might think, involved in a piecemeal perception of individual letters and words. The process whereby the clues are selected and the messages are fashioned is one of the more challenging questions in the investigation of the way people process information. (ibid.: 91)

Goodman elaborates that we think breaking written language into pieces for learners facilitate learning to read. He says, 'Instead, we turn it from easy-to-learn language into hard-to-learn abstraction' (cited in Moon 1984: 21). Moon summarizes his understanding on reading as follows:

> Written language acquisition is now deeply embedded in an overall communication model where the previous experience of the learner bears upon meaningful and important messages transmitted in the case of writing and received in reading. The provision and promotion of written language which is relevant and memorable is of the utmost importance, otherwise opportunities to learn and become motivated are diminished. (ibid.: 21)

Thus the process of reading is understood as a process of pattern recognition, relying largely on guessing and predicting the meaning. The synthesizing process of building up the word, letter by letter, is in fact rarely used, probably when a totally unfamiliar word crops up for the first time. Very often, if the new word bears any resemblance to a previously familiar word, tendency is to 'misread' the new word as the familiar one. We all experience this is our own reading and identify these as mistakes.

The difference between mistakes and natural steps in reading process perhaps needs further elaboration. Once in a JSA class, a young girl was 'reading' the alphabet chart. She was saying, *kaa kilam kaa*, (*Kaa* for pencil), *Khaa khapre kaa* (*Khaa* for tile), and so on. Other children were repeating with her. The teacher thought that the girl was not able to 'read'. In the chart, with *kaa*, the picture was that of a lotus flower (*kamal*) and with *khaa* of a rabbit (*khargosh*), and so on. The girl was not paying any attention to the pictures and was 'reading' from her memory. She was so confident that the teacher was not able to intervene and 'correct' her.

Later, during discussion among the team members the question raised was whether the girl was making mistakes or moving a step ahead of the alphabet chart, which in any case had pictures alien to her? Wasn't her reading making the chart more familiar, comprehensible based on her linguistic knowledge and engagement with the process instead of drawing blank seeing unfamiliar things? Other teachers also reported similar experiences. They emphasized that people unconsciously replace many words by their local equivalents while reading. For example they read: *machhar* (mosquito) as *bagdar; alag* (separate) as *agal; garib aurat* (a poor woman) as *garibini; baras* (year) as saal; *beta* (son) as *laraka; bilkul* (exactly) as *bilkum; ped* (tree) as *jhaad; khokhal* (hole) as *pulang; bakari* (goat) as *chhiriya;* and so on. While discussing such substitutions or 'miscues', a term coined by Kenneth Goodman to signify that deviations readers make from text are not necessarily negative—can become windows into students' mental processing. In fact, research in reading shows that all readers make some miscues in order to read fast enough to overcome the limitations of short term memory. Readers catch their miscues when the text stops making sense to them, and then they self-correct.

In JSA, until the issue was discussed with the teachers and the resource person in the context of the role of pattern recognition and prediction in reading process, many of them categorized these as mistakes and kept on correcting them. Acutely aware of such practices in classrooms, Smith (1990) lists out 12 easy thumb rules for making learning to read proactive rather than difficult. One of the rules is 'discourage guessing'.

JSA'S UNDERSTANDING

These research-based insights that were available to CAP team and later to JSA group helped in developing a radically different approach to literacy. Uniqueness, however, was that both these programmes were carried out among people who possessed a rich treasure of oral literature but little formal literacy and written resources. Most of the children in CAP and JSA were first generation learners and had no or little access to the kind of 'reading' opportunities that most of the researchers of the previous section have taken for granted. So, the 'natural' process of reading that is, a print environment, constant exposure and encounter with print and formal or informal guidance to negotiate with print was unavailable to these children. However, the rich oral literature—legends and folklores, traditions of storytelling, constructing poems and songs, and interaction among peers provided strong base for literacy work. Street's strong contestation of the theory of great divide between literate and non-literate societies and bringing the writing practices of so-called 'non-literate' societies in the ambit of formal literacy further helped in understanding and valuing the available resources. Such practices exist in all societies, argued Street, and so transition to formal education is not a break but a continuum. The CAP and JSA group also drew upon such practices. Thus, the JSA group arrived at the following understanding of the process of learning literacy:

1. Viewing reading in a dichotomous manner, that is, children can either read or they cannot, this all-or-none understanding undermines their linguistic accomplishments that play an important role in reading and writing. One of the most important emergent literacy accomplishments in primarily oral societies is children's constant effort to pretend reading, guessing, and drawing connections between oral and written forms.

The emergent literacy paradigm informs that people do not need didactic and sterile primers; they need interesting books to read. People learn to read only by reading; just as children learn to speak only by speaking. While learning to speak, children are allowed a lot of time, freedom, and opportunities to experiment and make 'mistakes'. All such virtues are denied when they learn reading and writing. Acknowledgement of this discrepancy demands a wide variety of interesting contextual reading material with differing levels of complexity to create and sustain interest in reading.

Children's tremendous response to CAP and JSA's mobile libraries demonstrated this as even non-literate children who became members of these libraries, selected books on their own, changed them every week, even if rarely borrowed the same book it was always a conscious decision, never a mistake due to inability to 'read'. They actually flipped through the pages, engaged in pretend reading, and were helped by the library-in-charge just as the literate members were.

2. If what children read is of intrinsic interest to them, they will be motivated to 'read' and will try to make sense of print without needing drills. By breaking each word and with emphasis on pronouncing alphabet, a reader tends to lose touch with meaning. Thus, reading is reduced to a mechanical chore instead of an engaging exercise of meaning construction.

Here, it is instructive to read Holt's experience of a young black man of about 17 who was a student in an Upward Bound summer programme in England. Holt says that he was at the absolute bottom of all his regular school classes, and tested, judged, and officially labeled as being almost illiterate. At the meeting, which Holt was part of, the students, some black, some white, all poor, had been invited to talk to their summer-school teachers about what they could remember of their own school experiences and how they felt about them. Holt says that until quite late in the evening, Leon, the young black man, didn't speak.

> When he did, he didn't say much. But what he said I will never forget. He stood up, holding before him a paperback copy of Dr. Martin Luther King's book 'Why We can't Wait', which he had read, or mostly read, during that summer session. He turned from one to another of the adults, holding the book before each one of us and shaking it for emphasis, and, in a voice trembling with anger, said several times at the top of his lungs, 'Why didn't anyone ever tell me about this book? Why didn't anyone ever tell me about this book?' What he meant, of course, was that in all his years of schooling no one had ever asked him to read, or ever show him or mentioned to him, even one book that he had reason to feel might be worth reading. (Holt 1989: 27)

Furthermore, Holt (1989) points out that this book:

> [I]s full of long, intricate sentences and big words. It would not have been easy reading for more than a handful of students in Leon's age or any

other high school. But Leon, whose standardized Reading Achievement Test scores 'proved' that he had the reading skills of a second grader, had struggled and fought his way through that book perhaps in a month or so. The moral of the story is twofold: that young people want, need, and like to read books, that have meaning for them, and that when such books are put within easy reach they will sooner or later figure out, without being 'taught' and with only minimal outside help, how to read them.... (ibid.: 27)

And that, 'The books that most children are compelled to learn to read from are beyond belief boring, stupid, shallow, misleading, dishonest, and unreal' (ibid.: 28).

3. It is important to understand people's own language resource, whether oral or written, which Street calls local literacy and the reasons for their silence and withdrawal. Properly and respectfully handled people's oral traditions become powerful tools for initiating them into the world of written word. As Moon (1984) emphasizes, initial mastery of reading is best achieved in the context of, 'reconstructing meanings from texts that are interesting in themselves'. But he also warns that, 'Such texts must also be sufficiently close in content and form to the spoken utterances with which the child is familiar for him to be able to adopt strategies already developed for the comprehension of speech' (ibid.: 20).
4. Literacy and its sustenance crucially depend upon teachers' own interest in reading and writing, attitude towards illiterate people, motivation to communicate with them, and their ability to locate and use new written materials and oral literature creatively.
5. The current research on reading process tells us that its acquisition is closely related to the desire to communicate through the written words. It has now clearly emerged that mature reading is a complex and high speed process of pattern recognition and guessing rather than a very high speed process of decoding the text into a sound system via the phonological, syntactic, and semantic components. This pattern recognition is easier/faster if familiar and/or relevant 'text' is used in the beginning. This also means encouraging the children to 'read' poems, songs, and stories they already know and enjoy reciting or singing.
6. The CAP experience established that children take a lot of interest in copying. It is amazing to watch how meticulously they copy

matter from any book. It is a long string of words that they begin their writing with where they don't identify words or even sentences separately. However, as the reading progresses, with the help of a teacher, they do start identifying words and alphabet. Matured and skilled hands in themselves, they seldom need a prior drill to develop simpler strokes before going on to writing letters and then words involving more complex strokes. As Holt also asserts,

> Only a few basic shapes and pen strokes are needed to make letters, and all these pen strokes are easily and quickly made by the hand and fingers. On the whole, I see no reason to make children waste their time practicing these shapes. If they write, as they speak, in order to say things they want to say to people they want to say them to, and if they have good models of printing to look at, they will improve their writing just as they improve their speech. (Holt 1989: 41)

This helps in building up writing skills in pace with reading and thus writing and reading go hand in hand.

7. In all predominantly non-literate societies, there is a treasure of oral literature some of which can become text of the reading material in the beginning. Being familiar text this not only facilitates the reading and writing process but also helps in building positive self-image of the learner. Oral literature does have its own class, caste, and gender biases, and limitations and so how these can be modified, changed or evolved would depend entirely upon the social context and the teachers as orality is also as much embedded in it as literacy is.
8. It is a prevalent notion among the educationists that fewer words and short sentences make reading easy. Holt, in his chapter on 'how not to learn to read', wonders why publishers keep restricting the vocabularies of their books.

> One possible explanation… is that as the readers became more boring, children hardly learned to read well. The conclusion drawn from this fact was not the obvious one that as text books became more boring to children and teachers alike; children would have a harder time working up an interest in learning to read. Instead, it was concluded that the books were too difficult for the children and that things should be made easier for them, by asking them to read fewer words! (ibid.: 29)

CLASSROOM PEDAGOGY

Interpreting the above understanding into pedagogic practice has turned out to be an involved multi-faceted creative exercise in research and communication. The major highlights of the evolving pedagogy are summarized in the following paragraphs.

Clearly, the above understanding made the literacy work far more demanding and challenging—intellectually and otherwise. Moreover, we were dealing with the first generation learners who did not have access to print materials and opportunities for literacy practice. School going children also had only their textbooks that were invariably didactic and poorly produced. Therefore, here, more resource material was needed in the classroom to build up the required literate ambience as Holt says, 'What children need to get ready for reading is exposure to a lot of *print*. Not pictures, but print. They need to bathe their eyes in print, as when smaller they bathe their ears in talk' (Holt 1989: 11).

Therefore, it was necessary that every centre had posters, a collection of books, access to cyclostyling/copying facility, and a reasonable 'library'. Each centre was therefore stalked with about a hundred children's titles with multiple copies. To generate and maintain interest in reading and create a literate environment, a series of cycle-borne mobile libraries were also an integral part of this endeavour. JSA ran about 50 such libraries in far off villages. During the training programmes, all the teachers were encouraged to make posters of selected poems, slogans, and quizzes for their centres. Thus every teacher equipped his/her centre with sufficient number of JSA publications, posters, and Hindi and *bundeli* story and poetry books. Interest and passion for books, even among illiterate non-schoolgoing children of remote villages, was well established by mobile libraries. One of the crucial activity of the mobile libraries also ensured that children got an opportunity to read aloud as their home environment did not provide such scope.

A two-pronged approach was found to be useful. Beginning with collective reading of interesting songs, poems, and stories, provided it was ensured that each one of the learners had a cyclostyled or printed copy of whatever was being read followed by separate sessions where interesting books, articles, and newspapers were read aloud by the teacher. 'Read aloud' from books on every day basis was a must. Highlighting the difference between story telling and reading them aloud was crucial.

The formal beginning of a class was made with reading aloud the poems from the poetry books while drawing students' attention towards charts of the same poem displayed on the walls. The idea was to recognize the posters on the wall and associate them with the poem in their book. This process was repeated many times over a period of a week or so. The teacher first read the poem either from the poetry book or from the chart. It was important that the teacher actually read and finger tracked on the text of the poem in the book or the poster. After repeated retelling of the poems and the stories, they begin reaching towards text reading. Thus, begins the association between the written matter and the spoken words. The selection of poems and stories and their order was worked out carefully in such a way that small, easily memorable poems with repetitive and rhyming words appeared first; the vocabulary was familiar and the poems were interesting. These selections were made after several trials. Some were from printed books while others were drawn from their oral forms. The first sense of achievement came with recognizing these poems on the posters and in the poetry books. The first few days were spent in reading aloud, reciting poems, identifying charts, writing names, date, and so on, in their notebooks and sometimes copying poems from the charts or the books. Gradually, this process helped in the identification of the specific poems, different lines of a poem, and subsequently its words and alphabet.

While the teacher read from the book or a chart, each student tried to 'read' by finger tracking the text either on the chart or in the book. Finger tracking of the print helped in coinciding the beginning and the end of spoken sentences with the print. The teacher also drew attention towards words that were repeated and rhymed. These words were written in the notebook and on the blackboard. Slogans and puzzles were also 'read' in a similar fashion. Children were also encouraged to 'read' other books kept in the small library of the centre. Every visitor visiting the centre also read aloud for the children. Also, children on their own engaged in 'pretend reading' for their peers or younger siblings or parents at home. Books became their prized possession.

Experience was that if poems and stories were carefully selected, children enjoyed 'reading' them. They often made their own poems and stories and 'wrote' them inventing their own spellings. At this stage their reading resource was also enriched by providing them a cyclostyled booklet containing material drawn from their oral resource, including quizzes, slogans, *doha*s, riddles, and so on. To pose new challenges, some innovative teachers used to alter the order of the posters or replace them with new posters every week so that the poems were not identified by memorizing the location of the posters. The experience of such exercises was illuminating. The teachers reported enthusiastically that such challenges further activated the students as they immediately noticed those changes and took more interest in 'reading' the new posters.

It was established in JSA that if the above process of engagement with the written text and active support from the teacher continued for two to three months, on a regular basis, students gained confidence in not only reading and writing but also in engaging with unfamiliar text. The introduction of multiple reading resource from the beginning was an important aspect which encouraged the learners to engage in 'reading'. The reading resource and the reference material grew with the active involvement of the teacher and the pupil. Pretending to read aloud to each other was encouraged and was a very popular reading activity among them, which entailed discussion, making 'corrections', and invention of substitute syllables and words.

Here, perhaps it is significant to share the experience of one centre, which was started in November 1992. The centre was located in a *mohalla* of *kabeer panthis*, Dalits, near Pipariya in Hoshangabad district. Two teachers who were in charge of this centre had a fairly good understanding of the sociolinguistics and psycholinguistics. However, they were developing the classroom methodology for the first time. Their class had about 25–30 children and adults. They had barely started their classes in a well lit but dilapidated hut a few days before when the news of Babri Masjid demolition came in. They held discussions on this issue in their class and selected a few posters, which had slogans and *bhajans* by Kabir, Raidas, Rahim, and other *sufi* poets. The whole class got involved in reading and writing such slogans in their notebooks and on charts. Some printed posters were also displayed on the walls of the hut. These posters used to be read aloud, songs were sung and discussed during the off class hours. Finally, it was decided that such songs and slogans should be written on the walls of the village houses. Thus the JSA team, consisting of illiterate and neo-literate children and adults, did a hectic wall writing campaign in many villages. This further emphasized the role of a teacher. If the teacher was keen, motivated, and ingenious, she made use of various opportunities and enriched the class. On the other hand, reading material was not of great help if the teacher was not motivated.

To continue the discussion on the methodology, a game similar to scrabble was introduced after a few months of 'reading' exposure and practice. The 'real' scrabble is based on the underlying synthesizing principle. But here the game started with the identification of the words of a given sentence from a collection of word cards or making new sentences from the same collection. It was only at a later stage that alphabet cards were introduced. Ability to identify patterns in new content was also regularly assessed. It was observed that once the logic of reading was caught people started taking initiative, that is started 'reading' the new content. And once the confidence to 'read' (which may have started by merely flipping through books and/or identification of a few words) a new content was achieved, it opened floodgates. Helping individual student at this stage was crucial since a little more guidance and encouragement had tremendous impact on their confidence. It needs to be emphasized that all educational effort requires sustained input until a threshold is reached from where people can pick up on their own. Some of these issues could be better understood by looking at the diaries of the visitors or resource persons. The following two accounts from the diaries are particularly illustrative.

> One of the JSA teachers looked hassled for many days as the progress of one of his elderly woman student was not satisfactory. She was hardworking, regular, and invariably sat in the class beyond the regular hours. 'But she forgets', said the teacher. 'She had read poems and stories from the JSA publications many times but felt that she could do it only by memorization. She had not yet acquired the confidence to deal with the new text, which she thought was the real test of the reading ability. She is definitely lagging behind, and that is making her suspicious of her capability. What to do? Where did we gone wrong? While others have started reading new story books, slogans, poems, writing one or two line letters, film songs, and so on, she is stuck with her reading', said the exasperated teacher.
>
> From his own experience, the teacher knew that 'reading', that is, identification of words in the familiar sentences and then in the unfamiliar text happens by continuous engagement with new text. It was suggested to him that he just needs to keep motivating and helping her in reading new poems and stories, and make the process creative instead of going through repetitive drills. And after about one week, during one of the classes, she started 'reading'. She read a children's book. According to another teacher, 'once this breakthrough occurs. It is difficult to hold them back. They start reading whatever comes their way: names of peers, stations, government posters, and so on and so forth'. In her case she could not believe that she was actually reading. She tested her skill by reading from various books and was overwhelmed.[4]

Another observer's diary recorded the following experience.

> When I entered the class, a 6–7 year-old girl was reading aloud a poem from the chart. The chart was too high for her but that had not dampened

Empowering Pedagogy: Potentials and Limitations

her spirits and enthusiasm. Other children of the class were also participating in the chorus. I stopped the girl to ascertain if she recognized any of the words or sentences. Quickly and confidently she identified a few sentences. Thereafter, one by one, I called many children and asked them to 'read' instead of just finger tracking and reciting. It was quite hearting to see that there were many children who could do that. Most of them could identify all the charts displayed on the walls. How could they achieve this level of 'reading' ability, I asked the teacher. 'They are coming regularly for the past three months or so and have been "reading" from the first day', was the answer. The teacher excitedly informed me that:

In the initial stages I used to read the poem and they followed me. They never got tired of listening to the poems and constructing the new ones and trying their writing skills. At times, due to pupil's excitement, it was difficult to get down to doing other things. They would pester for more songs and poems. In the next phase there were writing sessions or reading in the real sense of the word that is, children would open their books and start 'reading' and finger-tracking on the text. In the beginning, speed of the fingers was much faster than intended but it got conveyed to them that whatever is being spoken has correspondence with print. This was repeated for a few days and gradually, by itself, speed slowed down and they started noticing patterns. The first breakthrough came when similar words got identified. Children were so thrilled and excited with these achievements that they started searching for these patterns on the charts or whatever other written material was available to them. It became a challenge for them and thus a new arena of written world was unfolded as an exciting and challenging experience, not as a boring exercise. First few words were identified in two to three day's time. It was not necessary to identify each and every word in a sentence. The emphasis was on building up familiarity with the written codes and in this process association with the pattern and the spoken words started taking place slowly.[5]

While the teacher was still busy talking with me the children went on merrily from one poster to the next till we realized that they were out of the room, in the verandah, standing in front of their favorite poster, chanting at the top of their voices, and a new girl was leading the reading activity.

CONCLUSION

And finally, a note of caution, the objective here is not to undermine or trivialize the structural constraints, which restrict people's participation in education efforts. In fact, it was very difficult to run the classes regularly. Disruptions were due to various political (as stated in the first section) and practical compulsions. For instance, during winters children did not come for the classes, as they did not have enough clothes. They preferred to remain at home, sit around the fire in their huts. Also, during monsoons attendance used to drop considerably. This was either due to illness or inaccessibility of the place where the classes were held. For instance, in 1994, prolonged monsoons played havoc in the lives of the people in rural Madhya Pradesh. There was an outbreak of Cholera and gastro-enteritis epidemic in many parts, a regular occurrence during monsoons. Cholera claimed many lives in the remote villages. In Bankhedi block, one of the worst affected villages was Kotri, where the flooding of drains had cut-off this village from the surrounding areas for weeks. With no access to any medical assistance, one death occurred in almost every household in this small village. Burning the dead, in pouring rains, was a hard job. Many houses collapsed during monsoons, including the one where the JSA centre was located.

Yet the experience establishes, beyond doubt, that despite odds a theoretically informed approach generated interest due to inherent intellectual challenge. Still it is important to understand how social context, in which the educational effort is situated, not only influences its consequences but strongly moulds the content also.

NOTES

1. Kishore Bharati (1970–89) was a voluntary organization based in the Bankhedi block of Hoshangabad district in Madhya Pradesh. KB did pioneering work in the field of school science education, non-formal education, adult education, and people's health. It was also engaged in rural development work, and based on its rich experience in running development projects, it arrived at a sharp political critique of mainstream, government and non-government, and rural development programmes and policies. Through its adult education work, based on the principles of awareness creation and conscientization, KB got involved in the issues of landless labourers and small farmers.
2. CAP was run in a few primary schools to strengthen the teaching of mathematics and literacy. Along with this, the programme ran its own children's night centres, and cycle-borne, weekly mobile libraries in villages and a daily children's library in Pipariya centre. Intensive academic inputs and observations of the children's learning process were the main thrusts of this programme. To encourage reading and writing, CAP published *Bal Chiraiya* (a children's cyclostyled newsletter) regularly for a few years.
3. *Bal Chiraiya* and *Gulgula* were the two cyclostyled newsletters of the children's writings and drawings that were published under CAP. The writings and drawings for the *Bal Chiraiya* were collected from schools in Pipariya and elsewhere, and from

the villages covered by the mobile libraries. About 40 issues of this publication were brought out before KB shut down the programme. About 1000 copies of each issue of *Bal Chiraiya* were cyclostyled and sold at a nominal price of 25 paise. Several other groups which were working with children were inspired by CAP's various activities, especially *Bal Chiraiya* and *Gulgula*, and started their own versions under different names.

4. Field Note 1. 1990 (from the diary of the JSA Resource Person One).
5. Field Note 2. 1990 (from the diary of the JSA Resource Person Two).

BIBLIOGRAPHY

Bourdieu, Pierre. 1991. *Language and Symbolic Power*. Cambridge: Polity Press.

CAP (Children's Activity Programme). 1991. *CAP (Children's Activity Programme) Final Report—March 1991*. Report submitted to Kishore Bharati.

Gumperz, J. Cook. 1985. 'International Socio-linguistics in the Study of Schooling', in J. Cook Gumperz (ed.), *The Social Construction of Literacy*, pp. 47–67. Cambridge: Cambridge University Press.

Holt, John. 1989. *Learning All the Time: How Small Children Begin to Read, Write, Count, and Investigate the World, Without Being Taught*. New York: Addison-Wesley.

Ilaiah, Kancha. 2003. *Main Hindu Kyon Nahin Hun*. New Delhi: Arohi Book Trust.

Kolers, Paul K. 1972. 'Experiments in Reading', *Scientific American*, pp. 84–91.

Mason, Jana M. and Shobha Sinha. 1993. 'Emerging Literacy in the Early Childhood Years: Applying a Vygotskian Model of Learning and Development', in B.Spodek (ed.), *Handbook of Research on the Education of Young Children,* pp. 137–50. New York: Macmillan.

Moon, Cliff. 1984. 'Recent Developments in the Teaching of Reading', *English in Education*, 18(9): 20–27.

Ngugi, wa Thiongo. 1994. *Bhasha Sanskriti Aur Rashtriya Asmita*. New Delhi: Saransh Press.

Sadgopal, Anil. 1981. 'Jan Andolan Mein Vigyan Ki Bhumika', *Dinman*, 8, 15 and 22 November.

Saxena, Sadhna. 1993. 'Politics of Language', *EPW*, Vol. 26 (Nov.): 2445–2445.

———. 1998. 'Education of the Poor—A Pedagogy of Resistance', in Sureshchandra Shukla and Rekha Kaul (eds), *Education, Development and Underdevelopment*, pp. 265–92. New Delhi: Sage Publications.

———. 2000. *Shiksha aur Janandolan*. New Delhi: Granthshilpi.

———. 2002. 'Nellore Revisited: Locating the Anti-arrack Agitation in its Historical Context', in Aditi Mukherjee and Duggirala Vasantha (eds), *Practice and Research in Literacy*, pp. 73–89. New Delhi: Sage Publications.

Smith, Frank. 1990. 'Essays on Literacy, from Hindi translation', *Palash*, Februray 23.

Street, Brian V. 1984. *Literacy in Theory and Practice*. Cambridge: Cambridge University Press.

Teale, William H. and Elizabeth Sulzby. 1986. 'Introduction: Emergent Literacy as a Perspective for Examining How Young Children Become Writers and Readers', in W.Teale and E. Sulzby (eds), *Emergent Literacy; Writing and Reading*, pp. vii–xxv. Norwood, NJ: Ablex.

9
Squaring National Pride with Tolerance: A Lesson for School Textbooks

Narayani Gupta

TOWARDS A 'COMPREHENSIVE HISTORY' OF INDIA

The countries of South Asia have in the last century gone through the exhilaration of achieving independence and also the anguish of fragmentation. When the subcontinent became two independent countries—India and Pakistan—their resources, material, and intellectual, also got divided. School and university courses were not changed, but it was clear that the contents of history textbooks would have to be modified. Indian history should be written from an 'Indian' point of view. A decade earlier, in the 1930s, South Asian historians had launched an ambitious 'comprehensive history' in many volumes, as an indigenous response to the multi-volume *Cambridge History of India*.[1] This project dragged on, and even today the *Comprehensive History of India* (not including Pakistan by name, though it *is* included in geographical terms) has not been completed.[2] In the area of research monographs the situation was different—the challenge was to produce works of history qualitatively different from books by British historians, described as 'imperial' and 'colonial'. Indian economic and social historians have produced a body of work which has gained international recognition.

To write history textbooks for school students presented a third kind of challenge. Till 1947, Indian children read histories to which most of them did not relate—the history of Britain, and the history of India (essentially that of the north, of the Ganges plain, with the rest of the subcontinent figuring as postscripts). In the 1950s, the most urgent task before the new regimes was that of developing a sense of nationhood. In Pakistan, this meant forging a spirit of nationality among people speaking different languages and inhabiting two widely separated geographical areas—west and east Pakistan—tribal people in sparsely populated mountainous regions, urban dwellers in cities, people in rich agricultural belts, and poor peasants in riverine flood-prone areas. History here went against this effort because the basis of nationalism was neither region nor language, but religion. Pakistani nationalism was only a few decades old, and the roots of its uniting religion lay further west. India was similar in that it consisted of people speaking many languages, belonging to varied regions and social groups, but also following many religions, including Islam, which had been adopted by many in the subcontinent by choice. Though there was no one uniform culture, as in Europe, India, *unlike* Europe, was confident of creating a sense of subcontinental nationalism, rising above nascent linguistic nationalisms.

At its simplest, nationalism could be equated with patriotism. (Bernard Shaw had defined a patriot as one who loved his country because it happened to be the one he was born in!) The symbols of the nation, including the flag and the national anthem, can be evocative, but are not essential. This is seen by the fact that Indian teenagers today for most part do not know the words of the national anthem but do have a vigorous sense of patriotism. The sense of nationalism is based on the country's common social and cultural features, which in recent decades found expression in seeking to forge political unity.

NARRATIVES OF HISTORY AND NATIONALISM, 1947–2004

Popular nationalism usually creates 'others'—the former colonial rulers, or present-day neighbouring countries, who become enemies when territorial demarcation makes frontiers into matters of dispute. In the case of India, 1947, the year of Independence, is the cut-off date for 'history'. Wars (which figure in detail in school textbooks) are seen differently for different periods. There is a repeated use of the notion of the 'invasion of India' from the 11th century, in some cases even for earlier conflicts. This is inaccurate, since there was no state called 'India' till 1947. Wars fought from the late 18th century are seen as 'imperial/colonial' wars.

The wars between India and Pakistan, and India and China are not studied as part of History in Indian schools, but are seen in simple terms as the 'invasion' of India. If Pakistan is seen only as a country of Muslims, the wars between India and Pakistan (1947, 1965, 1971, and 1999) can be read as a continuation of the 'invasions of India' by Muslims from central Asia. This blurs history and geography. This is aggravated by the fact that Indian students in the last half-century have become more and more distanced from 1947. Only very recently was a supplementary textbook of *Contemporary History* introduced for senior secondary classes.

In contrast, the textbooks in Pakistan, which dwell more on the years after 1947, see the wars as part of the behaviour of the big bully, India. This helps to build up a sense of anti-Indian nationalism. At its most simplistic, patriotism is the negative, and very potent, value of hating neighbouring countries. Unlike India, however, this image of India as a bully cannot be projected backward into history, since the historic conflict lines in the sub-continent were not between the regions of present-day India and Pakistan, but between north Indian empires centred in Delhi or Patna, and eastern India or southern India. The difficulty of teaching the history of an artificially united nation without too much reference to the other people of the sub-continent has led to the progressive diminishing of the volume of history taught in Pakistan.[3]

After 1971, the same problem faced the newly independent Bangladesh. Cutting off its links with Pakistan did not mean it forged new links with India, or even with Indian Bengal, to which it was united by language but not by religion. At the academic level, there was cordiality and interchange of ideas between the two, but Bangladesh was determined that it was not going to exchange one big brother for another. In its anxiety to signify its independence, it too reduced the quantum of history and the narrative of the sub-continent.

It is clear, therefore, that these three countries purvey to children only the sections of history that they choose to. (By contrast, the little country of Bhutan for many years taught courses of Indian history where, the name of their own country did not even figure!)

The three subcontinental countries are united in their perception of their history as consisting of three chronological periods, as had been set out by British historians. This is in part due to inertia, in part because it suits their sense of how the past should be presented. For nationalist and Marxist Indian historians, the past was thus 'ancient' India, a long period when different regions of India went through the stages of history to feudalism, 'medieval' India, a feudal economy moving towards enlightened absolutism and to the development of trade, the 'modern' period when India became modern not by choice, as did Japan, but via colonial rule, overthrown by the evolution of a modern sense of nation. For Pakistan and Bangladesh the 'medieval' period was synonymous with the coming of Islam to the sub-continent, Islam the great leveler which helped people escape the tyranny of the caste hierarchy. The brief period of 1905–11 was seen as specially significant by Bangladesh because in those years Bengal Presidency was divided, along the lines of geography, into two— Indian West Bengal and East Pakistan/Bangladesh.

Since India is the only one among these countries which has been a democracy continuously after 1947 (except for 1975–77, the years of the Emergency), the ideologies of different parties are likely to be reflected in the policies on content of the textbooks. The following section of this paper will analyze how far this has been the case, and what lessons we can learn from the history.

In the 1950s and the 1960s the main concern was that children should get a sense of the nationalist movement (till then imbibed from the liberal British point of view as given in Thompson and Garratt's *Rise and Fulfilment of British Rule in India* (1934).[4] A second concern which was central to the ideology of Prime Minister Jawaharlal Nehru was that of secularism, the tolerance of all religions which was the special feature of India.[5] It was believed that religious education should not form part of school syllabi, but history books could refer to the rise of different religions. The result was that the textbooks did not describe Hinduism, Christianity, or Islam. They did, however, give a sense of Jainism and Buddhism, of the *bhakti* and *sufi* cults, and of Sikhism, all of which had strong strains of egalitarianism about them. Among the unanswered questions was that of how India had such a large population of Muslims—had they been converted voluntarily or 'by the sword', or were they all the descendants of west and central Asians? It was only later appreciated that this meant that children were exposed in many cases to two narratives—the official one at school, which glorified nationalism, implicit or explicit, and the family one, where religion, caste, and region were valourized.

The National Council of Educational Research and Training (NCERT) was set up in 1964, in order to give a sense of like objectives to education policy, which was in danger of being fragmented, since in the Constitution of 1950, education was a 'concurrent' subject, over which the new states (based on language) had as much control as did the central government. The National Council prepared *model* textbooks, written by some of the best scholars. The schools took the easy way out, and used these as *prescribed* texts; some enterprising publishers produced clones of these. None of them gave much thought to the language and the relevance of the material to children of the ages they were meant for. Most of these books were good miniaturized adult books, produced cheaply, with little that was attractive to children.

Meanwhile the state councils prepared their own syllabi and textbooks. Many of them followed the National Council's pattern. Some of them struck out on independent paths, usually to give more time and space to their own regional culture. West Bengal decided that children needed to know the history of Bengal and of the world, and that the history of India was not essential. Maharashtra wanted to play up the history of their hero Shivaji and downplay the Delhi-centric narrative that dominated the National Council's textbooks. These texts were in the regional languages. As far as language and design were concerned, these books were a little better than the National Council books.

From the 1970s, regional and a few national political parties gained strength, and made inroads into the huge majority that the Congress party had enjoyed all through the Nehru years. One now heard criticism of the textbook accounts of the nationalist movement, which saw it as synonymous with the Congress party. At the academic level, the 'subaltern school' of historians questioned the simplified account of the 'freedom struggle' and identified many tensions of class and sub-region within it.

From the 1970s, also, the Hinduist party (which went through several changes of name, from Jana Sangh to Bharatiya Janata Party[BJP]) was gaining ground. This was a national party which also claimed to be nationalist. It stressed on Hindu-ness, Hindi, and the north of India (Hindustan). As time went on, it also took up positions on sacred sites and argued that the Gods of Hinduism were historic figures, who could be located at particular points of the past, and were not myth or legend. They saw the middle centuries as dominated by the struggle between Indian Hindus and foreign Muslims; where the latter won, foreign rule was established. By this logic, parts of India had been ruled by 'foreigners' from the 8th century. This was different from the secular argument that 'foreign rule' began with the British victories of the 18th century. It implied that the large population of Muslims living in independent India were descended from invaders and were themselves foreigners. It became easy to taunt them by saying that they did not belong to India, and should go to Pakistan.

Linked to the Bharatiya Janata Party was the Rashtriya Swayamsevak Sangh (RSS), an organization which acted on the principle that good Hindus needed to be made, and it was never too early to start. Arguing that Muslims were allowed to have *madrassa*s where children were taught about their religion and used the Urdu language (very similar to Hindi but written in the Persian script), and that Christian missionary schools gave Bible lessons, they instituted a chain of schools which today number many thousands. The senior classes had to conform to the syllabi of the National or State Councils, but the junior classes' syllabus had a heavy dose of religious education, and history was taught selectively and in a distorted fashion. Pre-Islamic India was seen as a society which enjoyed the virtues of high moral standards, social harmony, a high status accorded to women, and achievements in the sciences, literature, and philosophy. Much of this, by their argument, was destroyed with the coming of the Muslims, a sorry state that continued with the coming of western imperialism. 'We' and 'them' were clearly defined.

Hate and prejudice is so much easier to imbibe than tolerance— this has become clear from the 1980s, when Muslim 'invaders' of the 12th century, the Muslims of Kashmir fighting for freedom, and the Muslim state of Pakistan were all linked in the minds of the young as people to be hated. Very few of those who referred to Muslims with hostility in reality knew any Muslims. Hardly any of them take note of the irony in enjoying west and central Asian cuisine and dressing in costumes associated with Muslims, while at the same time speaking of them with dislike. Also from this time, prosperous Indians settled in Western countries were seeking to recover the religion they had in their youth been quite careless about. Internet sites, tapes, eager gurus, brand-new temples in British and American cities, fed into this new angst. In India, the Hinduist leaders chose to obfuscate things by projecting Hindus as the 'majority' in India, when in a democracy the term 'majority' referred to the political party which had most seats in parliament.

The basic framework of school textbooks did not have to be changed— the three segments of Indian history were retained. The 'achievements' of ancient India were glorified, and it was suggested that these anticipated developments in other parts of the world. Even the story of the Aryans moving in successive migrations from central Asia was modified, and India was explained as having been their 'homeland'. The 'foreign rule' of Muslims in the medieval period is given as the explanation for India not going through a European-type 'renaissance' (this also meant that much of the recent research on the 'Renaissance' is ignored). This is ahistorical, is dismissive of much excellent and nuanced research on Indian history, and can be very dull. But, for the passive reader, it can be a very comfortable view of India's history.

In 1998, the BJP won the elections and formed a government at the Centre. Within months, this Hinduist ideology gained official endorsement. It was transferred from the RSS schools to the national level. Endorsed by the NCERT, it was possible to carry the ideology to the level of secondary and senior secondary classes. It found expression in a new set of textbooks published by the National Council, which reached the schools in 2002. After 26 years, the history syllabus and the history textbooks were changed. The books also underwent some change—the quality of paper and design were far better than before. This was a strong reason for parents and students to commend the books even before reading them.

Textbooks are not read by students for pleasure, nor seen as works of literary quality. They are a means to an end—to write an examination and to get high marks. Some of the teachers who had to use the new books grumbled because they had been shaken out of inertia. For the students these were just textbooks. The books would probably have enjoyed a quarter-century of use, like the earlier ones, but for a strong reaction from historians, mostly university teachers. This had been sparked off two years earlier, when the *National Curriculum Framework* had been published, which gave a sense of what the textbooks would be like. Their criticism was of the tone of the curriculum, which projected an 'Indian' identity which was Hindu, Hindi, upper-caste, and male. The earlier textbooks also had been very unimaginative on gender issues, and had ignored many regions of the country. But in the 2000 *Framework,* it was expressed more blatantly, suggesting different curricula for girls, for 'rural' children, and for the underprivileged. The Hinduist bias was not stated explicitly, but was implicit in the choice of 'leaders' whose biographies would be studied, and the period of history which would be highlighted.

While reiterating that textbooks are not read for pleasure, it is also important to understand that biases can be communicated by textbooks, both by what is written and by what is omitted. In many schools, students are asked to memorize sections of the text, and repeated memorization, without discussion or debate, converts opinions and biases into 'facts'. One of the themes in history which suffered was the 'national movement' (for a long time 'national' and 'nationalist' were used interchangeably). The nationalist movement in India had been not just an anti-colonial struggle;

it had worked to build an overarching sense of nationhood, at the same time diversities were celebrated. This sense can be destroyed by pushing a unicultural story, to which 'upper caste' north Indian Hindus can relate, but which for students from the south, the northeast, from 'minority' religions and 'lower castes', will confirm a marginalization that many of them experience in daily life.

INCLUSIVENESS, DIVERSITY, AND LOCAL HISTORIES

Politics can take unexpected turns. In an unexpected reversal of the political balance, the elections in 2004 brought the Congress and the Left parties back to power. This had an immediate effect on the education policy. The National Council, with a new director, Professor Krishna Kumar (in place of Mr Rajput, who had just retired) went into overdrive again. A new Curriculum was worked out in a year, and published in 2005. This was different from the earlier National Curriculum Framework (NCF) in three important respects. It was not put together by a small group, but with the enthusiastic collaboration of a vast number of focus-groups. Second, the inclusiveness emphasized in this Curriculum is in complete contrast to the NCF of 2000. Diversity and local histories are to be encouraged. Third, and more importantly, the child's needs have been addressed—how to make him/her a participant in the learning process, not merely a passive recipient. If teachers and students work together, if children are encouraged to discuss their cultural and social differences instead of some of them cringing because they are not in some standard 'Indian' mould, mutual tolerance can become a way of life. If India's neighbours can be seen as people who share many common histories with India, the long history of the sub-continent acquires meaning. It will then be possible to think of a project for writing textbooks which can be used in all the three countries, just as China, Japan, and Korea have done, and as France and Germany plan to do—and this is just what the National Council is now planning to work on.

Petty prejudices and a sense of being superior to others will not vanish from people's minds, but a rigorous policy of respecting and celebrating cultural differences, while seeking to reduce economic and social differences, in the long 12 years of confinement in school, can significantly reduce these negative emotions. This is what the National Council, the State Councils, and the school teachers have to work towards.[6]

NOTES

1. *Cambridge History of India,* a chronological account in many volumes, published between 1922 and 1937, not to be confused with the ongoing *New Cambridge History of India*, again in many volumes, each on a different theme, the first of which appeared in 1988.
2. *The Comprehensive History of India* was proposed in 1940 by the Indian History Congress, and supported by the Bharatiya Itihas Parishad in 1946. Its first volume came out in 1958.
3. A. H. Nayyar and Ahmed Salim (compilers) 'The Subtle Subversion: A Report on Curricula and Textbooks in Pakistan'. The subject 'Pakistan Studies' is taught in universities and in senior school. It is a mix of geography, history, political science, economics, foreign relations, and literature.
4. Edward Thompson and G. T. Garratt's *Rise and Fulfilment of British Rule in India* was published in 1934.
5. Jawaharlal Nehru's very popular *Discovery of India* was published the year before Independence, in 1946.
6. Twenty-one position papers based on the discussions of the National Focus Groups set up in 2004 by the NCERT have been printed in 2007 (Vol. I—Curricular Areas, Vol. II—Systemic Reform, Vol. III—National Concerns). These are also available on their website.

BIBLIOGRAPHY

CUP (Cambridge University Press). 1922–37. *Cambridge History of India*. Cambridge: Cambridge UP.
———. 1998 . *New Cambridge History of India*. 1988. Cambridge: Cambridge UP.
Gupta, Narayani. 2002.'A Battle over History: A Discussion', *Social Action,* 52(4).
Indian History Congress. 2003. *The Comprehensive History of India*, new edition. New Delhi: Sterling.
Ministry of Education. 1966. *Education and National Development, Report of the Education Commission 1964–66* (popularly called the 'Kothari Commission Report'), Ministry of Education, Government of India
NCERT. 2000. *National Curriculum Framework for School Education*. New Delhi: NCERT (National Council of Educational Research and Training).
Nehru, Jawaharlal. 1946. *Discovery of India*. Delhi and New York: The John day Co.
Rosser, Yvette. 2003. *Islamization of Pakistani Social Studies Textbooks*. Delhi: Rupa.
———.2004. *Indoctrinating Minds: the Politics of Education in Bangladesh*. Delhi: Rupa.
Thompson, Edward and G. T. Garratt. 1934. *Rise and Fulfilment of British Rule in India*. Delhi and London: Macmillan.

10
Indian School Textbooks

Teesta Setalvad

IDEOLOGIES OF HISTORY

History, as a subject, has always been of critical importance to political ideologues and ideologies of all hues. The historian, however, especially in the 20th century has emerged distanced and independent of the political project. Therefore, historical learning and theory, especially in the last century, have made significant progress in assimilating and developing data and knowledge distanced from the influence of direct politics.

These developments worldwide came with the spread of the notion of democracy and democratic function, approaches that recognized the motivations of the rulers and theocracies of the past who employed 'official chroniclers or historians'. As knowledge and academics matured to independence, history as a discipline too benefited. In India, the academic breakthroughs afforded by historians like Maharashtra's D. D. Kosambi are significant, paving the way for the widely recognized works of Romila Thapar, Sumit Sarkar, K. N. Panikkar, Irfan Habib, and R. S. Sharma of recent times.

The manner and slant of historical interpretation, especially in official history texts has, to some extent reflected the thrust and ideology of the government in power. Within this, however, less democratic political dispensations, dictatorships, and authoritarian regimes have had in the past and present greater tendencies to control thought, ideas, and interpretation.

Like other facets of individual and collective human lives, religion which is both a personally and spiritually empowering source also becomes, in its institutionalized, hierarchical form, a source of the exercise of power. A history of religions show their empowering and dark sides as is true of all human history. As students of history, we need to have the courage to face the shadows and silences of our collective pasts. The stranglehold on economic power, production, or spiritual power through knowledge and education that Brahmanical (caste) Hinduism had on the masses in this country oppresses and denies 20–25 per cent of our population even today. During the dark, medieval ages, the fate that befell Galileo is well known. What is not known is the fact that one million women were burnt at the stake in the space of 400 years through an avenging Christianity. The history of the spread of Islam is complex: it happened through *sufi* saints, traders, and an exchange of knowledge as much as by military campaigns that were often brutal and violent.

The subtle demonization of Islam and Muslims, the evasive treatment of the subject of partition, the lack of exposure or development of the movement of Dalits against injustice during the struggle for independence and their serious differences with Gandhi and Nehru, the scant treatment on the subject of the assassination of the father of the nation, Gandhi, are some of the most obvious examples. Which facts will we reveal and which shall we conceal? Who will decide the basis of the inclusions and deletions?

According to certain political world views, especially those of the narrow right, these uncomfortable facts of history simply need not be told. It is better that our children and our adolescents grow up distanced from the knowledge of human impulses and lifestyles, cultures and their formations, of injustice and poverty, of deprivation and denial, and imbibe instead a goody-goody brew that is myth, not history. We can collectively thereby deny any assiduous and creative questioning. We would then produce, non-questioning minds. Good cadres for the ranks of authoritarian political parties but a disaster for questioning minds and history.

While the world attempts to move in the direction of reconciliation and dialogue, we through the moves of such mind-sets are harking back to medieval denials. There is no need to know of the evils that the system of rigidified caste deteriorated into and the conditions of life it means for 240 million people in South Asia. The sub-continent is a bitter example of the shattered images that we try to draw through a distortion of history. If we leave aside Nepal, Myanmar, and Bhutan and look closely at

Pakistan, India, Bangladesh, and Sri Lanka, we have a sorry record to show the future generations. In Pakistan, the Indus Valley Civilization that the Right wing in India are busy claiming 'Hindu' lineage for is not taught in schools; in Bangladesh there is a desire to deny the history between 1947 and 1971; in Sri Lanka, Tamil and Sinhala-speaking children are taught diametrically opposed histories.

INTERWEAVING CONFLICTING HISTORICAL NARRATIVES

Indian history textbooks have contained a curiously centralized and linear way of approaching the subject that has not seriously engaged in weaving the complex realities of local and regional histories within and without the 'national' or 'centralised' frameworks. The conflicts and contradictions between the 'nationalised' and 'regional' view often have been glossed over and avoided. Hence, the tensions and dichotomy between central history and regional historical inquiry and interpretations have not really gotten rigorously and creatively resolved. For example, Maharashtra's history texts written by the regional educational board have not been able to de-personalize the persona of Shivaji and the depiction of his encounter with Afzal Khan retains both communal and aggressively violent overtones. Conversely, in centralized and national historical lingua, however, the fiery ruler from the peasant castes who symbolized the breakaway from latter day feudal (Mughal) rule has been reduced to a less than honourable place.

Similarly, the necessity of decommunalizing medieval history, especially given its overtly anti-Muslim portrayals in the past cannot be undermined and has been achieved through the works of renowned historians. But the tendency to look at even medieval India in an entirely centrist, 'national' perspective without examining—or portraying—the struggle of Kashmiri rulers against Mughal domination or the campaigns of the kings of Assam (also driven by similar motivations) have limited the growth of a rich and dynamic 'Indian' history further.

The regional histories of regions that we today identify as the 'states' of Kerala, Orissa, Manipur, and Andhra Pradesh are rich, complex, and varied. They deepen the understanding of the economic, social, and political processes that resulted in actions in both the distant and not so distant past; at the same time they challenge the 'modern' 'Indian' mind attuned to viewing the reality of this country in the context of political realities of the past 60–150 years.

The treatment of the struggle for freedom from the British suffers most from this linear treatment. 'Regional freedom fighters' suffer exclusion or scant mention. This has been an issue and cause for debate for some decades now. The different streams within the struggle against the colonial powers are not given just treatment; the desire not to deal with the complexities of means and methods has ignored the revolutionary stream; the need to be politically 'correct' has failed to record that Savarkar was a fiery leader from Maharashtra who fought for freedom—fought against the indignities of caste—but who also, soon, evolved a sectarian and militarized vision of a 'Hindu Nation' (*Hindutva*). After the formation of the Hindu Mahasabha, the emphasis on fighting colonial powers declined.

In 1947, India made a historic tryst with destiny. Independent yet partitioned, after extensive and careful deliberation, we opted for a democratic structure outlined in the Indian Constitution. The education project, state-driven or autonomously ensured, should have, under such a democratic structure, been committed to free enquiry, the fair and equal access to information, both quantitative and qualitative, the imbibing of the right to debate and dissent, at all times, providing the young mind with the richest possible access to information. The only restrictions and limits to when and at what junctures what kind of information could be shared with the child should have been pedagogical.

What is being argued is that the equality project in any democracy simply must extend to education. In quantitative terms, this means the right of every Indian child to primary and secondary education. The United Nations Children's Fund (UNICEF) figures shamefully record how we have failed. We have 370 million illiterates (1991), half a century after we became independent. But qualitatively too, the equality principle within the Indian education syllabus, especially related to history and social studies teaching, in state and central boards, is sorely wanting.

Wedded to the equality principle, the democratization of our history and social studies syllabus should have meant a critical revision of both the periodization, approach, and content of the material taught because pre-Independence, history writing under the British was infested with colonial biases. This has failed to happen so that in most of our texts and syllabi we continue to perpetuate the colonial legacy of portraying ancient India as synonymous with the Hindu and the medieval Indian past with the Muslim. We have, over the years, further accentuated the colonial biases with sharp and more recent ideological underpinnings that can be clearly linked with the sharp emergence in the political sphere of the Hindu Right.

These dangerous patterns we weave through the syllabus in general and the history and social studies curriculum in particular, for the young mind, need to be traced carefully. They reveal how the average Indian text looks at the historical and the present question of caste-based discriminations, community-driven stereotypes and as significantly how we 'teach' students about the issue of the status of women, then and now.

These patterns, distorted and prejudicial as they are, will open our eyes to the process that has actually contributed to mainstream secular space being dominated by the discourse and dictated by the Right. We will then begin to understand how certain manipulated discourses and imageries that have been pulled out for public consumption over the past decade-and-a-half find instant and widespread resonance in civil society. There were crude allusions to Muslims as *Babar ki aulad* in the mid-1980s and the charge of 'forced' conversions against Christians in the late-1990s. How come these find a silent acceptance in the marketplace of popular ideas, and even dominate the media?

TOWARDS A HOLISTIC AND MULTIDIMENSIONAL VISION OF THE PAST

This is because many of post-Independent India's textbooks have been unable to offer a clean, holistic, rational, and multidimensional vision of the past that includes a historically honest portrayal of how different faiths arrived on the shores of this subcontinent. Our textbooks are similarly suspiciously silent on the motives behind thousands of Indians converting to different faiths over the years. Instead, through allusions and exclusions, they lend credence to the false claim that in a vast majority of cases these conversions happened under force.

Hate-language and hate-politics cannot be part of the history project in a democracy. What we unfortunately do find is that prejudice and division, not a holistic and fair vision, has been the guiding principle for our textbook boards and the authors chosen by them. Over the years, our history and social studies texts, more and more, emphasize a prejudicial understanding and rendering of history, which is certainly not borne out by historical facts. What is far more worrisome and needs careful and equally studied examination is how the textbooks in use in most of our states under the ambit of the state textbook boards as well as the texts of the prominent national board, too, echo the same historical precepts, misconceptions, and formulations.

If, as citizens, we are concerned about the route of the creative thought processes that our learning system encourages—the actual quality of thinking that is developed in the mind of our young, the processes of enquiry that we engender through our attitude to learning and teaching (the contents of the texts in particular)—we also need to explore how our texts tackle the question of free enquiry, dissent, and debate. We also need to pay attention to specific inclusions and exclusions within the content of these texts. Other crucial questions also need to be raised. How do Indian texts specifically deal with the fundamental question of race, origin, culture, and faith on the sub-continent?

It is surely neither possible to speak about apartheid in the world context without linking it to the birth of South Africa as an independent nation under Nelson Mandela nor understand slavery in the modern context without knowledge of the role of colonial powers in Africa or equally pertinently, the whole phenomenon of the American War of Independence and Abraham Lincoln. But do Indian textbooks reflect the ability to examine social inequality, specifically the caste system, as it emerged and was legitimized historically and how it continues to exist today, perpetrating an exploitative and unjust social order? Can a young student of social studies really seek to understand the caste system without first of all, being informed of modern-day social and economic apartheid that 16–20 per cent of the Indian population continues to be forced to live under today? There is hardly in existence any Indian text that honestly and candidly sketches out the indignities that continue to be perpetuated on Indian Dalits even today.

The life-sketch of Dr Bhimrao Ambedkar is restricted to his contribution as the 'architect' of the Indian Constitution. The serious challenges he posed to the pre-independence struggle and the Brahmanical order, or his radical conversion to Buddhism as a method of 'social and political emancipation' (one million Dalits converted to Buddhism on 14 October 1948) find scant or no reference at all in 'secular' Indian textbooks.

This blinkered vision of Indian social disparity extends to the fashion in which Dr Ambedkar is portrayed to the young and the struggles that he led. On 25 December 1925, Ambedkar burnt copies of the *Manusmruti* at Mahad village in Maharashtra. This was a strong political statement against the domination suffered by Dalits, epitomized in this Brahmanical text that had laid down the code of a social order which regards *shudra*s and 'women' together as deserving of no rights. The incident finds no mention at all in any Indian school textbooks, revealing a sharp upper caste bias that has excluded real enquiry into these events and move-ments. There is no attempt at a critical look at texts like the *Manusmruti* that have, since their being written nearly a 100 years ago, reflected the attitudes of vested interests. In fact, this Brahmanical text itself receives favourable mention in Indian school textbooks.

As an extension of the same argument, some of our average Indian textbooks continue to label Christians, Muslims, and Parsees as 'foreigners', and moreover depict 'Hindus as the minority in most states of the country,' selectively speak about the 'immoral behaviour of Catholic priests in the middle ages' while exonerating the Brahmins and the Indian ruling classes (Gujarat state social studies texts). What is the message that we send out to the growing child with these factual misrepresentations coupled with deliberate exclusions about the Brahmanical elite of some historical events and modern day social realities?

The same college textbook in Maharashtra that speaks at length and with a fair degree of venom about Islam and its violent orientation is silent on what many ancient Indian kings did to Buddhist 'monasteries' and *bhiku*s during the ancient period (King Sashanka of Assam is reputed to have destroyed several monasteries). What then are the conclusions that a critic needs to draw about the motivations behind these selective inclusions and exclusions?

Exclusion is a subtle but potent form of prejudice. If, therefore, the average Indian textbook is silent on the motivations of many 'Hindu' kings who employed their officials to raid and destroy temples in the ancient and medieval periods, simply because they could be certain to find wealth there (King Harshadev of Kashmir is one such, referred to by Kalhana in his *Rajatarini*), is there a not-so-subtle attempt to allow the popularly cherished belief that temple breaking was the 'Muslim' rulers' favoured prerogative, to fester and grow?

Rabid observations on Islam and Christianity are overtly visible in excerpts of the books conceived by the Rashtriya Swayamsevak Sangh (RSS) which are used for 'teaching' in the *Shishu Mandir*s. For discerning observers and educationists, this commitment to indoctrination that presupposes injecting small yet potent doses of poison against an 'enemy other' is not really surprising when we understand the true nature of the ideological project of these outfits. Take for instance a textbook recommended for the final year Bachelor of Arts students in history, in Maharashtra. The chapter titled 'Invasion of Mahmud of Ghazni' is cleverly used by the author to launch a tirade against Islam itself. The content of this textbook could favour chapter and verse with sections of *Shishu Mandir* texts that are in other parts, far more direct, having nothing positive to say about Islam or Christianity.

Critically, how do our history and social studies' textbooks approach the complex question of gender? What is the underpinning of analysis on critical gender issues within these books? How do our textbooks explain notions of *pativrata* (worship of the husband), *sati* (widow burning), child marriage, burning of women at the stake (called 'witch hunting' during the medieval ages), polygamy, polyandry, and so on, to the child? What were the varied facts behind the emergence of different faiths on the sub-continent?

The tale of the often ruthless methods that the Portuguese Christians took to effect conversions in Goa may be more recent but it is by no means the whole story of how Christianity arrived on the shores of the sub-continent and found deep and abiding routes. That is an enquiry that is more complex, and far richer in detail.

The record of persons opting to convert to different faiths whether it be Buddhism, Jainism, Christianity, Islam, or Sikhism is a worthy exploration in itself. Honestly told, it could offer vital insights on the impulses of ideas and motives as they have driven humankind over the ages. It is however a subject that has been significantly ignored except through banal references to 'syncretism' and 'synthesis' that are left thematically and conceptually unexplored.

The subject of shifts and changes to different faiths is educative, simply because if fairly approached, the process will throw up different sets of reasons and varying motivations for these actions—these changes of faith that people opted for. The differences and variety would depend upon the period when the change took place, the region within India that we would be looking at, and finally the method employed for the conversion itself.

None of the mainline Indian textbooks, however, really do this subject justice. There is to be an often found, single sentence reference to the fact that Islam first came to the shores of the Malabar Coast through the regular visits of Arab traders who enjoyed a long-standing relationship of trade and commerce with India. But the next sentence immediately shifts gear to the other way that Islam came to the Indian sub-continent—through the 'invasions' in Sind. From thereon, our children are told in graphic detail of the numerous 'invasions' but nothing of the coming of Islam through trade and the formations of communities that resulted.

Many conversions to Islam or Christianity in the modern period of history have also coincided with the passage of emancipatory laws liberating bonded labour that allowed oppressed sections the freedom to exercise choice in the matter of faith. These sections, then, exercised this choice, rightly or wrongly, perceiving either Islam or Christianity to be more egalitarian than Hinduism's oppressive system of caste.

There were several instances of conversions during the second half of the 19th century in Travancore, for instance. Educational endeavours of missionaries and the resultant aspirations to equality of status encouraged many persons of 'low' caste to change faiths and through this to a perceived position of equality. For example, the first 'low' caste person, to walk the public road near the temple in Tiruvalla, in 1851, was a Christian. Around 1859, many thousands converted to Christianity in the midst of emancipatory struggles that were supported by missionaries in the region—the struggle of *Nadars* on the right of their women to cover the upper part of their body, opposed by the upper castes!

There are so many fascinating examples. Large scale conversions to Islam took place on the Malabar Coast not during the invasions by Tipu Sultan but during the period, 1843–90. These were directly linked to the fact that in 1843, under the British, slavery was formally abolished in the region. As a result, large numbers from the formerly oppressed castes, bonded in slavery to upper caste Hindus moved over to Islam, which they perceived, rightly or wrongly to preach a message of equality and justice.

Trade and commerce finds dry and peripheral treatment in our texts as do the impact of technological developments through history. Religious interpretations and explanations often predominate, with little attempt to explain how ideas and thought processes travelled across continents and borders; the means and modes of communication, and so on, are hardly explored.

Democratic and secular India has had 54 years of independent schooling to groom and develop. Quite apart from the critical failings listed above, little or nothing has been done to develop a sense of individual civil rights or liberties short of reciting the Preamble to the Indian Constitution by rote or often learning the section of the fundamental rights by heart! What are the critical liberties that an individual enjoys within a democratic state that have evolved through history, that are essentially modern in nature, and are therefore antithetical to critical aspects of India and the world's ancient and medieval past? How does a high school student of civics develop an understanding of the Indian Constitution or civil liberties if the whole desire and objective behind the creation of our educational syllabus is to foster unthinking and uncritical minds and also develop pride in only ancient (read Hindu) India? The student is repeatedly told through text and syllabus that he must develop respect for ancient India and her traditions. But there is no similar guideline or entreaty made to our young by the educator or the textbook to develop an abiding respect and sense of democratic values and freedoms.

History, in India, needs to reflect the rich and diverse sections of its people. Why should a Bhil Tribal be interested in the kind of history being dished out today? Is there anything of the history of the artisan, the fisherfolk, the weaver, the tiller of the land in our current history? Have we asked ourselves why there is not? When we speak of India, the rich, the poor, the rural, the urban, the tribal, the non-tribal, the Dalit, the Hindu, the Muslim, the Christian, the Keralite, the north Indian, the Gujarati, the Assamese, the task becomes even more awesome.

The legend of the Bhil tribal boy, Eklavya, may or may not have the same emotive element for a Muslim or Christian youth living on the margins of acceptability in a deeply polarized Indian polity. However, as a profound comment on the denial of education to lower castes in a rigidly caste-ridden society and tradition, it surely has lessons for any student or teacher attempting to grapple with notions of social equity, justice, and deprivation in the days of yore?

The vivid account of Gandhari's curse on Lord Krishna—the mythical image of a mere woman cursing a God—after the great war (*Mahabharata*) that left millions, including her eldest son dead, immortalized in Indian literature, may not have deep significance to the rigid follower of *Hindutva* cannot but have profound meanings for women today grappling with more and more indignities—familial and societal violence included—in a violent, modern world.

The history of the first Arab settlers on Kerala's shores may or may not be perceived to be of interest to students of history in the rest of India; nor the fascinating fact that 5,000 years ago when this land that we now dub not just India but Hindusthan, gave the King of Persia a copy of the book, *Kalilavadamana*, that contained vital information on a medicine for immortality.

But the business communications and trade links that this development lead to, and the uniquely mixed communities that these associations engendered are critical in understanding the lives and cultures of these communities that line our vast shores.

The near-mythical intellectual association of the Shaivite *jogin*, Laleshwari and the *sufi Sant* Nooruddin have echoed through the folklore of Kashmir. They both help and baffle us while grappling with the ethos and understanding of *Kashmiriyat*. The students and teachers of history in India, while looking at the *Ramayana* as a political epic will need to grapple and thereafter, reconcile to the fact that over 200 versions of the *Ramlila*—village-level performances of the epic—have dotted this land where some venerate Ram and others Ravana.

What we learn and teach about history shapes our understanding of the events of the past. This understanding of the past influences our ability to grapple with the present and therefore, also the future. Such knowledge, if both rich and varied, can break limited ways of understanding our past and present and demonstrate to us the variety and wealth of the culture of the sub-continent as a whole. This will help us forge new ties for its people in the future.

BIBLIOGRAPHY

Ali, M. Athar. 2006. *Mughal India: Studies in Polity, Ideas, Society, and Culture*. Oxford: Oxford University Press.
Chakravarti, Uma. 1998. *Rewriting History: The Life and Times of Pandita Ramabai*. New Delhi: The Book Review Literary Trust.
Linda Beth Hess and Shukdeo Singh (eds and trans.). 2002. *The Bijak of Kabir*. Oxford: Oxford University Press.
Lal, Chaman (ed.). 2007. *Bhagat Singh: The Jail Notebook and Other Writings*. Delhi: Left Word Books.
Mani, Braj Ranjan. 2005. *Debrahmanising History: Dominance and Resistance in Indian Society*. Delhi: Manohar Publishers.
Mohanty, Manoranjan. 2004. *Class, Caste, Gender*. New Delhi: Sage Publications.
Mokashi, Digambar Balkrishna. 1987. *Palkhi: An Indian Pilgrimage*. Translated by Philip C. Engblom. New York: SUNY Press.
O'Hanlon, Rosalind. 2002. *Caste, Conflict and Ideology: Mahatma Jotirao Phule and Low Caste Protest in Nineteenth-century Western India*. Cambridge: Cambridge University Press.
Robertson, Bruce Carlisle. 1999. *The Essential Writings of Raja Rammohan Ray*. Mumbai: Oxford University Press.
Sadgopal, Anil. 2004. *Globalisation And Education: Defining The Indian Crisis*. Delhi: Zakir Husain College.
Setalvad, Teesta. 1998. 'Teaching to Hate', *Communalism Combat*, pp. 5–14.
———. 1999. 'How Our Textbooks Teach Prejudice', *Communalism Combat*, pp. 5–15.
———. 2005. *Constitutional Mandate and Education*. CABE (Central Advisory Board of Education Committee), Government of India, pp. 5–35.
Sikand, Yoginder. 2003. *Scared Spaces: Exploring Traditions of Shared Faith in India*. New Delhi: Penguin.
Thapar, Romila. 1995 [1992]. *Interpreting Early India*. Oxford: Oxford University Press.
———. 1998. *A'soka and the Decline of the Mauryas*. Oxford: Oxford University Press.

PART IV
ETHICAL PATHS TO GLOBAL CITIZENSHIP

PART IV

ETHICAL PATHS TO GLOBAL CITIZENSHIP

11
Global Ethical Options in the Framework of Development: Gandhian Perspectives

Neelakanta Radhakrishnan

GLOBALIZATION AND COMMERCIALIZATION OF EDUCATION

Two parents can't raise a child any more than one. You need a whole community to raise a child. And the little nuclear family is a paradigm that just doesn't work. It doesn't work for white people or for black people. Why we are hanging onto it, I don't know. It isolates people into little units—people need a larger unit. (Angelo 1989)

In the present age where the primary concern of humanity appears to be the tackling of the various aspects related to globalization and its wily cousins such as *liberalization, market-driven economy*, the driving spirit is more or less couched in what Prof. Huntington described as 'Clash of Civilizations'. What kind of ethical considerations do we envision from the parched terrain of human existence? The whole world has become a village or market, thanks to communication explosion and economics of liberation. As Mathew Arnold pointed out in *Dover Beach*, we have been reduced to the status of ignorant armies fighting by midnight. Whose battle are we fighting out? We do not know. By which ever nomenclature we are known, whether as professors, lectures, teachers, administrators, we are bridges, facilitators, interpreters, guides, and friends to seekers of knowledge.

In humanity's onward march for survival and the relentless search for truth with the aid of science and technology, many of the old concepts irrespective of their validity and utility became outmoded and hence discarded. Values and precepts when called upon to quantify and qualify in the wake of new scientific truths and discoveries were gradually relegated to the background, perhaps, not gradually but too soon and convincingly. The Hi-tech messiahs and champions of the newly fashioned philosophy, 'when it is tough, only the toughest get going', supported by the multinational corporations and prophets of globalization, liberalizations, market economy occupied the centre stage of our life since the last quarter of the last century. The emergence of the unipolar world and the helplessness of former giants in the emerging scenario only compound the already confused situation. Religion is dead—they shouted at the top of their voice. Then what is not dead? Markets! Money!

All talks now are around shares, automobiles, computers, import, export, liberalization, globalization, Sensex, and Forex. Where are human beings? His or her voice gets drowned in the din of all these voices and the worth of a human being is measured gradually on the basis of his/her purchasing power. Human being has been relegated to the position of a commodity, whose 'value' is being decided by market trends.

Gone are the days when a human being was respected and admired or allowed to live in society based on achievements, his/her caliber, or scholarship. Now, everything is decided by the markets. Gone are the days when we talked about skill-based or knowledge-based society. The acquisitive and competitive tendencies have been encouraged feverishly and sharpened their edges to the extent that it is the spirit of going for the 'kill'—both physical and managerial—that is stressed and evoked in most of our endeavours. Even in the field of education, instead of values and character building, what is sought to be encouraged now is the spirit of competition. It is forgotten that too much of emphasis on competitive spirit generates aggressive tendencies in the child. Commercialization of education has also led to a sort of 'commodification', where survival and profit become the guiding principles. All talks in this commercial era are centred around profit generation. Ethics, morality, and all such considerations are nowhere in the reckoning. It is all about time marketing strategies.

Marketing of what? Obviously, what is produced and certainly not the producer. It is even forgotten that human beings who are behind the production and marketing also need care and consideration. We have reached a situation were the value of a human being is lost in the midst of marketing activities, and education, unfortunately, is no exception.

Commercialization of education and mushrooming of education institutions have added a new dimension. Though the spread of liberal education and compulsory state-sponsored education have been found to be of use in the general context, a certain kind of gulf seems to be developing between the schools directly under state control and those run by private institutions. Schools have become 'Information Pumping Centres' (IPC) rather than centres which shape the character of children. One is tempted to ask a question: how is education viewed and treated today? As a commercial activity or as a process to enable children and teenagers acquire knowledge and skills required in their life? A seeming contradiction of ideas and a lurking selfish motive is discernible in the present system.

Let us remember we are living in a new society. We have a new kind of family life where dialogue among the members has become rare or minimum. Tension mounts in the family for various reasons. Estrangement between partners is increasing. Divorce rate has been steadily increasing. Alcoholism has also registered an all-time high. Joint family system is becoming a thing of the past. Television and other media which is on air round the clock have been steadily contributing to the emergence of a situation whose cumulative impact on the traditional behavioural pattern and values are yet to be assessed. Schools and colleges are no longer the sole repositories or centres of learning.

If one looks at education from capital and revenue point of view, then students invariably become commodities and institutions reduced to commercial establishment. This development is dangerous and a paradigm shift is very essential before it is too late. Veering away from the commercial angle, education has to focus on character building, value creation, and rearing of future citizens thereby making it more than a mere 'revenue spinning' arena or activity. What the distinguished Japanese philosopher and peace activist, Dr Daisaku Ikeda said assumes importance in this context:

> The problem of education goes far beyond the basic task of learning to read and write. We must also find ways to draw out the latent potential of people who have not yet acquired even the basic know-how of survival and to channel that potential towards the building of the global community. (Radhakrishnan 2006: 225)

Neelakanta Radhakrishnan

TOWARDS A HOLISTIC VISION OF EDUCATION

Though it might be provocative, I cannot but remember what a student said at the Brown University in U.S.A, during a seminar I was leading there in 2000; 'Satan is the greatest teacher in humanity, Eve, his first student, Adam, a reluctant second. And education began with the coaching Satan offered unsolicited to Eve to disobey God.'

Let us agree or disagree with this observation. But can we ignore this? To provoke you further, I would like to invite you to another observation by Daniel Cottom who in his recently published book *Why Education is Useless* argues:

> Education is useless because it leads us away from practicality.
>
> Education is useless because it leads us away from idealism.
>
> Education is useless because it isolates us from the rest of humanity.
>
> Education is useless because it hardens our hearts. It makes people think so much that they forget to feel.
>
> Education is useless because it lowers our spirits.
>
> Education is useless because it weakens our bodies.
>
> Education is useless because it dulls our personalities.
>
> Education is useless because it makes us slaves.
>
> Education is useless because it makes us rebels.
>
> Education is useless because it impoverishes us.
>
> Education is useless because it pampers us.
>
> Education is useless because it makes us optimists.
>
> Education is useless because it makes us pessimists.
>
> Education is useless because it leads to dogmatism.
>
> Education is useless because it leads to doubt.
>
> Education is useless because it distances us from real life.
>
> Education is useless because it mires us in real life.
>
> (2003: 2–5).

It all depends on how one looks at education. Do we look at it as a process, an invitation, a method, a strategy, or as a tool? The role of education played all through the history of humanity cannot be ignored and as *Caliban* in Shakespeare's *Tempest* would say to his master, Prospero, 'You taught me language, I am using it. If it hurts you, I am sorry.'

Gandhian Perspectives

Gandhi had a holistic view of life and education was considered by him as a tool of character development, habit formation, a source of nourishment to hand, heart, and head, and an instrument of transformation which will usher in non-violent, non-exploitative social order. Gandhiji said:

> By education I mean an all-round drawing out of the best in child and man—body, mind, and spirit. Literacy is not the end of education or even the beginning. It is only one of the means whereby man and women can be educated. Literacy in itself is no education. I would therefore begin the child's education by teaching it a useful handicraft and enabling it to produce from the moment it begins its training. I hold that the highest development of the mind and the soul is possible under such a system of education. Every handicraft has to be taught not merely mechanically as is done today but scientifically, i.e., the child should know the 'why' and the 'wherefore' of every process. (Prabhu and Rao 1945: 379)

By defining the goal of education thus, Gandhi comes close to Bertrand Russell who considers that the four virtues education should foster are *vitality, courage, sensitivity, and intelligence.*

According to Gandhi, parents have a very significant role to play in forming the character of the children and their future destiny. He wrote:

> Children inherit the qualities of the parents, no less than their physical features. Environment does play an important part, but the original capital on which a child starts life is inherited from its ancestors. I have always seen children successfully surmounting the effects of evil inheritance. That is due to purity being an inherent attribute of the soul. (Ramachandran 1964: 24)

The real property that a parent can transmit to all equally is his or her character and educational facilities—parents should seek to make their sons and daughters self-reliant, able to earn an honest livelihood by the sweat of the brow. He, thus, stressed again and again that the education of the children is primarily a duty to be discharged by the parents. Therefore, the creation of vital educational atmosphere is more important than the founding of innumerable schools. Once this atmosphere has been established on a firm footing, the schools will come in due course. Gandhiji suggested the following system for educating the children, which was also practiced in the Ashram, and schools started by his disciples during his life-time.

1. Young boys and girls should have coeducation till they are eight years of age.
2. Their education should mainly consist of manual training under the supervision of an educationist.
3. The special aptitudes of each child should be recognized in determining the kind of work he (or she) should do.
4. The reasons for every process should be explained, when the process is being carried on.
5. General knowledge should be imparted to each child as it begins to understand things. Learning to read or write should come later.
6. The child should first be taught to draw simple geometrical figures, and when he has learnt to draw these with ease, he should be taught to write the alphabet. If this is done, he will write a good hand from the very first.
7. Reading should come before writing. The letters should be treated as pictures to be recognized and later on to be copied.
8. A child taught on these lines will have acquired considerable knowledge, according to his capacity, by the time he is eight.
9. Nothing should be taught to a child by force.
10. He/she should be interested in everything taught to him/her.
11. Education should appear to the child like play. Play is an essential part of education.
12. All education should be imparted through the mother tongue.
13. The child should be taught Hindi/Urdu as the national language, before he learns letters.
14. Religious education is indispensable and the child should get it by watching the teacher's conduct and by hearing him talking about it.
15. Nine to sixteen constitutes the second stage in the child's education.
16. It is desirable that boys and girls should have coeducation during the second stage also as far as possible.
17. Hindu Children should now be taught Sanskrit and Muslim children Arabic.
18. Manual training should be continued during the second stage. Literacy education should be allotted more time as and when it is necessary.
19. The boys, during this stage, should be taught their parents' vocation in such a way that they will by their own choice obtain their livelihood by practicing the hereditary craft. This does not apply to the girls.

20. During this stage, the child should acquire a general knowledge of world history and geography, botany, astronomy, arithmetic, geometry, and algebra.
21. Each child should now be taught to sew and to cook.
22. Sixteen to 25 is the third stage, during which every young person should have an education according to his or her wishes and circumstances.
23. During the second stage (9–16) education should be self-supporting, that is, the child, while learning should also do some productive work, the proceeds of which will meet the expenditure of the school.
24. Production starts at the very beginning, but during the first stage it does not still catch up with the expenditure.
25. Teachers should be inspired by a spirit of service. It is a despicable thing to take any Tom, Dick, or Harry as a teacher in the primary stage. All teachers should be men of character.
26. Big and expensive buildings are not necessary for educational institutions.
27. English should be taught only as one of the several languages. As Hindi is the national language, English is to be used in dealing with other nations and international commerce (Ramachandran 1971: 378).

In sharp contrast to Macaulay's concept of education which prepared half-baked *babus* for *sarkari naukari*, Gandhi offered a revolutionary concept of new education, *Nai Talim*. He called it *Jivanna-Sikshana* or Basic Education. He said:

> This system is meant to transform village children into model villagers. It is principally designed for them. The inspiration for it has come from the villages. Basic education links the children, whether of the cities or the villages, to all that is best and lasting in India. It develops both the body and the mind, and keeps the child rooted to the soil with a glorious vision of the future in the realization of which he or she begins to take his or her share from the very commencement of his or her career in school....The object of Basic Education is the physical, intellectual, and moral development of the children. Any scheme which is sound from the educational point of view and is efficiently managed is bound to sound economic. For instance, we can teach our children to make clay toys that are to be destroyed afterwards. That too will develop their intellect. But it will neglect

a very important moral principal, viz, that human labour and material should never be used in a wasteful or unproductive way. The emphasis laid on the principle of spending every minute of one's life usefully is the best education for citizenship and incidentally make Basic Education self-sufficient. (Gandhi 1949: 62)

Gandhi viewed the fundamentals of basic education in the following manner:

1. All the education to be true must be self-supporting, that is to say, in the end it will pay its expenses excepting the capital which will remain intact.
2. All education must be imparted through the medium of the provincial language.
3. In this, there is no room for giving sectional religious training. Fundamental universal ethics will have full scope.
4. This education, whether it is confined to children or adults, male or female, will find its way to the homes of the pupils.
5. Since millions of students receiving the education will consider themselves as part of the whole of India, they must learn an inter-provincial language. This common inter-provincial language can only be Hindustani written in Nagari or Urdu script. Therefore, pupils have to master both the scripts (Gandhi 1953b: 16).

He believed that:

[M]anual training will serve a double purpose in a poor country like ours. It will pay for the education of our children and teach them an occupation on which they can fall back in their later life, if they choose, for earning a living. Such a system must make our children self-reliant. Nothing will demoralize the nation so much as that we learn to despise labour. (Gandhi 1955: 60)

In this scheme, the hand will handle tools as it draws or traces the writing. The eyes will read the pictures of letters and words and also will know other things in life; the ear will catch the names and meanings of things and sentences. The whole training will be natural, responsive and, therefore, the quickest and the cheapest in the world.

Gandhi believed that values can be instilled in a person only through a conscientious practice and in children unless it is woven in their education process it will be of no consequence. Education as practiced in the various schools and colleges funded by Mahatma Gandhi since the 1920s aims at developing three aspects of the child: the mind, the heart, and the skill to use one's hands. The child knows with his mind, loves with his heart, and creates with his hands. Unless we provide outlets for all these three, and training in all these areas, the child has a lopsided education.

Gandhi did not want to accumulate learning as many people accumulate assets or riches—learning should not be for the purpose of being first or winning a competition, at the expense of others. Rather than being acquisitive/competitive, Gandhi wanted education to become cooperative. It should prepare the individual to be lifted into a non-exploitative social structure.

The Basic Education (or New Education—*Nai Talim*) in its essential form fosters self-sufficiency. With that aim in mind, students do their own laundry, work in the kitchen, sweep and scrub, practice gardening, weaving, pottery, and carpentry as well as learn the three R's and acquire knowledge of essential academic subjects. In summation, Basic Education is:

1. Child-centred or learner-centred;
2. Dynamic;
3. Cooperative;
4. Non-violent; and
5. Geared toward the acquisition of self-sufficiency.

Vinoba and other Sarvodaya Thinkers developed it further as follows:

1. *Nai Talim* is the integration of *Jnana* (knowledge) and *Karma* (Action) resulting in *Ananda* (Joy).
2. *Nai Talim* cannot be pursed keeping the social order of today as it is. *Nai Talim* is based on the principle of bread labour. It is a revolution in social values.
3. *Nai Talim* is the education for non-violence. It is founded on freedom and mutual cooperation. The aim is freedom from fear.
4. *Nai Talim* is based on *Swavlamban* or bodily needs, for independent critical thinking and acquiring complete knowledge and for spiritual development.
5. Education should develop social consciousness among the students, the attitudes and habits of doing work in cooperation with others.
6. The social principle of *Nai Talim* is that all human lives are to be respected equally.

7. Education should be intimately and harmoniously related to life and nature. Life without association with agriculture is incomplete.
8. The school should be organized on the model of a good family.
9. The goal of education is discipline and character; not self-indulgence but self-control.
10. *Nai Talim* is a never-ending continuous process, always fresh. It varies from day-to-day, and from region to region.
11. *Nai Talim* is not meant for the elementary grades only. It is the character of every education. It's not meant only for the villages, but for everyone at all stages of life.
12. *Nai Talim* is not an education method. It is not 'activity education'. It is a creative idea, a way of life. It is a new approach. The alpha and omega of education is the quest for truth (Gandhi 1950: 93).

Gandhi had the vision of 'a true system of education' which he had advocated in *Hind Swaraj*. He was sure that the family should be the starting point, and Tolstoy Farm, the historic settlement was run like a big joint family. Tolstoy Farm was one of the communities started by Gandhi in Transvaal, South Africa, in 1910. The other was Phoenix Ashram. These two communities became the headquarters of Gandhiji's satyagraha campaigns (non-violent resistance for justice) which he led at that time. There was a common kitchen, which was possible because those who were habitual meat eaters voluntarily gave up meat during their time there. The women took charge and the children regularly helped them in turns. The whole community, adults and children alike, were set to work on the farm, in the vegetable gardens, and in the workshops. Everyone shared in the sanitation work, and there was carpentry and sandal making also. With all this bodily exercise and simple healthy food, the children grew well and there was very little sickness. It was the rule there that children should not be asked to do things that their teachers did not do; teachers would work with them at every kind of labour, so things went fairly well, even though it was completely a new experience for all the children. Gandhi was clear about three things: the children should live at home, they should not be separated from their parents and sent to a residential school; they should learn in their own mother tongue; they should not have any privileges which other children could not share. They live at home because 'the education that children naturally imbibe in a well ordered household is impossible to obtain in hostels'.

'The intimate relationships of the home were', Gandhiji believed, 'the foundation of all social and moral education' and that was what he regarded as of central importance. 'I had always given the first place to culture of the heart and the building of character,' he wrote (Gandhi 1953a: 9).

Later, when Gandhi looked back on these years, he felt that his children have been able to learn the meaning of 'simplicity and a spirit of service' by growing up in a home where these things were being explored and practiced. It is exactly these things the young children of today are deprived in the name of modern education. Unfortunately, in a country like India, education becomes the first casualty with every change at the political level. This explains why we have had so many education commissions during the last 40 years since independence. And it has assumed the level of a national tragedy when we painfully realize that after 48 years of experiments we are back to square one, re-examining the Gandhian alternatives now. Alas, that too half-heartedly!

THE TEACHER AS VALUE CREATOR

In the present age where the teacher–student equation has undergone a tremendous change, teachers have to realize that in all departments of human life, all over the world, may be in varying degrees and pace, the rhythm of human life is undergoing changes. Teacher as a value creator, teacher as a bridge between community and children, teacher as a facilitator of learning, teacher as a signpost of change in society, teacher as a knowledge bank—which role are we assigning to him or her in the cyber age?

A person enters the world of teaching as a profession. Despite all her/his efforts to be a good teacher, he/she will remain an outsider until the teacher becomes a missionary to the cause. Teaching has to become a mission. The moment it becomes a mission, the teacher becomes a value-creator, simple and direct. It all depends on what the teacher wants to become and how he/she is able to fit into the evolving mould. The mould could remain static because of the fixed notions and non-mobility of the teacher, psychologically and spiritually. A dedicated teacher instead of quarrelling with the system would naturally try to identify herself/himself, making the job, a mission. In the gradual emergence of the teacher, students also certainly have a big role to play. Just like all teachers are not good teachers, all models are not worth emulating either.

In the emerging scenario, the teacher's role is very difficult. He/she is caught between competing schools, ambitious parents, unrealistic syllabus, orthodox methods of examinations, and helpless students. We are creating a generation of children or young people who forget to laugh. The truck-load of books a student is forced to carry to school every day in the morning reflects his/her anxieties over the awaiting uncertainties in the schools. When the child returns home in the evening he/she returns heavier with the doze of home work which puts additional burden on the parents who in large numbers very often have to depend on tuition masters. If the child survives the ordeal, he/she might be a very brave one.

The general condition makes the teacher helpless. For argument's sake, can a teacher take this scenario as a challenge?—as a challenge to his/her creativity, ingenuity, capacity to innovate and offer leadership? Do we love our profession? Have we entered this field by accident or by choice? The general situation in the school, the content of the syllabus, the attitude of Parent–Teacher Association (PTA) or Management, or the education authorities might not be to the liking of the teacher. He/she might feel that all this should change. But then the reality of the situation is the difficulties confronting a teacher. The question is how is he/she going to face the situation? He/she has to become a good teacher before donning the garb of a reformer.

The paradox of present-day society is that while there is an explosion of communication and the world has shrunk in size and has come together to become almost a global village, the distance between individuals, individuals and families, and families has increased resulting in an unfortunate situation where intimacy has given way to cautious and impersonal kind of relationships.

The teacher alone cannot be the torch-bearer of values and morals. Yet, it has to be borne in mind that he is an important player. In India, Gandhi drew our attention to this. But the Gandhian Model of education was not given even a fair trial before it was condemned and thrown out.

'My life is one indivisible whole and all my activities run into one another, and they have their rise in my insatiable love of mankind,' said Gandhi (Gandhi 1979: 184).

It is time those who are in charge of human destiny ask whether the development models we have at present, the education systems we practice, the political order we assiduously seek to establish, the ethical and moral framework we trample upon, the family and social values we propagate are conducive to fostering of any healthy vision of society which will nurture the essential ingredients of what Dr Daisaku Ikeda identified as Global citizenship:

1. The wisdom to perceive the interconnectedness of all life and living.
2. The courage not to fear or deny difference but to respect and strive to understand people of different cultures and to grow from encounters with them.

3. The compassion to maintain an imaginative empathy that reaches beyond one's immediate surroundings and extends to those suffering in distant places (Ikeda 1996).

Should not humanity take these aspects seriously when Global Ethical Options for development are debated?

BIBLIOGRAPHY

Angelo, Bonnie. 1989. 'The Pain of being Black', *Time*, 22 May.
Cottom, Daniel. 2003. *Why Education is Useless*. Philadelphia: University of Pennsylvania Press.
Gandhi, M. K. 1949. *To the Student*. Ahmedabad: Navajivan.
———. 1950. *Educational Reconstruction*. Wardha: Hindustani Talimi Sangh, Sevagram.
———. 1953a. *Basic National Education*. Wardha: Hindustrani Talimi Sangh, Sevagram.
———. 1953b. *Towards New Education*. Ahmedabad: Navajivan Trust.
———. 1955. *Basic National Education*. Ahmedabad: Navajivan Publishing House.
———. 1979. *The Collected Works of Mahatma Gandhi*. Volume XIII.
———. 1994. *Collected Works*. Vol. XII. New Delhi: Publications Division, Government of India, 1960–1994.
Ikeda, Daisaku. 1996. University Speeches, Lecture at Columbia University, June 13.
———. 2001. *For the Sake of Peace, Seven Paths to Global Harmony*. Santa Monica: Middleway Press.
Lawrence E. Carter, George D. Miller, and Neelakanta Radhakrishnan. 2001. *Global Ethical Options in the tradition of Gandhi, King and Ikeda*. Tokyo: Weatherhill.
Mani R. S. 1995. *Educational Ideas and Ideals of Gandhi and Tagore*. New Delhi: New Book Society of India.
Prabhu. R. K. and U. R. Rao. 1945. *The Mind of Mahatma Gandhi*. Ahmedabad: Navajivan Publishing House.
Radhakrishnan. N. 1992. *Gandhian Perspectives of Nation Building for World Peace*. New Delhi: Konark Publishers.
———. 1995. *Gandhi the Quest for Tolerance and Survival*. New Delhi: Gandhi Smriti and Darshan Samiti and Gandhi Media Centre.
———. 1998. *Ikeda Sensei: The Triumph of Mentor Disciple Spirit*. New Delhi: Gandhi Media Centre.
———. 1999. *Gandhian Perspectives on Education*. Trivandrum: G. Ramachandran Institute of Nonviolence.
———. 2006. *The Living Dialogue: Socrates to Ikeda*. Trivandrum: Gandhi Media Centre.
Ramachandran, G. 1964. *The Man Gandhi*. Gandhigram.
———. 1971. *Gandhi's Views of Education* (speech delivered), Gandhigram.

12
Reconciling Identity and Citizenship: A Case for Moral Cosmopolitanism in a Divided World*

M. Satish Kumar

INTRODUCTION

This year has been marked with increasing polarization between communities in UK in particular and the world in general. While terrorist threat levels have sea-sawed through the seasonal changes in the direction of the westerlies, inevitably as global citizens we find ourselves increasingly imbricated into the ever mounting justification for and against the *veiled* Muslims—be it in France, the UK, or Europe. The point is, do we want to engage with the politics of *veil* or a *turban*? Why is a veil so critical to our existence, our identity? Or is this only an assertion of a political position that group identity is far more important than our individual identity. The only interregnum in this saga of assertion and counter assertion is the alarming discourse around global warming, of international migrants pouring in from Romania, and the rise of overcrowding in British prisons. Invariably politics, religion, ethnicity, culture, and philosophy tend to get entangled when we attempt to define ourselves in relation to our position in the world in which we live. The dissolution of the erstwhile Soviet Union and the eastern Europe has led to the pre-eminence of capitalism and its democratic liberal principles in place of the ideal of socialism.

*Reprinted from permission from *Social Change* (Volume 36, No. 3, September 2006).

'Cultural turn' and its assertion of rights, representation and affirmation of group difference have reinforced new forms of cultural politics and have overshadowed the primacy of individualism and their rights too. Indeed, identity is a complicated issue and does not lend itself easily to a generalist interpretation. Thus, to be identical is very different from sharing an identity (Sen 2006: xi). The complexity of the term is further compounded when we introduce group versus individual identity.

This chapter attempts to evaluate the current debates on identity and citizenship informing our society. It will assess how far global citizenship as a rallying point is capable of informing issues of identity, social, political, and thereby infuse a sense of global responsibility to the citizens in the present context. Daisaku Ikeda's assertion that the foundation of all education is learning the path of true humanity will be contextualized in the current debates. This chapter makes a case for enforcing the significant ideals of moral citizenship based on the profound respect for each other's common moral platform. It asserts that universal human values can only be cultivated through a conscious application of value-based education, which recognizes the universality of human rights, of mutual understanding and appreciation of diverse civilizational order, ethnicity, and cultures. Is there a space for cultivating a more humane social order based on mutual dialogue, infused by democratic ideals?

COMMUNITARIAN VERSUS LIBERAL THINKERS

Benhabib (1992: 1) notes that 'specific aspects of our social, political, and symbolic universe have been irretrievably transformed', and in this context the ideas of identity and citizenship too have become highly charged and contested. Over time, three perspectives can be identified which can be associated with identity and citizenship. These relate to communitarianism, liberalism, and civic republicanism. Communitarians actually adhere to a strong sense of community. Communitarian ideas relate to a critique of the liberal conception of self or the sovereign individual. They believe that an individual, as a self-centred being cannot contribute to the common good of humanity. However, it does acknowledge that the individual is the sole bearer of rights in any given society. Liberalism on the other hand asserts that an individual precedes the polity, and citizenship is there to protect the rights of the individual. Therefore, liberalism as a concept is far more utilitarian and functional in its engagement with the citizens. In this respect, all political systems render a service in order to protect the rights of an individual. Kymlicka (1995) notes that modern liberalism has not been very forthright in its dealings with rights of the group.

Protagonists of both communitarian and liberal persuasion appear to be at odds in their conception of the 'individual'. Adherents of liberalism speak about self-promoting individuals, who are constantly ensuring that their rights are protected. Communitarians, on the other hand, believe that all individuals are situated and embedded and not totally independent and isolated from the community as claimed. Sandel (1982: 150) notes that identity is defined by being a member of a community, just as members of a society are associated with the sentiments and communitarian principles of a given community. In a way, communitarians have always asserted the rights of a group in the making of an identity. They insist that all individuals relate to and imagine themselves to be part of the larger community. In other words, an individual's identity is a derived identity dependent largely on their affiliation and indeed their membership to a group. The point is how far individual actions are motivated and transformed by their membership to a community. Individual preferences, that is, being a practicing Muslim or a Jew or a Buddhist can help transcend individual ego to encompass the community of Muslims or Jews or a Buddhist, especially when they face or sense persecution. We have seen this being deployed in the case of Palestinians, Iraqis, Israelis, or Burmese. As Sen (2006: xi) notes, '[T]he idea that one's communal identity is that of self-realization and not of choice is hard to accept given that we as individuals are constantly making choices and prioritizing those choices regarding our affiliations and associations in the society. Identity, therefore, is a complicated matter.'

IDENTITY

Identity is extremely personal, reinforcing an intense sense of self. At the same time, it is associated with our sense of belonging to a group or community and the way one is recognized, classified, and acknowledged. Our language and food habits form the cultural markers to distinguish one from the other, that is, us from them. While this gives a sense of cohesiveness, it also reinforces a sense of collective identity. This automatically instills a sense of empowerment and links naturally to political and social power. Identity has a special and contentious place in social, political, and religious theories. It helps us to present a unified sense of unique self, sharing a given set of beliefs and values. At the same time these very attributes force us to seek recognition as members of a group in a very political sense. The deliberation for a new found sense of identity calls for the excavation of hitherto silenced and fragile subjectivities. Thus, identity does not necessarily have to be rooted in stable social constituencies within the human community. Today identities have become far more ambiguous and hybrid in nature and character. The question is when does identity become an issue? According to Bauman (1996: 18–36), this becomes an issue when as individuals we are confronted with a sense of uncertainty of our existence. I remember after the Sikh riots in Delhi in 1984, most of the clean-shaven Sikhs took to wearing their turbans and growing their beards to reassert their Sikh identity. Travelling to and fro in the public transport, I was acknowledged as a Sikh because of my beard and *kara* (bangles) even though I was not born a Sikh. Thus, identity has 'always remained a work in progress' (Taylor and Spencer 2004: 4), and we negotiate this identity every time we meet a new person, or a group, constantly reasserting the spaces of our interaction. It is fair to say that groups who have faced intense cultural and political marginalization have always attempted to reinstate their identity and citizenship. No matter how 'political' or 'rational' one may appear, it affects us the way we present ourselves, in the way we dress, speak, and how we socialize.

TYPES OF IDENTITY

Our affiliation to a given group, community, or an order, influences our identity. Having settled down in the UK, I seek allegiance to my country of origin, India. So I am a person of Indian origin, being born into a Hindu family, and believe in the philosophy of Buddhism. I am an academic and as an intellectual, work across a range of social science disciplines, namely, history, economics, and geography. As a person born after India's independence, I am conscious of my postcolonial leanings and have no problem engaging with issues of environmentalism, human rights, and peace. I am not explicitly opposed to globalization and would prefer its regulation both in the short and long-term across nation-states. So my identity is both simultaneous and collective. It helps to pluralize the perception of my self. Thus, my identity impinges on my gender, class, profession, politics, and indeed my moral choices. In many ways, we may have different kinds of affiliation or membership to societies and groups, which manifest on our identities. A common membership, for example, with the United Nations, highlights our responsibilities as effective citizens and our relation and responsibilities in dealing with members of the same group. Likewise, we may also have membership of exclusive groups, such as professional associations (football clubs), and at the same time may belong to a particular class or gender. Here our identities are very specific and not generic to our membership as a global citizen.

The social capital or a sense of belonging to a community can reinforce our identity and thereby our acceptance and participation in the society. Indeed, we are constantly making choices about our membership to a particular group at all times. When we become victims of a particular form of politics, we tend to revert back to our primordial affiliation and thereby reinforce our identity as a Hindu, Sikh, or a Muslim. The advantage of adhering to a plural identity is that one need not deny an identity for the other. Rather, we tend to make informed choices of the relative importance of a given identity particularly during conflictual situations. Consider the following: For the forthcoming UK university-wide Research Assessment Exercise (RAE), I am putting forward my identity as a historical geographer, though I write and teach in the area of development studies too. This is my choice which I am forced to make in the UK higher education system, to be dovetailed into a pigeonhole. This was not my experience in India and I am sure even outside of the UK. As Sen (2006: 19) suggests, 'identities are robustly plural and that the importance of one identity need not obliterate the importance of others'. As Sen (2006) and Craib (1998) argue, in other words there is no singular identity, which can be ascribed to any one of us. Thus, one may be a housewife, a mother, a daughter, a wife, and a senior manager in a firm or a historical geographer, or a development economist or a philosopher.

Historically, individual identities were always subsumed under the stable moorings of tradition/conventions and were believed to be divinely ordained. This was true of the British monarchy, as of the Japanese or Indian kings in the early 19th and 20th centuries. The transformations of modernity ushered in by Renaissance of the 16th century and of Enlightenment in the 18th century clearly helped the individual identity to break free from the shackles of the high church and to a great extent, of the state. For now, the individual identity came to occupy the position of primacy and became the touchstone for all forms of scientific progress and transformations in the human society. As Hall states, 'rather than see identity as a finished project, we should speak of identification in process, always being formed' (Hall and Du Gay 1997: 122). Globalization has once again de-centred this individual identity fragmenting it further as a postmodern subject.

GLOBALIZATION AND IDENTITY

The radical shifts in transnational diasporic migration in the postcolonial world of Chinese, Indians, or of members of the Northern hemisphere suggest that globalization has transformed the way we relate to and interact with each other. Identities are about the strategic use of resources, such as language (be it English, French, or even Dutch), history, and culture, in order to seek access to the new world. It is very rare that we find instances of someone seeking to learn Hindi or Chinese to emigrate to India or China particularly when the potential migrant is from the developed world. In fact, we have come to accept universally that English is the global lingua franca, much to the chagrin of the French. The analysis of transnational migration is always about flows from the developing world. As a result, the main outcome of these types of flows is that it raises questions of not just who they are and where they come from, rather it is also about where they are going to and what they represent as a collective, not simply as an individual. Thus, the construction of an identity takes place before they are actually represented in any given space. As Laclau (1990: 3) points out, construction and the subsequent representation of a given identity is an 'act of power' made either out of consensus or decreed as given.

In post 9/11, George W. Bush can decree that a given identity and all individuals associated with it are the *axis of evil*. Of course, this form of rhetoric does not help one to distinguish a brown skinned Indian from a brown skinned Pakistani or a Bangladeshi or a fair skinned Sikh with a customary turban from a Taliban. In many instances, mistaken identity has led to disastrous consequences in USA and UK. I would prefer to be a British Indian than the customary British Asian in order to sit apart from those adhering to a particular faith or code of conduct, or even dress. The conflict we see today is between stable identities trying to come to terms with the constantly changing and fragmented identities in a global world. Modern identities while emphasizing uniqueness are no longer unified or wholesome. They come in various shapes and sizes, choreographed to represent specific politics of culture. In this sense, all identities are socially, culturally, and historically constructed. Within the Bourdieu inspired *habitus*, we share common conventions, values, ethics, and practices, which help reinforce our identity and indeed our common citizenship. As Hall and Du Gay state, it is only in the process of engaging with or giving legitimacy, that is, recognition or non-recognition, which helps bring to the fore our sense of identity.

IDENTITY FORMATION AND ITS LINK TO CITIZENSHIP

In making an analytical distinction between identity and citizenship, it is easy to state that identity can be applied to both sentient and insentient beings. Thus, we can label nation-state with an identity, just as we can do for a person or even the various regions of the world. A bar code helps to distinguish the identity of a product in a supermarket, much as it would be true for a credit card. Indeed cats, dogs, and indeed all mammals are said to have a personality or an identity unique to their genes. These identities are complex in nature and content. However, overtime slippages in these identity formations have come to the fore when there is a perceived threat to identity. The current debate of the *veil* or *hijab* in Belgium and in the UK relates to this quandary over identity.

Citizenship as a concept suggests universal entity, which is not tied down to any particular form of identity. As Donald (1996: 175) notes, 'it is identity-less'. The state guarantees the perception of citizenship as enshrined in our constitution and laws of the land. Therefore, national identity gives rise to a common ground for citizenship. A sense of belonging to the nation helps develop what Anderson has called the 'imagined community'. One identifies with being British or American or Indian based on one's allegiance to the flag, national anthem, and cultural symbols of territorial solidarity. However, citizenship and rights of a citizen can easily be extended beyond the boundaries of the nation-state. The fluidity of landscapes, in particular 'urbanscapes' in both the developing and the developed world allows the formation of such citizenship. Globalization, as Graham and Marvin (2003) suggest, and its attendant transformation of Information Technology (IT) infrastructure have also led to greater splintering of identities and thereby that of common citizenship. It has also aided the closing of the gap across regions of the world in helping form a common and more urgent form of identity.

Global citizenship, therefore, implies active engagement of concerned citizens and goes beyond the narrow confines of identity. A potential global citizenship transcends nation-state (Taylor and Spencer 2004: 56). In many ways, deliberate exclusion of individuals from the polity and society leads to a fracture in the common identity of a citizen. Inclusiveness has always been extremely critical in bridging the fault lines in identity formation and its related representations. This naturally links to Kant's notion of civil society and of cosmopolitanism. To be able to think of oneself as an individual and at the same time having the capacity to respect others and have empathy for the distant strangers is critical in the formation and establishment of world citizens. As Habermas (1971) notes, only when the last human being is free and responsible can we be free too. Therefore, we have a stake in democracy for all to be free, thereby recognizing the freedom of others too. Such a citizenship, which calls for participation has a broader remit than mere political participation within the boundaries of nation-state (Van Steenbergen 1994: 2). It goes beyond the notion of civil and political rights. Despite the erosion of welfare state over time, we see what Falk (1994: 127–40) calls a 'rise of global citizenship', Turner calls 'cultural citizenship' (1994: 153–68), or what Beck names 'technological citizenship', Weeks 'sexual citizenship', and Clarke 'deep citizenship' (Taylor and Spencer 2004: 57).

What are the issues which help bind people together? It may be the appeal for digging deep into our pockets to support the *red nose* charity for Africa or it may be a collection for the victims of tsunami. What forms the basis for these associations to emerge? Is it faith, love, compassion or a feel good factor or even a determination to be a step ahead of the Jones'? Invariably it is a common tragedy, which galvanizes us to act. What space will these associations inhabit? It can relate to any region of the world, be it the Amazon forests, the G8 Summit, or even the dying victims of HIV in Africa. What emotions and concepts will it appeal to? It may appeal to our sensibility, our emotions of a common humanity, our empathy for those who do not necessarily have the same comforts as us. This goes beyond mere religion, though religious organization has been active since time immemorial in supporting endeavours during famines and earthquakes (India, Africa, or China) or during more recent months in Indonesia and remote parts of Pakistan. Thus, the perceived conflict between identity and citizenship can be reconciled with an emphasis on common humanity.

CITIZENSHIP AND IDENTITY

Citizenship therefore involves multiple and overlapping perspectives, which cuts across religion, politics, ethnicity, identity, and indeed boundaries and territories. Here the rights of a global citizen, of the individual and of the representative group, both of ethnic and religious affiliations can be reconciled if based on a common touchstone of social purpose for a common humanity. For once citizenship is underscored by the fact that we have to take the rights of groups seriously. Both Isin and Wood

(1999: ix) refer to the 'right to have rights…' as opposed to the passive right of status, which involves a re-conceptualization of the meaning of identity and citizenship and indeed the means and the ways by which we allocate and recognize the rights of a citizen. Thus, the concept of citizenship gains a wider berth with the recognition of a progressively greater inclusion of various embedded rights in every democratic institution in the world. This also means giving rights to women, gays, and the largely dispossessed citizens of the world, either due to the infringement of their political and cultural rights, for example, of Tibetans or Kurds or due to natural disasters being rendered homeless and destitute, for example, victims of earthquakes, tsunamis, flash floods, and of poverty in Africa and South Asia. Today, we have to recognize the victims of global warming, that is, victims of hurricane Katrina in New Orleans or those battered by endless cycle of cyclones in Bangladesh.

Indeed cultural politics and politics of identity can provide little respite and common nostrum for all the injustices, inequality, and oppression facing the world at large. Perhaps a life philosophy, which engenders respect and empathy for the global citizens, will help moralize the actions of self and the others. Citizenship and identity are indeed two sides of the same coin. 'The conflict between citizenship and identity arises from a specific conception of each where citizenship is seen as universal and identity as particular' (Isin and Wood 1999: 2–3). Citizenship entails 'loyalty, duties, and rights, not always in relation to another human being, but in relation to an abstract concept, the state' (Heater 1990: 2). As long as citizenship is construed on a common pledge, a common platform of ideals and goals for the happiness of oneself and for the distant others, as much as for one's immediate family, will we be able to transcend the conflict between citizenship and identity. Citizenship therefore transcends conflicts of identity based on a moral imperative of empathy, compassion, and global justice for the rights of others. The binding glue here is that rights are as important as duties and global responsibilities. Therefore, actively participating as global citizens is more important than flagging it as a status symbol.

According to Weber (1927), there is a general belief that citizenship as a concept originated in the West and that civilizations of China, India, and Middle East lacked any notion of citizenship. This is a highly ethnocentric, biased viewpoint because each of these ancient civilizations had their own understanding of citizenship. The enshrinement of rights and duties of a citizen in these societies was politically and communally determined.

Throughout recent history, we have evidenced the scaling down of civil and political liberties and rights in human societies. The main casualty in all of these, argues Turner, has been the notion of citizenship, which has always remained contested as a concept. Debates on citizenship have now been polarized along two axes, one, which asserted that individual, is sovereign with inalienable rights and freedom, and the other that political association created the rights of the individual. Therefore, the individual was seen to be subservient to the state. Today, rapid integration of global economic space, what Friedman calls *The World is Flat*, has resulted in a blurring of the boundaries of modern citizenship debate. Increasingly ideas of citizenship as a status and as political entity, embodied within the sovereign individual are being contested. There are increasing attempts to undermine the viability of citizenship by subscribing and confusing it to the narrow sectarian interests of individual rights and associated liberties. The way forward from this imbroglio is that of 'civic republicanism' (Beiner 1995: 8) which goes beyond quibbles around issues of liberalism and communitarianism.

CIVIC REPUBLICANISM

Civic republicanism suggests that citizenship can be effective only if there is a common vision and purpose for action. This action has to be for a common good while pursuing one's individual agenda. The coupling of altruism with individuality becomes the key factor for change. In this respect we could consider the blueprint adopted by Ikeda in *A New Era of the People: Forging a Global Network of Robust Individuals* (2006) and *Humanity and The New Millennium: From Chaos to Cosmos* (1998) as examples that reinforces this dynamic form of civic republicanism. The moral scope for this civic republicanism is immense and provides hope for the millions who attempt to contribute to the creation of value and ethics in their given society and community, based on their sense of purpose and absolute happiness. This helps transcend differences of gender, age, ethnicity, religion, and indeed nationalities. Citizenship as a concept has to be more than a simple political agenda. It has to be cultural and educational, which reinforces rights and justice in the global world.

Ikeda's philosophy attempts to bring to a closure the debates on identity and citizenship by focusing on democratic equivalence among individuals and groups without necessarily eliminating differences among individuals (Mouffe 1995: 38). This stresses not the indifference of self-proclaimed individualists, which has caused great deal of problems for the runaway liberalism of the west. In fact, Mouffe suggests that the priority of community in civic republicanism is also problematic in that it does not acknowledge the novelty of modern democracy with its principles of pluralism, individual liberty, and the separation of church and the state. No doubt that this is a strong reaction against western concepts of liberalism, and translating these very ideas of 'civic republicanism' into reality and practice has to be rooted in society and community.

Global citizenship is not incompatible with individual liberty if there is a common purpose and so long as the pursuit of the goal of world peace is based on the dignity of life and common interest of humanity. The advantage from such a philosophy of global citizenship in praxis is that this allows fostering a universal bond among relative strangers and whose primary allegiance to their ethnic, political or indeed religious affirmation need not be seen as conflicting with their membership in civil association. Here the citizen is neither one who is a passive bearer of rights (as in liberalism) nor someone who accepts submission to the rules prescribed by the political association (as in civic republicanism). This reinforces recognition of multiple subject positions in a society, for example, demanding minority rights be it gay or green/ecological rights, as critical for fostering radical global citizenship for effective political and civic identity, citizenship, and leadership.

Following Mouffe (1992a, 1992b, 1995) and unlike Isin and Wood (1999), rather than conflating identity and citizenship, the starting point is one of distinctiveness of identity before accepting the membership in a global community. Citizenship can be understood as a more radical social, cultural global identity and not necessarily a political one. Race, ethnicity, religion, or racial identity can be made subservient to the global identity.[1] Ikeda's notion of citizenship converges with Mouffe's perception that race, religion, and identity can be subsumed under a global identity without making a special case.

Global collectivism is based on a common purpose of working for the happiness of self and that of others. Ikeda's global citizenship has provided a collective basis to mediate through conflicting institutional interests and polity, such as opening up humanity-based dialogues with China, Korea, Soviet Russia, and erstwhile eastern Europe from late 1960s and 1970s.

Indeed today the concept of a common global purpose is unfortunately missing while focusing on the highly politicized concept of multiculturalism, political correctness, and inclusiveness, prevalent in the UK and the West. Value-based philosophy espoused by Ikeda relates to the sovereignty of an individual and the primacy of individual happiness. Thus, debates of citizenship inevitably spill over questions of identity. The tension is between those who purport that there are no durable group attributes or those who believe in the need to establish essential attributes of groups. The point we need to remember is that all identities are socially constructed. It is also recognizing that stable identities are giving way to fragmented ones and that these new identities are part and parcel of the process of globalization. Carter identifies three models of citizenship: *(a)* which seeks to maximize individual freedom and choice; *(b)* which emphasizes moral and political responsibility towards a shared society; and *(c)* which focuses on the individual obligations as well as the rights and the value of political activism. All three can be considered as an extended version of global citizenship. I am interested in the third element because it is compatible with a focus on global civil society and cosmopolitan values, which reinforces human rights, global justice, and peace. All of these are attainable only if we shun oppression, cruelty, and violence. Adherence to international law, to the principles and charters enshrined in the United Nations and our tolerance to religious and cultural diversity will allow space for this moral citizenship to take root in this society.

MORAL CITIZENSHIP

Martha Nussbaum, world-renowned moral philosopher, has been one of the key supporters of the concept of 'world citizenship' built on the notion of Kant's *moral cosmopolitanism*. Based on a cosmopolitan approach to education, she encourages us to think about our obligations of respecting distant strangers, as also our own citizens who appear culturally different. She argues for a moral community, which ensures empathy for the common humanity rather than fulfilling mere political agendas. This moral community is 'one made up of humanity of human beings'. These ideas find an echo in Linklater (1996: 77–103) and Ikeda's writings, urging us to focus on our ethical obligations to the globalized world. Here compassion is an integral part of the rights and responsibilities as a global citizen. Thus, moral citizenship and cosmopolitanism reaffirms the rights of individual citizens as much as of the general humanity. How to deal with distant neighbours and strangers? A fully developed morality can embrace universal human issues of solidarity and in this sense, morality is a universal concept (Walzer 1996: 105). Our commitment with our neighbours is as important as it is with the distant strangers. Therefore, fostering of a global citizenship enables a sense of duty towards future generations. Growing cosmopolitan consciousness engages with the issue of rights and justice at a global level and not confined to a handful few. Such cosmopolitan aspirations have been expressed and practiced in the non-Western world for many generations and have now moved outside the boundaries of Japan, India, and China. Ikeda, along with Nussbaum, believes that global citizenship and indeed the movement for peace, culture, and education can be fostered through the medium of education. Individuals working in conjunction with various non-governmental organizations and their initiatives help to reaffirm not only their identity as an individual, but also bring forth their sense of global consciousness and moral responsibilities. This helps to reiterate commitment at both the global, local, and community levels.

GLOBAL CITIZENSHIP

Ikeda constantly reiterates a perspective of global citizenship in all his writings and speeches that sovereignty resides with the people and not nations alone. In a sense, humanistic education calls for the establishment of solidarity of altruism and the widening of a network of truly global citizens, as I have shown elsewhere. Humanistic solidarity therefore implies friendship based on a spirit of equality and respect for each other's customs and traditions. This concept of global citizenship has its roots in the writings of Tsunesaburo Makiguchi, who died as a defender of his conscience and faith during the war. He stressed the importance of human rights and morality as well as peace and coexistence. Global citizens in a sense are people capable of value creation on a global scale. The essential elements of a global citizen as enumerated by Ikeda relate to developing wisdom, perceiving the interconnectedness of all life and living beings. This calls for courage not to fear or deny differences, but to respect and strive to understand people of different cultures and to grow from interactions with them.

Therefore the all-encompassing inter-relatedness is the crux of global citizenship and moral cosmopolitanism and reinforces Buddhist ideals of compassion and global justice. The experimentation with the internationally recognized Soka (or value-based) educational system, represented in primary, secondary, and tertiary education in Japan,

Malaysia, Hong Kong, Singapore, and the United States, helps in laying the conceptual and ethical foundation for these qualities. It is a vital project in which all are participants and all are accountable for the outcome. Humanistic, value-based education, therefore, provides a guide to such an exchange and the formation of global citizenship. Ikeda calls for 'the development of a robust character that can confront the changes in our society without becoming ensnared in greed and selfishness. This kind of robust individuals is rooted in society, in relationship with others and in shared and mutual concerns' (Ikeda 2006: 3). Nussbaum (1996) states that only 'through cosmopolitan education, we learn more about ourselves', thereby reiterating what Ikeda states that education is a noble project to establish a fundamental human attitude of being a world citizen.

ACKNOWLEDGEMENTS

To Anastasia and Taisha for helping me identify and adapt the text to the theme of the book. Thanks to Helen Sharkey and Colin Bird for being around during the 'monsoons of Northern Ireland' and helping me bounce off ideas during the drafting of this paper and to my students, David Zou and Mathew Kenny for assisting me with key references and discussing the key ideas of 'identity and cosmopolitanism'.

NOTE

1. An example of the application of Ikeda's ideas can be found in the Soka Gakkai International (SGI), which, following the footsteps of Daisaku Ikeda, reinforces this dynamic form of civic republicanism in over 190 countries. In India, SGI has members from most of the dominant religious groups be it Hindus, who religiously attend to fasting every Tuesday, yet manage to engage with their Buddhist practice on a daily basis and at the same time involve themselves in the movement for peace, culture, and education.

BIBLIOGRAPHY

Anderson, B. 1991. *Imagined Communities*. London: Verso.
Bauman, Z. 1996. 'From Pilgrim to Tourist-or a Short History of Identity', in S. Hall and P. Du Gay (eds), *Questions of Cultural Identity*, pp 18–36. London: Sage Publications.
Beck, U. 1996. 'World Risk Society', *Theory, Culture & Society*, 13(4): 1–32.
Beiner, R. 1995. 'Why Citizenship Constitutes a Theoretical Problem in the Last Decade of the Twentieth Century', in R. Beiner (ed.), *Theorising Citizenship*, pp. 1–27. Albany: State University of New York.

Benhabib, S. 1992. *Situating the Self: Gender, Community, and Postmodernism in Contemporary Ethics*. New York: Routledge.
Bourdieu, P. 1990. *In Other Words, Essays Towards a Reflective Sociology*. Cambridge: Polity Press.
Carter, A. 2001. *The Political Theory of Global Citizenship*. London: Routledge.
Clarke, B. 1996. *Deep Citizenship*. London: Pluto.
Craib, I. 1998. *Experiencing Identity*. Boston: London.
Davis, J.E. 2000. *Identity and Social Change*. New Brunswick: Transaction Publishers.
Donald, J. 1996. 'The Citizen and the Man About Town', in S. Hall and P. Du Gay (eds), *Questions of Cultural Identity*, pp.170–90. London: Sage Publications.
Falk, R. 1994. 'The Making of Global Citizenship', in B. van Steenbergen (ed.), *The Condition of Citizenship*, pp. 127–40. London: Sage Publications.
Friedman, Thomas. 2005. *The World is Flat: A Brief History of the Globalized World in the Twenty-first Century*. London: Allen Lane.
Graham, S. and S. Marvin. 2003. *Splintering Urbanism: Networked Infrastructures, Technological Mobilities and the Urban Condition*. London: Routledge.
Habermas, J. 1971. *Theory and Practice*. London: Heinemann.
———. 1994. 'Citizenship and National Identity', in B. van Steenbergen (ed.), *The Condition of Citizenship*, pp. 20–35. London: Sage Publications.
Hall, S. and P. Du Gay. 1997. *Questions of Cultural Identity*. London: Sage Publications.
Hanagan, M. 1997. 'Recasting Citizenship: Introduction', *Theory and Society*, 26(4): 397–402.
Heater, D. 1990. *Citizenship: The Civic Ideal in World History, Politics and Education*. London: Longman Group.
Hurst, J. 2000. 'A Buddhist Reformation in the Twentieth Century: Causes and Implications of the Conflict between the Soka Gakkai and the Nichiren Shoshu Priesthood', in D.W. Machacek and B. R. Wilson (eds), *Global Citizens: The Soka Gakkai Buddhist Movement in the World*, pp. 67–96. Oxford: Oxford UP.
Ikeda, Daisaku and Mikhail Gorbachev. 2005. *Moral Lessons of the Twentieth Century*. London: I. B. Tauris.
Ikeda, Daisaku. 1992. SGI News Letter, No.117: 4.
———. 1996a. SGI News Letter, No.159: 161–164.
———. 1996b. SGI News Letter, No.159: 65–66.
———. 1998. *Humanity and the New Millennium: From Chaos to Cosmos*. Tokyo: SGI publications.
———. 2006. *A New Era of the People: Forging a Global Network of Robust Individuals*. Japan: SGI publications.
Ikeda, Daisaku and Arnold Toynbee. 1989. *Choose Life*. Oxford: Oxford UP.
Ikeda, Daisaku and Majid Tehranian. 2002. *Global Civilization. A Buddhist-Islamic Dialogue*. London: British Academic Press.
Isin, E.F. and P.K. Wood. 1999. *Citizenship and Identity*. London: Sage Publications.
Kumar, M.S. 1996. 'Civil Society and the State: A Case for Religious Versus Secular Rights in Contemporary Japan', *Bulletin of the Institute of Oriental Studies*, (12): 135–49.
———. 1998. 'An Approach Towards World Citizenship in the Context of Soka Educational Perspective', *Bulletin of the Institute of Oriental Philosophy*, (14): 100–14.
Kymlicka, W. 1995. *Multicultural Citizenship*. Oxford: Oxford UP.

Laclau, E. 1990. *New Reflections on the Revolution of Our Time*. London: Verso.
Linklater, A. 1996. 'Citizenship and Sovereignty in the Post-Westphalian State', *European Journal of International Relations*, 2(1): 77–103.
Machacek, D.W. and B.R. Wilson. 2000. *Global Citizens: The Soka Gakkai Buddhist Movement in the World*. Oxford: Oxford UP.
Marshall, T. H. 1977. *Class, Citizenship and Social Development*. Chicago: University of Chicago Press.
Mouffe, Chantal. 1992a. *Dimensions of Radical Democracy: Pluralism, Citizenship, Community*. London: Verso.
———. 1992b. 'Democratic Citizenship and the Political Community', in Chantal Mouffe (ed.), *Dimensions of Radical Democracy: Pluralism, Citizenship, Community*, pp. 60–73. London: Verso.
———. 1995. 'Democratic Politics and the Question of Identity', in J. Rajchman (ed.), *The Identity in Question*. New York: Routledge.
Muller, F. Max. 1884. *The Saddharmapundarika: The Sacred Books of the East*, H.Kern (trans.), 21(1989). India: Motilal Banarasidass.
Nussbaum, Martha, C. 1996. 'Patriotism and Cosmopolitanism', in M.C. Nussbaum (eds), *For Love of Country: Debating the Limits of Patriotism*. Boston: Beacon Press.
Oakeshott, M. 1975. *On Human Conduct*. Oxford: Oxford University Press.
Sandel, M. J. 1982 [1998]. *Liberalism and the Limits of Justice*. 2nd edition. Cambridge: Cambridge UP.
Seager, R.H. 2006. *Encountering the Dharma: Daisaku Ikeda, Soka Gakkai, and the Globalisation of Buddhist Humanism*. Berkeley: University of California.
Sen, Amartya. 2006. *Identity and Violence: The Illusions of Destiny*. London: Allen Lane.
Taylor, G. and S. Spencer. 2004. *Social Identities: Multidisciplinary Approaches*. London: Routledge.
Turner, B.S. 1993. 'Contemporary Problems in the Theory of Citizenship', in B.S. Turner (ed.), *Citizenship and Social Theory*, pp. 1–18. London: Sage Publications.
———. 1994. 'Postmodern Culture/ Modern Citizens', in B. van Steenbergen (ed.), *The Condition of Citizenship*, pp. 153–68. London: Sage Publications.
Turner, B.S. (ed.) 1993. *Citizenship and Social Theory*. London: Sage Publications.
van Steenbergen, B. 1994. *The Condition of Citizenship*. London: Sage Publications.
Walzer, M. 1996. 'Spheres of Affection', in M.C. Nussbaum and J. Cohen (eds), *For Love of Country: Debating the Limits of Patriotism*, pp. 125–27. Boston: Beacon Press.
Watson, B. 1992. *The Lotus Sutra*. New York: Columbia University Press.
Weber, Max. 1927. 'Citizenship', *General Economic History*. London: George Allen & Unwin.
Weeks, J. 1998. 'The Sexual Citizen', *Theory, Culture & Society*, 15(3/4): 35–52.

13
Islam and Liberal Peace

Farid Mirbagheri

The question of liberal peace and Islam requires a clear definition of three principal terms: Islam, liberalism, and liberal peace. For, in spite of much writing on them, there remains some confusion, at least in the Islamic world, as to what we really mean by liberalism and liberal peace and in the West as to what in fact constitutes Islam. The media representation of these precepts has somewhat produced a distorted version of each in the other camp to the extent that misunderstanding may have replaced no-understanding. The aim of this chapter is not to focus exclusively on these definitions, but to attempt to provide a brief but unambiguous narrative of these discourses which would allow them to be explored in relation to one another. The emphasis on these definitions is more than just an academic exercise, for our assessment and conclusions will be largely based on our understanding of these terms. Therefore, our first task is to attend to the question of definitions. The first term requiring clarification, however, is 'peace' itself.

WHAT IS PEACE?

To many the term peace, like other concepts, is understood through its antonym, war—the absence of which clearly indicates the presence of peace. More liberal thinkers, however, such as Kant, tend to make a distinction between mere suspension of hostilities and peace, which in their view is an end to hostilities (Kant 1983: 107). Both these camps consider war as 'state of nature' and view peace as a necessary constituent of civil life (Hobbes 1955: 80–84; Kant 1983: 111). There is clearly a sort of strong association between peace and security as the most basic human security of all, which is survival, is threatened by the absence of peace; that is, war. But note should be taken that they are not synonymous. The security of the world in 1939, for instance, required engaging in war with Germany. Therefore, peace and war are generally viewed as defence and military terms. It is normally military prowess, albeit for political ends, that breaches peace and establishes the condition of war. However, a deeper definition of peace requires us to look beyond military conditions that define these two concepts. This would mean peace embedded in the very nature of human affairs, past the silence of the guns.

This perspective views peace as the main constituent of human nature and the condition sought by mankind at all times even in times of war. Wars are attempts by some to create a different peace but no peace is sought to arrive at war. As enunciated by St Augustine, peace is 'tranquility of order', order being 'the disposition of equal and unequal things in such a way as to give to each its proper place'.[1] So, although war can be explained in terms of peace, the reverse is not the case. In Islamic tradition also, the precept of peace goes beyond the absence of physical violence. One of the terms meaning peace and peacemaking in Arabic, *solh*, which is used in the Quran, is also the root of the word *islah* denoting development and improvement. Verse 9 of Sura 49 is an instance, where this term is used to refer to peacemaking. *Moslih*, the subject noun of *solh*, means a person who engages in the act of peacemaking and development. In fact, Verse 11 of Sura 2 deems *moslihoon* (the plural of *moslih*) as antonym to wrongdoers and corruptors—*And when they are told not to commit wrongdoing and corruption on earth, they respond, 'but we are only moslihoon (peacemakers)'.* The direct and unambiguous conclusion from this Verse in the Quranic discourse is that peace stands opposed to corruption and wrongdoing. Peacemakers are agents of good and those who breach it are elements of corruption and sin. In short, peaceful development of humanity is in line with Islamic discourse on the ontology of mankind. Another Verse (11: 117) postulates—*And your Lord would never destroy towns wrongfully while [as if] their people were moslihoon (peacemakers).* Another compelling support for peace can be seen in Verse 28, Sura 70—For their Lord's displeasure is the opposite of peace and tranquility. It is therefore observed that peace and peacemaking are seen in Islamic tradition as part and parcel of human development. In other words, peace and peacemaking are seen as Godly acts, worthy of praise and reward.

In this connection the story of creation, and the deception of Adam and Eve by Satan is significant. Narrating the story of eating the forbidden fruit the Quran states:

> *Then did Satan make them slip from the (garden) and get them out of the state (of felicity) in which they had been. We said: 'Get ye down, all (ye people) with enmity between yourselves. On earth shall be your dwelling and means of livelihood—for a time.'*

Enmity therefore is a condition to be associated with earthly living and temporal affairs. It is not present in paradise; for otherwise, God would not have told Adam and Eve about enmity on earth. Enmity takes root within and is the cause of conflict among humans without; 'wars start in the minds of men', reads the United Nations Educational, Scientific and Cultural Organization (UNESCO) Charter. Therefore, the main ingredient and instigator of much of armed conflict in history, enmity, and hatred, befell mankind as a result of having succumbed to satanic temptation and deception. This can be inferred from the story of creation, but it is also stated directly in the Quran—*Satan's plan is (but) to excite enmity and hatred between you*...reads Verse 91 of Sura 5 in the Quran. There is also the very first example of enmity and violence in human relations according to the Quran (shared by the Old and the New Testament) on Adam and Eve's two sons Cane and Able, where Cane murders Able. The inference is clear: enmity, murder, and war (large-scale and organized killing) are satanic; they have no place in paradise, but are an earthly condition of life. By extension, peace and peacemaking must be Godly and Divine. The original dwelling of mankind, paradise, appears to have been immune to the condition of enmity and war.

The commonality with Kantian as well as the Hobbesian perspective in considering enmity and war as a 'state of nature' (outside of the original dwelling), is all too clear. However, there is a striking difference in man's approach to the 'state of nature'. Whilst both Hobbes (1955) and Kant (1983) believe that peace is a better way of life and thus prescribe an artificial state of peace to promote human security, progress, and stability as a rational discourse.[2] In Islam, peace is advocated as a divine quality to be pursued in order to achieve the state of felicity that we were in paradise, our former dwelling. It is not only a human attempt to regulate human affairs in an orderly fashion in order to escape the scourge of war, but also seeking transcendental guidance on how to eradicate the effects of the original sin by rejecting the satanic condition of violence and returning to the original and divinely devised condition of peace.

Another difference here from the current liberal, secular understanding of peace is that peace is not treated in isolation, unattached to other precepts. It is very much associated with the nature of mankind and is based on justice. Verse 9 of Sura 49 earlier referred to states—*...make peace between them based on justice and equity...God loveth just doers.* Justice, as outlined in the Quran, refers to balance and is the foundation upon which creation stands. Verses 7 to 9 of Surah 55 may clearly refer to this point—*And the Firmament has He raised high and He has set up the balance (of justice). In order that ye may not transgress (due) balance. So establish weight with justice and fall not short in balance.* Ali, the son-in-law and the cousin of the Prophet, the fourth Caliph after the Prophet and the first Imam of Shi'as, has an incisive definition of justice. He considers justice to be the placement of everything in its proper order. The issue of proportionality and relativeness is thus an indispensable part of justice (Motahhari 1982: 59–67). Peace based on justice, therefore, would mean a balanced, fair, and tranquil state of affairs, where all concerned would enjoy their due rights and protection.

In this regard, the old English School and the Realist dictum that order should precede justice can be critiqued. It is based on the premise that justice cannot be sought or implemented in a state of chaos (Bull 1977: 86). Any order is thus preferable to chaos as it is the former that can possibly provide us with an opportunity to seek justice.[3] However, based on the Islamic definition of justice given above, a wrong order itself constitutes injustice. Looking for justice within an unjust framework then turns into an impossible task. For any establishment of justice would require, in the first place, deconstruction of the unjust framework and replacing it with a just one. The argument therefore of order preceding justice appears to be a fallacy, at best derived from a shallow understanding of the two concepts and at worst attempting to justify 'status quo' in international relations.

WHAT IS ISLAM?

It is particularly difficult to talk of Islam when so much has been written and said about it. To unlearn much of what has been broadcasted by the media and reported by the press internationally about Islam and replace it with a more reflective version is no easy task.

Islam, the last of Abrahamic traditions, was born in the city of Mecca and founded by Mohammad, its messenger. In a short period of time, it captured the whole of Arabia, toppled the Persian, and penetrated the Roman empires. It grew in political success in a manner far beyond the imagination of the bedouin Arabs and past the projections of global rulers at the time. It is the only Abrahamic tradition where the messenger actually established and governed a society; hence, the more than familiar claim of contemporary radical Islamists that Islam is in fact political.[4]

The rules of Islam known as *shari'a* were compiled nearly two hundred years after the death of the Prophet. The Quran itself was put together and given a final version during the rule of the third caliph, Othman (Watt 1997: 44). The Quran and the Sayings of the Prophet, *hadith*, are the basis upon which *shari'a* is devised. There is, however, a simmering dispute between various sects in Islam as to the admissibility of rationality and the requirements of the modern age influencing *shari'a*. While some subscribe to the adaptability of *shari'a* to modern age without compromising its essence, others believe in the comprehensiveness of *shari'a* as it stands and see no need for adaptability. The important point, however, is that *shari'a* nowadays claims supremacy over all other aspects of religion, including the spirit of Islam, a point, which is now challenged by many liberal Islamic thinkers.[5]

How one views Islam determines how one approaches the question of peace in Islamic discourse. For the purpose of this paper, we can have two main categories on Islamic thinking: epistemic and jurisprudential. The two stand opposed to each other. Whereas the first treats Islamic knowledge like any other branch of human knowledge, the second appears to proffer a historical nature to Islamic teachings. For epistemic Islam, change and exchange, views and reviews, vision and revision, are all part and parcel of the advancement of mankind and no branches of human knowledge can stand independent of all else and claim saturation and completion. Religious knowledge is no exception. It can only advance through a dialogue with reason and other branches of human knowledge continually. That is the epistemic nature of all knowledge to humanity. To jurisprudentialists, however, that is heresy. To them, the word of God does not require perfection; it is already perfect. All we need is proper implementation of Divine Directives as revealed in the Quran and in the deeds and words of the Prophet. Occasionally, some sects within Islam admit that they have to introduce adjustments or new rules clarifying the position of Muslims with regard to their religious duties. But nothing can be said or advised to suggest adaptability or reinterpretation of religious rules and regulations.

The subtle point, which epistemic Islam emphasizes, is that religion and religious understanding are two separate categories.[6] Even though God's words are perfect and immune from mutation or historicity, understanding His Words, which is an entirely human affair, is subject to change and reinterpretation. Unless we claim complete, perfect, and absolute understanding of revelation—an act which is in itself heretic for it elevates mankind to the status of the Divine—we are bound by changes in time and place, and impressed by historical developments; all of which naturally affect our ability to understand and interpret. Just as physics now has a different explanation for and perspective of the material world from a thousand years ago, so should religious sciences attempt to continually critique themselves for better and more complete understanding of religion. All aspects of religious learning, theology, jurisprudence, philosophy, and so on, are subject to this epistemic rule. Classification of religious sciences as historical renders them irrelevant and carries the risk of imprisoning the Absolute Word of Perfect God in the relative interpretation of an imperfect man.

Whereas jurisprudential Islam is preoccupied with do's and don'ts and addresses the question of human duties more than human rights, the epistemic Islam is more concerned with the spirit of Islam and interacts with its environment, accepts the historicity of man and that of his interpretation of religion; epistemic Islam does address the issue of human rights and does not consider the subject taboo. The question of war and peace can also be seen from these two different perspectives in Islam. The jurisprudential system by ideologizing religion has managed to set aside debate on these important concepts, moving them into the exclusive domain of the clerical hierarchy. It introduces concepts, such as Islamic peace, Islamic justice, and Islamic *jihad*, all of which are decided by religious leaders and handed down to followers.

The term *jihad* has been propounded in Muslim societies and translated to non-Muslims, as war. The actual meaning of *jihad* is to struggle. Even though it has been used in places in the Quran to refer to armed struggle, its main point of reference is the internal struggle to triumph over 'state of nature' within all of us. Armed struggle has been deemed by the Prophet as the lesser *jihad* and the inner battle with 'state of nature' within us is regarded as the greater *jihad*.[7] This internal 'state of nature' can also be the accumulation of endless desires within, besieging man, as outlined by Plato, and man's tireless efforts to fulfill them, as propounded by Hobbes. Greater *jihad* could therefore be viewed in the same light as the self-constraint prescribed by Plato (McClelland 1996: 24). When the Quran does talk of war the word it uses is not *jihad*; usually it is either *harb* or *ghetal*. The inference is quite clear; *jihad* as armed struggle is only used when self-defence has been the focus as none of the Verses containing the word *jihad* or its derivatives directly link it with war or violence except in defensive terms. The internal battle against self, the main focus of *jihad*, however, is what gives this term its significance. The following prayer by a prominent Muslim thinker highlights the nature of greater *jihad*— *O Lord: Kill selfishness so much in me or distance it so far from me that I would not feel or see the selfishness of others, and would not suffer from it* (Shar'ati n.d: 99).

In the religiopolitical view of jurisprudential Islam, however, *jihad* is an implicit order to the faithful that you must either kill the enemies of Islam or get killed by them/or both. And in both cases the enemies are to be defined and decided by the radical clerical leaders and not by the people. It is very much an ideologed version of Islam, rigidified and frozen in time and place and in many instances out of context and oblivious to overall commands of Islam to protect lives, rights, and properties of the innocent (non-combatants).[8]

The debate between these two groups within Islam may be likened to the kind of debate that started within Christianity in Europe a few centuries ago that led to the Reformation. Although this paper does not wish to engage in this debate or its outcome, it will consider the two approaches on the question of liberal peace.

LIBERAL PEACE

The main thrust of liberal peace theory has to do with the link it establishes between the nature and the style of governance on the one hand and inter-state peace on the other. In this discourse, the advance of societies into a liberal phase would lessen the chance of armed conflict between them. Liberalism here, by and large, is meant to indicate the presence of a representative government. Although there are clear differences between the Kantian version of liberalism in the world and today's liberal government (Kant, for instance, did not include free market as a criterion for liberalism), it is normally assumed that accountability of democratically elected rulers to their electoral masters, free market, juridical rights of citizens, and the presence of externally sovereign entities form the core of a liberal administration (Doyle 1983: 212).

Three questions on the liberal peace project require attention if we are to look into peace in an epistemic way. Addressing these questions would allow us a deeper insight into some of the most important aspects of liberal peace problematique and assess it in view of Islamic discourse. They are:

1. Is liberal peace holistic or is it be sought and achieved in a fragmented way?
2. Is liberal peace a unifying or a divisive experience?
3. Is liberal peace an exclusive or inclusive precept?

A fragmented peace, as addressed by the first question, seeks peace only in separate fields, detached from one another. A holistic peace, however, focuses on a peace that permeates all levels of individual, social, and international life. The liberal peace theory appears to link certain socio-political order to the establishment and durability of peace. In that sense it is not concerned and impressed by what may happen in any part of the world that is outside its area of focus—the illiberal world. Moreover, it detaches itself from any foreign policy issue between the liberal and non-liberal countries. The foreign policy approach of liberal states appears to be irrelevant to the cause of peace between libertarian countries. If, for instance, liberal states happen to be the biggest exporters of means of violence to the illiberal world, little or no effect can transpire from such acts to the state of peace in the liberal world; and the liberal peace project does not seem concerned by the devastating and war-generating impact such foreign policy by liberal entities may have on the non-liberal communities. This detachment of domestic policy from foreign policy by the liberal peace discourse, as regards the liberal and the illiberal worlds, stands in sharp contrast to the link it provides between domestic and foreign policies of liberal countries vis-à-vis themselves. There appears therefore a sort of philosophical inconsistency inherent in the liberal peace project. Such fragmented peace can hardly be celebrated as the jewel in the crown of human achievement in political developments.

A deeper and non-fragmented approach to peace would enquire and deal with the internal peace within every one. It would not treat peace only in a certain field— international relations and between certain actors and liberal states—in a detached manner from society and the individual. Liberal peace appears to overlook the individual in its assessment of inter-state peace. This is a fragmented approach.

A holistic peace, to the contrary, would concern itself with all aspects of behaviour in domestic as well as foreign policy domains. It would be born out of a tranquil order that pervades all aspects of life, social, economic, cultural, and political, both domestically and internationally.

The second question asks if liberal peace theory recognizes peace outside of the West and if it does how does it actually explain it? If war is to be avoided through liberalism, then the illiberal world will inevitably be deprived of peace. And as liberal peace does not appear to universalize itself—because liberalism is simply not universalized—then what is to be done in the real world is a sort of introducing or imposing liberalism everywhere if we are to establish and preserve peace? However, experience has shown that liberalism as understood and practiced in the West is not always the best model for all societies with different culture and history that may be at a different stage of socio-political development. People's innate love for and appreciation of freedom must not be misunderstood for longing for Western liberalism everywhere, all of the time (note, however, should be taken that this is no prescription or justification for rulers who seek to justify their tyranny by simply adopting an anti-Western stance). The example of Iraq in the past few years (in spite of outside meddling like that of Al-Qaida) points exactly to this important maxim. A tribal society, where sectarianism, religion, and collectivism are the norms and where there is no history of freedom, cannot be expected to respond swiftly, favourably, and responsibly to calls for Western democracy (based on individualism, liberalism, and rationalism).

Explaining legitimating and accepting only one kind of peace as liberal peace project does, closes the door to the variety of human experiences by disallowing and delegitimating the liberty of difference and the factuality of pluralism in human development. Is that not a very illiberal approach in itself? That may indicate yet another philosophical inconsistency in the liberal peace theory. It may therefore be observed that liberal peace concerns itself with people within a limited geography and limited socio-political experience. Just as the advocates of the so-called socialist peace theory were ill-advised to propound a global kind of socialism claiming a universalistic status for their inter-state 'peace', it would equally appear to be difficult to suggest the same for the liberal peace theory. To be short, liberal peace theory advances at best an understanding and an explanation of the absence of war in the Western world, in a certain timeframe and under specific conditions. That is a far cry from suggesting the only way to achieve peace in the rest of the world and throughout history is through importing the Western model, something which it attempts to do (even if we set aside the questions of slavery and colonialism and wars of the colonies on behalf of the Western colonial powers for now). In this regard the categorization and graduations of the liberal peace project, in particular that of 'victor's peace' serves to highlight the point in question.[9] Also, liberal peace theory underscores sovereign statehood, a concept that has of late been much critiqued by critical theory.

The unifying or divisive nature of liberal peace therefore is the core of the second question. Peace as a 'virtuous' commodity, and as opposed to what Oliver Richmond calls 'virtual one', is deemed to unify people. Plato's unifying criterion for justice and the very assumption that peace as an ultimate end to all else must itself be just, leads us to conclude that peace ought to be a unifying experience. In other words, true peace brings people together irrespective of their differences, unlike liberal peace that seeks for the erosion of socio-political differences before peace could be achieved. A unifying peace does not mean dissolution of varieties in human governance. The disregard for variety in human experiences and tastes inherent in liberal peace theory inevitably leads to the classification of people into 'peaceful' and the rest as 'non-peaceful'. That is a travesty of justice, as true and just peace must be unifying and not divisive.

Based on the arguments above, the exclusive nature of liberal peace, addressed by the third question, is self-evident. If you seek, recognize, and legitimize peace only between specific communities and by doing so disunite humanity and categorize people on earth into 'incompatible' groups, then you are automatically establishing an exclusion zone for the few that fit in your category. That is what the advocates of liberal peace theory may inadvertently be promoting. Sovereign statehood, underwriting liberal peace theory, has already made many parts of human population indifferent, if not hostile, to one another. The liberal peace project goes a step further by suggesting that peaceful coexistence is the exclusive monopoly of liberal countries. In today's thinking in International Relations (IR), liberal peace dictum may appear to support the current status-quo in the world affording moral legitimacy to the underlying structure of international relations.

Therefore, the divisive, fragmented, and exclusive nature of liberal peace theory appears as unavoidable elements in its discourse. The huge export of arms by leading liberal countries to the illiberal world, as noted above, add weight to the claim of those who have doubts about the truth and the axiological aspects of liberal peace project. The Islamic response to liberal peace theory can partly be assessed in the light of the nature and the definition of peace in Islam as argued earlier. A few words, however, will be said now with regard to Islamic discourse engaging these specific aspects of liberal peace. Below, the approaches of jurisprudential and epistemic Islam to liberal peace projects are each briefly assessed in turn, bearing in mind of course that a fuller and deeper analysis would require greater length than presented the bounds of this chapter.

JURISPRUDENTIAL ISLAM AND LIBERAL PEACE

Jurisprudential Islam is the particular interpretation, which has given rise to the advent of Islamic fundamentalism and/or political Islam (there might, however, be a subtle difference between the two but not directly relevant to the present discussion) and has in some ways associated Islam, in the minds of some Westerners, with the acts of terrorism.

Peace in jurisprudential Islam is viewed as defined and codified by *shari'a*. As *shari'a* concerns itself mainly with the external aspects of religion (the internal and spiritual aspects are more focused on by Gnosticism), peace also is treated in the same manner. Just as realism and neo-realism in International Relations seem to treat peace as an instrument of policy, mainly at the service of greater national interests or hostage to the underpinnings of international structure, the holistic coverage of the concept of peace, as outlined earlier, appears less emphasized in the jurisprudential interpretation of Islam.

The establishment of *ummah* (the Islamic community) on earth based on the rules of *shari'a* is the ultimate goal of Islam according to the jurisprudential approach. The *ummah* is not confined to any particular geography, or limited to any specific race; rather it consists of all believers throughout the world from whatever background, language, creed, history, or geography. It is a step beyond nationhood in that it attempts to unite all Muslims through a conscious empowering act of accepting Islam as a religion. Unlike race, language, history, and other such involuntary criteria in nationhood, where the individual has no choice, and nationalism and patriotism ask for allegiance to a particular nation and state not chosen by him/her, *ummah* arms the individual by allowing a choice to be made by him/her in joining or rejecting it. It is therefore a conscious and informed choice that establishes *ummah* and allegiance to it rather than non-voluntary factors as in nationhood.[10]

In order to fulfill their mission (establishing *ummah* based on *shari'a* in their country and throughout the globe), the jurisprudential Islamists may sanction the use of violence; although this does not include every member of the group; there are those within this camp who are less hesitant to use violence for the promotion of their cause. Seyyed Qutb in Egypt and Maududi in Pakistan were two real-life instances of such class of people. More radical and more contemporary, of course, is Osama Bin Laden, whose network of Al-Qaida has engaged in a series of horrific acts of violence against innocent civilians throughout the world. The monopolistic trait of this group of the faithful renders all other versions and interpretations of the faith invalid in their judgement. As religious zealots, they believe that, if deemed necessary, shedding blood of the innocent can be justified in the eyes of the Almighty because of their final goal. Two Verses from the Quran commonly referred to by jurisprudentialists on the question of war can be found in the Second and the Fifth Suras; Verse 191 of the Second Sura reads—*Slay them wherever you find them and expel them from where they expelled you; persecution is worse than killing*. Verse 5 of the Fifth Sura states—*Then, when the sacred months have passed, slay the idolaters wherever you find them, take them and besiege them and prepare for them every ambush*. These two Verses are used as bases to justify war against non-Muslims or even against Muslim rulers who fail in their duty to establish the rules of *Shari'a*. Seyyed Qutb, referred to earlier, believed that violent challenge to such Muslim governments was not only justified but actually incumbent upon every true Muslim.[11] This violent challenge extended to all levels of government and to every field. The following quotation from a Muslim fundamentalist on attacking tourists in Egypt may shed light on the matter—*First many tourist activities are forbidden, so this source of income for the state is forbidden. Striking against such a major source of income will be a major blow against the state.*[12]

The concept of power lies at the heart of this interpretation of Islam. In order to implement the word of God one needs first to acquire power and once armed with hard power Muslims are duty bound, it is claimed to do their utmost, including entering physical battle with non-believers if necessary to ensure that God's Commands are properly executed. Ibn Taymiyya, the Muslim jurist of the Mongolian period, is usually the main scholarly figure quoted by Muslim fanatics bent on armed struggle against their governments. Ibn Taymiyya had ruled that

Mongolian rulers were not true Muslims and therefore had to be toppled by Muslims (Shadid 2002: 77).

Differences with the liberal peace projects are only too obvious. Liberalism as the foundation of liberal peace is very much contested in this version of Islam: the former celebrates and praises individual freedom whilst the latter dictates and expects human obedience to *shari'a*. Whereas, in one people are sovereign, in the other sovereignty lies with God and by extension to those, who are officiated as the interpreters of His Words. Liberal peace itself promotes liberal ideas that are in conflict with jurisprudential Islamic teachings. However, on the aspects of exclusiveness, fragmentedness, and divisiveness, ironically there may be some similarities between the two. The agents of peace in both cases are the constructs of their specific schools and thus there is an aura of exclusivity in both. Both appear to detach external peace from internal harmony and the fundamental nature of mankind and thus examine it in an isolated fashion. That is nothing but fragmenting peace. And finally both claim privileged position for themselves in humanity regarding others as less worthy, which is a very divisive approach indeed.

EPISTEMIC ISLAM AND LIBERAL PEACE

The word Islam means to surrender. It is through surrendering to the Will of the Almighty, it is claimed, that one can find peace and tranquility in life and afterlife (The Quran: Sura 13, Verse 28). It is therefore sometimes asserted that the state of peace and peacefulness is an indispensable part of Islam. The peace propagated and promoted by Islam appears to host elements that stand opposed to the three aspects of liberal peace outlined earlier—fragmentedness, divisiveness, and exclusion.

The people are one nation...reads Verse 213 of Sura 2 of the Quran. The unifying approach of the Quran to mankind is illustrated in this Verse, a salient and indispensable element of the Islamic discourse. The kind of peace that is sought by the youngest Abrahamic tradition is one that embraces the whole of mankind. Although divisions within humanity are acknowledged, no advantage is given to any unless based on virtue.

> O Mankind! We created you from a single (pair) of a male and a female and made you into communities and tribes that ye may know one another. Verily the most honoured of you in the sight of Allah is the most virtuous of you. And Allah has full knowledge and is well acquainted (with all things). (The Quran: Sura 49, Verse 13)

It is clearly observed that there is no superiority over others except in virtue. Peace also, as a praiseworthy quality in Islam, cannot be allowed to segregate humanity into camps where one camp by the virtue of claiming peace for its own independent system of governance can appear to delegitimize peace for others. The theology of pluralism in Islam accepts the pluralistic approach to truth and peace.[13]

Whether liberal or otherwise, peace is a valuable and praiseworthy commodity, but in Islamic tradition it is to be based on justice (The Quran: Sura 49, Verse 9). And justice is the quality which is strongly associated with virtue.

> *O ye who believe! Stand out firmly for Allah as witnesses to fair dealing and let not the hatred of others to make you swerve to wrong and depart from justice. Be just: that is close to virtue: and fear Allah for Allah is well-acquainted with all that ye do.* (The Quran: Sura 5, Verse 8)

A just peace, therefore, can be said to be a virtuous peace: a unifying peace that does not discriminate communities within humanity and utilizes divisions in order to promote completion in good deeds.[14]

The Persian Muslim philosopher Sa'adi of 13th century wrote: *Human beings are members in a body, whole related, from a single essence are they all created.*

This illustrates the non-fragmented and unifying approach of Islamic discourse in peace. Verse 213 of Sura 2 states, as the mission of all prophets is to reconcile the differences between people, that is making peace throughout the earth. However, this peace does not start and end between leaders of communities. If wars start in the minds of men, as UNESCO Charter states, then peace is also to be initiated and constructed within, before it is transposed to the outside world. In epistemic Islam such internal developments emanating from one's religious faith are essential underpinnings of externalizing the Will of the Almighty. In the words of one Muslim thinker, 'When law and faith merge in an individual's life, they create a sense of security and integrity about the great responsibility of pursuing justice for its own sake. And when this sense of security and integrity is projected to the collective life of the community it conduces to social harmony. Peace, then, is belief translated into action' (Sachedina 2001: 43–44). This philosophical foundation for internal and external peace has a universal dimension that does not divide, fragment, or exclude any members of human community. Submission to the Will of God, in this perspective, is to pursue justice and establish peace based on justice.

Differences with jurisprudential Islam, however, are most striking on the question of violence. Verse 32 of Sura 5 in the Quran reads:...*if anyone slew a person it would be as if he slew the whole of mankind; and if he saved a life, it would be as if he saved the whole of mankind*. This Verse is one of *mohkamat* in the Quran—unambigious Verses that do not need interpretation. Its relevance therefore to the concept of peace and the practice of peacemaking is uncompromising as epistemic Islam suggests. No Muslim is allowed to engage in violence against the innocent; in other words end does not justify the means here. If the aim of Islam is to spread peace, harmony, and tranquility on earth (Sura 2:213 states the mission of all Messengers is to reconcile differences in human community), one cannot cause chaos and wage war in order to achieve it. That would simply defeat the object of the exercise. To quote one Western scholar—*If Islamic rules were followed today, much of modern warfare would be impossible, and terrorism would be unthinkable. There would be no attacks on civilians, no retaliation against innocent parties, no taking hostages of non-combatants, no incendiary devices* (Stewart 1995: xx).

CONCLUSION

There are two main strands to Islamic thinking: epistemic and jurisprudential. Whilst the former seeks interaction and exchange with humanity and history, the latter views humanity from an absolute and historical vantage point, devoid of epistemological approaches that dominate the field of human knowledge. Peace, and in particular, liberal peace is nowadays and by and large a Western construct very much associated with the foundational underpinnings of today's system of power allocation in international relations. As such the theory and the practice of peace appear to link itself with the dominant discourse of the powerful in the world. It has in effect become divisive, fragmented, and exclusive. Islamic responses to the concept of peace, based on inferences from the Quran, however, inform a unifying, holistic, and inclusive precept. Without intending to undermine the importance and significance of peace, anywhere and any time, which Islamic discourse outlines as the mission of all prophets, a closer look at the Quran appears to root peace in justice and virtue. Without those foundations, however, peace may prove a very fragile commodity indeed.

NOTES

1. Quoted in Brown et al. (2002: 3). The similarity with an Islamic definition of Justice is remarkable; see note 4.
2. They, however, disagree widely on how to achieve that state.
3. It is interesting to note in this connection a statement by Ibn Taymiyya: 'Sixty years with an unjust imam is better than one night of anarchy'; see Ibn Taymiyya (1948: 172) quoted in Ruthven (2000: 171). Other views expressed by Ibn Taymiyya, however, appear to be at odds with this.
4. For one good source, see Shari' ati Ali (1968).
5. For a good source in this regard see Abdullahi Ahmed Al-Naim (1990). One argument advanced by subscribers to epistemic Islam is that spirit of Islam rejects slavery even though, in the context of society in early Islam, it was not banned. Now, however, slavery is rejected by Muslims. The same, it is argued, should be the case for women's rights. Any Quranic references to the contrary must be contextualized as the spirit of Islam strongly supports gender equality; see Dalacoura (1998: 45–47).
6. This was first put forward in an elaborate and systemic way in Soroush (1990).
7. This is a well-documented *hadith* quoted by many. For an English quotation see Esposito (2002: 28).
8. In this regard it is significant to note that upon the capture of Mecca by the Prophet, his arch-enemy, Abu Sufian, was granted a pardon by him; so were all members of his household and anyone else who chose to take refuge in his house or even stood in the shade of the perimeters of his house.
9. For an elaborate account of various graduations of peace, including 'victor's peace', see the "Conclusion" in Richard (2006).
10. For a full elaboration of this concept see Shari'ati Ali (1972).
11. For a brief but informed account of Qutb's views see Ruthven (2000): 307–22.
12. Interview with Hisham Mubarak in Beinin and Stork (1996: 321).
13. For an informed and elaborate debate on the issue see *Monazereh dar Bareye Pluralism e Dini* (Debate on Religious Pluralism) between Abdolkarim Soroush and Mohsen Kadivar, Tehran: Salam Newspaper Publications, 1999.
14. The Quran, Sura 5, Verse 48 reads, 'To every one of you, we have appointed a path and a way. If God had willed, he would have made you but one community…So compete with one another in good works.'

BIBLIOGRAPHY

Ali. Shar'ati, 1968. *Eslam Shenasi* (Understanding Islam). Mashhad: Toos Publications.
———. 1972. *Ummah va Emamat* (The Ummah and Its Leadership). Tehran: Hoseinieth Ershad Publications.
———. n.d. 'Niayesh' (Prayers). *Collection of Works No. 8*. Tehran: Hoseinieh Ershad Publications.
Al-Naim, Abdullahi Ahmen. 1990. *Toward an Islamic Reformation: Civil Liberties, Human Rights, and International Law*. Syracuse, NY: Syracuse University Press.

Beinin, Joel and Joe Stork. 1996. *Political Islam: A Reader*. London: I.B. Tauris and Co. Ltd.
Brown, Chris, Terry Nardin, and Nicholas Rengger (eds). 2002. *International Relations in Political Thought*. Cambridge: Cambridge University Press.
Bull, Hadley. 1977. *The Anarchical Society*. London: Macmillan.
Dalacoura, Katerina. 1998. *Islam, Liberalism and Human Rights*. London: I.B. Tauris.
Debate on Religious Pluralism between Abdolkarim Soroush and Mohsen Kadivar.1999. *Monazereh dar Bareye Pluralism e Dini*. Tehran: Salam Newspaper Publications.
Doyle, Michael. 1983. 'Kant, Liberal Legacies and Foreign Affairs', *Philosophy and Public Affairs*, 12(3) (Summer): 205–35.
Esposito, John L. 2002. *Unholy War: Terror in the Name of Islam*. Oxford: Oxford UP.
Hobbes, Thomas. 1955. *Leviathan*. Oxford: Blackwell.
Kant, Immanuel. 1983. *Perpetual Peace and Other Essays*. Translated by Ted Humphrey. Indianapolis: Hacket Publishing Company.
McClelland, J.S. 1996. *A History of Western Political Thought*. London: Routledge.
Motahhari, Morteza. 1982. *Adl e Elahi* (Divine Justice). Tehran: Sadra Publications.
Rashad Khalifa (trans.). 2001. *Quran The Final Testament* (Authorized English Version). Rev. III (ed.). Fremont: Universal Unity.
Richard, Oliver P. 2006. *Transformation of Peace: Peace as Governance in Contemporary Conflict Endings*. London: Palgrave.
Ruthven, Malise. 2000. *Islam in the World*. Oxford: Oxford University Press.
Sachedina, Abdlu Aziz. 2001. *The Islamic Roots of Democratic Pluralism*. Oxford: Oxford University Press.
Shadid, Anthony. 2002. *Legacy of the Prophet*. Cambridge, MA: Westview Press.
Soroush, Abdolkarim. 1990. *Ghabz o Bast e Teorik e Shariat* (The Theoretical Expansion and Contraction of *Shari'a*). Tehran: Serat Cultural Institute.
Stewart, P.J. 1995. *Unfolding Islam*. Reading: Garnet Publishing.
Taymiyya, Ibn. 1948. *Siyasa Shari'a*. Beirut.
Watt, Montgomery. 1997. *Introduction to the Quran*. Edinburgh: Edinburgh University Press.

About the Editors and Contributors

EDITORS

Anastasia Nikolopoulou is currently the Dean of the School of Humanities and an associate professor in the Department of English Studies at the University of Cyprus, where she teaches courses in theatre and cultural studies. She received her Ph.D from Cornell University. She co-edited (with Michael Hays), *Melodrama: The Cultural Emergence of a Genre* (St Martin's Press, 1996, 1999) and (with Savas Patsalides) *Melodrama: Ideological and Aesthetic Transformations* (University Studio Press, in Greek, 2001). In addition to her ongoing research on 19th-century theatre and culture, she has a growing interest in matters related to education and issues of peace, particularly in the ideas of Tsunesaburo Makiguchi and Daisaku Ikeda—whose work she has reviewed in the Greek-Cypriot Press. She is the recipient of two UNESCO Participation Program Awards (2007 and 2009) that enabled her to organize interconnected conferences on education for sustainable development in Cyprus.

Taisha Abraham is an associate Professor, Delhi University. She received her Ph.D from the State University of New York at Stony Brook. Her publications include a critical edition of Arthur Miller's *Death of a Salesman* (2008), *Introducing Postcolonial Theories: Issues and Debates* (2007), *Women and the Politics of Violence* (edited, 2002), *Feminist Theory and Modern Drama* (edited, 1998), and *Female Empowerment: Impact of Literacy in Jaipur District of Rajasthan* (co-authored, 1995). She is at present the general editor of *Shakti* series that focus on global issues and women in South Asia.

Farid Mirbagheri completed his secondary and tertiary education in the UK. He graduated in International Relations from Keele University, England, where he also earned his Ph.D in the same field. He currently holds the Dialogue Chair in Middle Eastern Studies at the University of Nicosia. Editor of the *Cyprus Review*, an internationally refereed journal by the University of Nicosia and the University of Indianapolis for seven years, he now serves on its advisory board. He is also an associate editor of *Global Dialogue*. He has written *Cyprus and International Peacemaking* (UK: Hurst & Co and USA: Routledge, 1998). His other publications *Historical Dictionary of Cyprus* (Scarecrow Press) and *War & Peace in Islam* (Palgrave) are due out in 2009 and 2010 respectively.

CONTRIBUTORS

Janet Chawla graduated from the University of California, Riverside, and earned a Masters of Theology degree with the Jesuits at Vidyajyoti Institute of Religious Studies in Delhi. She initiated and taught 'Gendering God: The Goddess in the Indian Traditions' at that institution. Janet taught natural childbirth classes in Delhi from 1980–95. As an activist, health educator, researcher, and founder-director of the NGO, MATRIKA, she has introduced a religio-cultural perspective to work on *dais*. She has written numerous articles for the popular press, scholarly journals, and contributed to academic collections. Her edited collection, *Birth and Birthgivers: The Power behind the Shame* focuses on birth in India. MATRIKA's website (matrika-india.org) details their research and cultural aspects of birth.

Anita Ghai teaches at the Department of Psychology (Jesus and Mary College) in New Delhi, India. She researches in the area of disability focusing especially on education, health, sexuality, and gender. She is the author of *(Dis) Embodied Form: Issues of Disabled Women* (New Delhi: Haranand, 2003/2006); *The Mentally Handicapped: Prediction of Work Performance* (with Anima Sen, New Delhi: Phoenix, 1996). She is on the editorial board of *Disability and Society* (Routledge); *Disability Studies Quarterly (Society for Disability Studies)*; *Disability, Education and Culture*

(Sage); and *Scandinavian Journal of Disability* (Routledge). Her distinctions include a U.G.C (University Grant Commission) deputation as a teacher fellow and career award from Indraprastha College (2000). She was appointed by The National Trust for Welfare of Persons with Autism, Cerebral Palsy, Mental Retardation and Multiple Disability, Government of India, to be a member of the local guardian committee for south-west Delhi. She has been recently elected as a President of Indian Association for Women Studies (IAWS).

Narayani Gupta retired in 2004 from the Department of History and Culture, Jamia Millia Islamia, New Delhi. She was a visiting faculty, teaching the history of architecture at TVB School of Habitat Studies, New Delhi, 1991–94. Gupta is a founder-member of the Conservation Society of Delhi, 1982, and a member of the Delhi Urban Art Commission (2005–08). She is on the Editorial Board of *Planning Perspectives* (Birmingham), *Urban History* (Cambridge), and *The Book Review* (Delhi). Gupta was the chairperson of the team that prepared Social Science textbooks for Classes 3–8 for government schools in Delhi (2003–04) and of the group that prepared a new curriculum and textbooks of history for the national-level NCERT (National Council of Education Research and Training) (2005). Her publications include *Delhi Between Two Empires, 1803–1931* (1981), an edited version of T.G.P. Spear's *Delhi, Its History and Its Monuments* (1997), and articles on Indian urban history and architectural conservation.

Ravi Kumar works as assistant professor at Department of Sociology, Jamia Millia Islamia, New Delhi. He completed his Master of Philosophy on 'Modernity and its Critics: An Analysis of Select Texts of Gandhi, Marcuse and Foucault' and his Doctorate on 'Dynamics of Identity Formation: The Political Economy of Backward Castes in Bihar.' His publications include *Global Neoliberalism and Education and its Consequences*, (co-edited, Routledge, *The Crisis of Elementary Education in India* (Sage Publications, 2006), and *The Politics of Imperialism and Counterstrategies* (Aakar Books, 2004). His other work includes a volume on status of untouchability in Bihar entitled *Dahleej Tak... Gawain Bihar Mein Chuachut par Taaza Adhyan* (Hindi, 2005). His areas of interest include identity politics, sociology of education, and political sociology. He is also an editor of the web journal *Radical Notes* (www.radicalnotes.com)

M. Satish Kumar is the Director, India Initiative at Queen's University Belfast. He is based at the School of Geography, Archaeology and Palaeoecology. He previously taught at Jawaharlal Nehru University, New Delhi and University of Cambridge, UK. He was the recipient of the prestigious Commonwealth Fellowship to Cambridge and was awarded the Bhoovigyan (Earth Scientist) National Leadership Award for contributions to *Population, Environment & Development Studies* (India, 2002). His research focuses on colonial and postcolonial spaces in India. He has edited two books, *Colonial and Postcolonial Geographies of India*, with S. Raju, and S. Corbridge, Sage Publications, (2006), and *Globalisation and North East India: Some Developmental Issues* (eds) A. Dubey, M. Satish Kumar, N. Srivastava, and Eugene Thomas, Standard Press, New Delhi (2007). He has contributed to national and international academic books and journals in India, UK, and Japan.

Archana Prasad is an Associate Professor at the Centre for Jawaharalal Nehru Studies, Jamia Millia Islamia, New Delhi. She is the author of *Against Ecological Romanticism: Verrier Elwin and the Making of an Anti-Modern Tribal Identity* (Three Essays Collective, 2003), *Environmentalism and the Left: Contemporary Debates and Future Agendas in Tribal Areas* (LeftWord, 2004), and has edited a collection *Environment, Development and Society in Contemporary India: An Introduction* (Macmillan, 2008). She finished her doctorate from Jawaharlal Nehru University, New Delhi, in 1994, and was a Rockfeller Fellow at the Department of Science and Technology Studies, Cornell University, untill 1996. She has been actively involved in the People's Science Movement and the women's movement. She is a member of the National Tiger Conservation Authority and played an active role in the campaign for passing the Forest Rights Bill. She has been working on contemporary tribal issues, biodiversity management, and the impact of Hindutva politics and neo-liberal globalization on tribal people. She has several popular and academic articles on these subjects.

Neelakanta Radhakrishnan is Hon. Ambassador, Soka University of America; Professor Emeritus at the Jain Viswabharati University (Ladnum in Rajastan); Secretary-General of the Indian Council for Gandhian Studies; Founder and Chairman, G. Ramachandran Institute of Nonviolence; Missionaries of Nonviolence Foundation India; Violence-free Society Campaign; Gandhi Media Centre; Centre for Development

About the Editors and Contributors

Education and Ikeda Center for value Creation in Trivandrum, Kerala. For over 20 years he was associated with Gandhigram Rural University. He has been a visiting professor at more than 20 universities and institutions around the world. His books include *Gandhi and Youth: The Shanti Sena of GRI*; *Gandhian Perspectives to Religious Intolerance*; *Gandhi: Quest for Tolerance and Survival*; *Gandhi and Global Nonviolent Transformation*; *Gandhi and the Challenges of the 21st Century*; *Ikeda Sensei: The Triumph of Mentor-Disciple Spirit*; and *Gandhian Perspectives on Education*. He is the recipient of Soka University (Japan) honorary doctorate award, University of Kerala Millennium Award, Gandhi, King, Ikeda Community Builders Award, Atlanta, and member of International Collegium of Scholars, Morehouse College, USA.

Sadhna Saxena is an Associate Professor in the Department of Education, University of Delhi, India. She has worked for more than one and a half decades in Kishore Bharati which was a voluntary organization based in Hoshangabad district of Madhya Pradesh, India. While at Kishore Bharati she did intensive educational work within the school system and outside with school drop-outs, adults, and women. She has also been associated with the Democratic Rights work in India. She has worked in the field of literacy with a research organization of the MHRD (Ministry of Human Resource Development) called the National Institute of Adult Education. Before joining the university, the major focus of her work has been in the area of mass education.

Michael J. Scoullos is a Professor of Environmental and Marine Chemistry and Director of the Laboratory of Environmental Chemistry at the University of Athens (UoA); Chemist (MSc, DSc), Oceanographer (Ph.D); responsible for the postgraduate course of Environmental Education (EE) and Education for Sustainable Development (ESD) at UoA. He is a member of the Executive Bureau of the European Environment Agency (EEA); founder and since 1992 Chairman of the Mediterranean Information Office for the Environment, Culture and Sustainable Development (MIO-ECSDE), the largest Federation of Mediterranean Organizations; coordinator of the International conference 'Environment & Society', Thessaloniki, 1997; member of the Task Group that drafted the UNECE Strategy on ESD for the UN Decade for ESD (2005–14). He is author of several books and more than 300 articles on Oceanography, Environment, Water, and International issues.

Teesta Setalvad is the editor of the journal *Communalism Combat*. Her activism has focused on the protection of human rights and democracy. She is the recipient of numerous awards, such as the Nana A. Palkhivala Civil Liberties Award (2006), the Siva Prasad Barooah Award for Journalism (2002), the Thomas National Human Rights Award (2004), and the Chameli Devi Jain Award for Outstanding Woman Journalist (1993). She has launched the country's first educational curriculum to help children engage with human rights. To spread her curriculum across India—and eventually across South Asia—she is training teachers to take up her approach in their schools. She is also building a national advocacy campaign on caste, religion, and gender biases in textbooks. The nationwide critique of social studies and history curriculae was pioneered by Khoj, the secular education programme which Setalvad is the director of and resulted in her being inducted into the Central Advisory Board of Education (CABE) an advisory board to the Indian Parliament.

Shobha Sinha is an Associate Professor in the Department of Education, University of Delhi. She has taught undergraduate and graduate level courses in language education in India and in America. She has worked for several years in an innovative elementary education programme in Delhi University where she was involved in designing courses in language education and school based experiences. Her research interests include various aspects of literacy development in children, especially from low socio-economic backgrounds. Currently she is doing research in Indian children's early literacy experiences in the school context.

Sukhadeo Thorat is Chairman, University Grants Commission, New Delhi; Professor of Economics, Jawaharlal Nehru University, and Director, Indian Institute of Dalit Studies. He has been a visiting faculty member for two years (1989–91) in Iowa State University, AMES, U.S.A. He has also been a consultant to International Food Policy Research Institute, Washington DC, U.S.A. Thorat's research is mainly on agricultural development, rural poverty, institution and economic growth, problems of marginalized groups, and economics of caste system. His publications include *Rural Development—Problem and Prospect* (edited March 2001), *Slum in Metropolies-Living Environment* (with Sudesh Nangia, Shipra, New Delhi 2000), *The Untouchability of Rural India* (co-author, Sage Publications, 2006), *Ambedkar on Social Exclusion and Inclusion* (with

Narender Kumar, Oxford, 2008), *Dalits in India: In Search of Common Destiny* (Sage Publications, 2009), and the forthcoming *Blocked by Caste-Economic Discrimination and Social Exclusion in Modern India* (Oxford, 2009). He is the recipient of numerous awards including the Dr Ambedakar Chetna Award (2001) and the Vidyalankara (Lifetime Achievement Award) (2008).

Index

Bal Chiraiya, 131

Cambridge History of India, 152
caste-based exclusion and discrimination, xxv, 5–6
   consequences of, 6
      conflicts, birth of, 7
      on economic growth, 7
      on poverty, 6
   economic discrimination, concept of, 5, 13
   evidence on, 13–14, 23–25
   occupation by birth, determination of, 5
   remedies for, 8
      reducing economic discrimination, 8
      state's interventions, need of, 8
   social exclusion, of untouchables, 5
   socio-economic condition of SCs and, 9
      disparities, persistence of, 14–15
      education and health, access to, 11–12, 21–22
      employment/unemployment rate, 10, 17–19
      occupation patterns, 9–10, 16
      ownership of agricultural land, 10, 16, 17
      poverty, 11, 20–21
      practice of untouchability and atrocities, 12–13, 23
   untouchables, exclusion of, 5
caste system, in India, 3. See also caste-based exclusion and discrimination
   Dalits, position of, 3
   elements in dynamics of, 14
   governing principles of, 4–5
      caste-based economy, 4

      caste-based rights, 5
      inequitable rights on graded hierarchy, 5
      untouchables as inferior human beings, 5
   hierarchical division of rights, 3
   low-caste untouchables, disadvantages of, 3
Central Advisory Board of Education (CABE), 36, 38, 96, 103
childbirth, xxviii–xxix
   biomedical and public health approach, 86
   caesarean rates, studies on, 82–84
   hospital services, in rural areas, 83–84
   indigenous skill and knowledge, 84–86
      need of, 86–87
   MATRIKA's research methodology, 87–88
   medicalization of, 81–84
   Narak and Bemata in, 88–90
Children's Activity Programme (CAP), 131
civic republicanism, 197–99

Decade of Education for Sustainable Development (DESD), xiii–xiv, 55
Development as Freedom, xxiv
disability, xxv–xxvi
   concept of, 30–31
   and existing educational scenario, 33
      Action Plan, by government, 37
      CABE, reconstitution of, 36
      funding, need of, 36–37
      ICDS programmes, exclusion from, 35–36

Index

inclusion in regular school, need for, 34
inclusive schooling, move towards, 37–40
NPE, on integrated education, 34
PWD Act, on education to disabled children, 34–35
rehabilitation of disabled, efforts for, 33
right to education, as fundamental right, 35
and gender, 40–42
and inclusive system of education, 41–42
and marginalization, 31
political economy of, 31–33
    capitalist system, and disabled people, 31–32
    education for empowerment, need of, 32–33
    low employment rates, for disabled, 32
District Primary Education Programme (DPEP), 29
Dover Beach, 175

Earth Charter Commission, xi
education
    education systems for Global citizenship, need of, 186–87
    Gandhiji view on, xxix, 179
        and development of concept of *Nai Talim*, 183–84
        educational atmosphere, need of creation of, 179
        fundamentals of basic education, 182
        goal of education, 179
        importance of family and home, stress on, 184–85
        manual training in education, need of, 182
        Nai Talim (basic education), concept of, 179–81, 183
        parents' role, in child education, 179
        system for educating children, 179–81
        values in education process, need of, 182–83
    globalization and commercialization of, 175–77
        consequences of, 176–77
        and need for change, 177
    role in global citizenship, 200–201
    teacher as value creator, role of, 185–86
education system, in India, xxiii–xxiv
    efforts for improvement of, 95–96
    globalization and
        benefits of globalization, Sen on, 96
        neoliberal capitalism in, 98–99
        role of market with uncontrolled freedom, 97
        Stiglitz argument on, 97–98
    impact of neoliberalism, 100, 103–104
        inability to buy education from market, 109–10
        inequality in education, creation of, 106
        mass suicides by farmers, 108–10
        nature and status of education in society, 104–105
        private capital in higher education, 106–107
        privatization, promotion of, 101
        quality education, state reluctance on, 110
        state interest in free education paradigm, lack of, 106
    reforming of system, efforts for, 110–11
Environmental Education (EE), xxviii. *See also* UNECE strategy, for ESD
    and Belgrade meeting, 47–48
    Earth Summit and, 48
    and Education for Sustainable Development (ESD), 50
        components of sustainable development, 53, 54

economic development, EE for, 50–51
education, as basis of three pillars of SD, 51
ESD, implementation of, 53, 54
Governance, as basis of SD pyramid, 52
role of governance, in implementation of SD, 53
role of tolerance, in ESD, 53
three dimensional representation, of SD module, 52
three pillars of SD, Rio concept of, 51
UN Decade of ESD, 55
UNECE strategy, 55–58
Stockholm Declaration on, 47
Tbilisi Declaration on, 48
Thessaloniki Conference, on sustainable development, 48–49

global citizenship
 Ikeda notion of, 200
 role of education in, 201
globalization
 definition of, 28
 and education of disabled, 29–30
 impact of, 28
 and neoliberal policies, 29
 and sustainable development, xxiii–xxiv
Gulgula, 131

Handbook of Reading Research, 125
history textbooks for school students, writing of, 152, xxvii
 in Bangladesh, 153–54
 history after partition, representation of, 154–55
 in India, 153–54
  bias in, 158–59
  change in NCERT books by BJP, 158
  and ideology of Hindu leaders, 156–58
  National Curriculum Framework on, 158

new inclusive Curriculum in 2005, 159
reflection of ideology of ruling party, 155
regional books, by state councils, 156
textbooks by National Council, 155–56
 in Pakistan, 154
sense of nationhood, development of, 153
for unity among sub-continent people, 159

identity, xxix–xxx, 189–91
 citizenship and, 195–97
 formation, and common citizenship, 194–95
 globalization and, 193
 types of, 191–92
indigenous knowledge, importance of, 81
Integrated Child Development Services (ICDS), 35–36

Jan Shikshan Abhiyan (JSA), xxvi–xxvii, 129
 classroom pedagogy, 145–49
 culture and language of learner, undervaluing of, 134–35
 emergent literacy, role of, 137–38
 investigation on JSA's activities, 129–33
 literacy development, before formal instruction, 138–39
 literacy learning process, understanding of, 141–44
 literacy programme, for non-school going children, 129–31
 pattern recognition and prediction in reading, role of, 139–40
 poems and songs, popular in classes, 132–34
 reading readiness paradigm, 136–37
 reading without comprehension, problem of, 134
 story reading by adult, role of, 138

Index

Kishore Bharati (KB), 130

liberal peace, and Islam, xxvii–xxviii, 204
Islam, concept of
  birth of Islam, 208
  epistemic Islam, 208–209
  jihad in jurisprudential Islam, 210
  jihad, meaning of, 209–210
  jurisprudential Islam, 209
  schools of Islamic thinking, 208
  shari'a (rules) of Islam, 208
  liberal peace, aspects of, 210–14
  and epistemic Islam, 216–18
  and jurisprudential Islam, 214–16
  peace, concept of, 204–205
  in Islam, 205–207
literacy in India, xxvi
  concept of literacy, 117–18
  drop-out rate in primary education, 120–21
  history of, 119
  literacy research, lack of, 125–26
  pedagogic inefficiency, as major problem, 125
  poor performance, of students, 121
  rate of, 119
  reading, theory and research on, 123–25
  role of school, 120
  teacher training, need of, 126–27
  textbooks, dependence on, 122
  traditional literacy pedagogy, 121–22

moral citizenship, 199–200
moral community, concept of, 199

National Curriculum Framework (NCF), 158, 159
National Policy of Education (NPE), 29, 34
neoliberalism impact on education
  privatization, promotion of, 101

Persons with Disabilities Act, 1995, 34–35

Rise and Fulfilment of British Rule in India, 155

Sarva Shiksha Abhiyan (SSA), 34, 73, 78, 96, 106
sustainable development
  and education for (*see also* Environmental Education (EE))
  economics of nature in, xv–xx
  UNECE strategy, on education for SD, 50, xiii
  universal language, use of, xi–xv
  WSSD initiatives on, 49–50
  politics of, xx–xxii
sustainable tribal development, education system for. *See* tribals, in India

textbooks on history, contents of, xxvii. *See also* history textbooks for school students, writing of
  bias and distortion, in social studies syllabus, 164–65
  conflicting regional and nationalised views in, 163–65
  deletions of facts in, 162–63
  Dr Ambedkar struggle, no reference of, 166–67
  holistic and fair vision of past, missing of, 165
  importance of, 161
  misrepresentations of religions and conversions, 167–69
  and need of understanding of past events, 170–71
  reflection of ideology of ruling party, 161
  regional freedom fighter, exclusion of, 164
  social inequality by caste system, exclusion of, 166
Thessaloniki Declaration, xii–xiv, 48–49, 51

tribals, in India, 64
  development and educational projects, in colonial time
    alienation from natural resources, 66
    craft education, imparting of, 69
    education for development of nationalist identity, 68–69
    education projects, by missionaries, 66–67
    Elwin's proposal, for tribal people, 68
    impact of, 69
    missionary activity and education, criticism of, 67–68
    policy of exclusion for tribals, 68
  globalization, impact of
    on education, 78
    on tribal livelihoods, 77–78
  goals of, sustainable development for, 65
  integration through formal education, status of
    drop-out rates of school children, 72
    enrolment pattern in higher education, 74–75
    enrolment rates at different levels, 72
    expenditure pattern on education schemes, 73
    government employment, 75–76
    impact of reservations on STs, 76
    number of beneficiaries for different schemes, 74
    school education, 71–74
    ST students enrolled at various stages, 76
    technical education, 74–75
  Nehru's plans, for tribal development, 69–70
  modern ideas of development, expenditure on, 70–71
  state monopoly, on natural resources, 70
  Tribal Welfare Department, setting of, 70
  uneven development of tribals, 71
  quality education by state, need of, 79
  traditional lifestyle
    impact of colonial capitalism on, 65
    in pre-colonial period, 65

UNECE strategy, for ESD, 55–58
  and framework for
    areas for actions, 58
    evaluation, 61–62
    financial matters, 60
    international cooperation, 58–60
    national state implementation, 58
    roles and responsibilities, 60
  implications for education, 57
  objectives of, 56
  principles of, 56–57
United Nations Economic Commission for Europe (UNECE), 49
United Nations Educational, Scientific and Cultural Organization (UNESCO), xii–xiv, xxii, 47, 48, 55, 206, 217

Why Education is Useless, 178
World Conference on Education for All, Jomtien, xiv
World Summit for Sustainable Development (WSSD), 49